The Dictionary
of Misinformation

The Dictionary of Misinformation

TOM BURNAM

Thomas Y. Crowell Company
New York / Established 1834

Library of Congress Cataloging in Publication Data

Burnam, Tom.
    Dictionary of misinformation.

    1. Errors, Popular.   I. Title.
AZ999.B87   001.9'6'03   75-15651
ISBN 0-690-00147-9

10 9 8 7 6 5 4 3

For Phyllis

Acknowledgments

There may be people in this world who could write a book like this without any help from others. If so, I am not one of them. First, I salute those who have blazed the trail: Bergen Evans and his *Natural History of Nonsense,* Ashley Montagu and Edward Darling and their *The Prevalence of Nonsense,* as well as *The Ignorance of Certainty* (marvelous title!), with a special bow to Edward Darling for his generous help. George Simpson. A. S. E. Ackermann. Vilhjalmur Stefansson (if you think he was just an explorer, read his *Adventures in Error* with its delightful introduction).

And let us not overlook those essential tools, the *Oxford English Dictionary,* the *Britannica,* the Merriam-Webster dictionaries, and everyone's friend, *Bartlett's Familiar Quotations.* Admittedly, it is a little late to be saluting John Bartlett, but surely Emily Morison Beck, editor of the fourteenth edition, deserves praise for providing a model for all who seek (as I do—with what success you must judge) both general interest and sound research.

A bow also to all those, from Perth Amboy to the Philippines, who have written me, upon hearing of this project, with helpful suggestions. Edmond Gnoza, Humanities Librarian at Portland State University, should have, and hereby gets, a special word of thanks.

I would like to acknowledge my indebtedness to Robert L. Crowell, Amy Kostant, Edwin Doremus, and Bernard Skydell. Without Mr. Crowell, the book simply could not have been done. Without the others—and, I am sure, many whom I don't know by name—it could have been done, if at all, only with much more difficulty.

Permit me also to express gratitude to Carlos Baker, Jerome Beatty, John Brown, and Helen McGuire of the Oregon Bank, Citizens Branch; Jack Capell, meteorologist with KGW-TV in Portland, Oregon; Elmer C. Case; Ralph Combs; John Gray; Robert Hammond of the Navy pre-commissioning detail, "Polar Star"; David Levin; Dr. Robert Mass; James Nardin; Edgar E. Renfrew, co-founder (with me) of RTSC, or "Remember the Sacred Cows"; Richard Sailer of the Goodyear Community Relations Department; Frederik Schuman; and—though slightly out of order alphabetically—George Savage, who had nothing whatever to do with this book. But he's the best teacher of writing I've ever known.

Many of my colleagues at Portland State University responded generously to my suggestion (which fortunately they chose to understand in the manner I intended) that a university faculty ought to be a rich mine of misinformation. In the English Department: Freeman Anderson, Tom Buell, John Cooper, Georgia Crampton, Ivan Curcin, Thomas Doulis, Philip Ford, Ross Garner (and also his wife Ann, daughter Margaret, and son Dave), Frederick Harrison, Michael Hollister, Robert Kelly, James Lill, Carl Markgraf, the late Branford Millar, James Nattinger, Stanley Radhuber, Shelley Reece, Ralph Singleton, Robert Tuttle, Donald Tyree, Frederick Waller (chairman of the department), Baxter Wilson, Anthony Wolk, and Samuel Yorks.

Others at Portland State are Evelyn Crowell of Interlibrary Loan, Nona Glazer-Malbin, John Hammond, Donald Hellison, Goerge Hoffman, the late Fred Holling, David Jannsen, Joseph Jones, Stephen Kosokoff, Miriam McKee, Thomas Palm, Dan Passell, Vera Petersen, Irene Place, David Smeltzer, Ralph Smith, John Trudeau, and Richard Wiltshire.

The following people were generous with help and suggestions: Seldon D. Bacon, Patrick Barrett, Jacques Barzun, Franklyn M. Branley, Muriel B. Crowell, Joseph A. Davis, Jr., Alan S. Pomerance, Hugh Rawson, Axel Rosin, Leonard L. Rue III, Nicholas

Slonimsky, Linda Stewart, John Terres, David L. Thomas, Edward Tripp, Chantal Veraart.

And special thanks to Richard Armour for his generous foreword; to Patricia Cooper, whose editorial eye was invaluable; to Sam Adolf Oakland, photographer; to Star Reierson for her help in research; to Mary Reece for her above-and-beyond typing; to Kathy Moeller, Lois Mock, and Cindy Walker; and my wife Phyllis, whose patience, understanding, and love go far beyond my power to praise.

All these have helped, and more.

Foreword

By Richard Armour

Collectors of information are numerous, and so are their collections: dictionaries, encyclopedias, almanacs, and all manner of reference works. But collectors of misinformation are rare. In fact Tom Burnam is the only one of this species (endangered, perhaps, but not dangerous) I have the pleasure of knowing personally.

Some years ago this unusual professor of English, a man who delights in errors while others are fooling around with facts, wrote me of his playful-serious search for commonly accepted fallacies. Since I too take a fiendish pleasure in correcting the mistakes of others, and am willing to admit I am sometimes (often) wrong myself, we began a long, if sporadic, correspondence. The reason our correspondence was so long was that his task turned out to be a lengthy and difficult one. Most of us, as Tom Burnam discovered, have been wrong about more so-called facts than even he at first thought.

But at last he has brought together some of the mistaken beliefs many of us have confidently expounded in speech and writing. What we thought true—the authorship of a famous quotation, the origin of a word, an episode in history, a scientific principle, a grammatical rule, who invented what, or such a widely accepted fact that drowning persons always rise three times—turns out to be false. Burnam, a seeker of truth, is vigorous in his condemnation of a falsehood. Thus in commenting on the above-mentioned belief that drowning persons always rise three times, his comment is "Absolute and utter balderdash." Then he goes on to explain why.

Some readers may be embarrassed to discover they have been wrong about something they were confident was right. Others will delight in catching even scholars and self-described intellectuals in error. Still others will enjoy joining the author in his search for the truth in both large matters and small. It is like playing a game, with nothing to lose but a little of your ego.

I, for one, salute Tom Burnam for bringing us fact and fun. I do this even as I many times stand, or sit (but I hope do not lie), corrected.

Preface

It all started with the publication by *Saturday Review,* in its
"Phoenix Nest" department, of a brief item of mine with a title
nearly as long as the piece itself: "One Hundred Percent Certified
True Information I Am Tired of Carrying Around Since Nobody
Believes It Anyway." It might have ended there had not Robert L.
Crowell seen the item and suggested that here might be the start
of something bigger. And so it was: *Dictionary of Misinformation.*

Along the way, however, we had to make certain decisions. This
was not to be another book of odd facts and little known truths.
Quite the contrary. This was to be a book of odd (or not so odd)
non-facts, of only too well-known *untruths.* And I early proposed
that we should make no attempt to deal with the nonrational;
only with the irrational. I have always tried to distinguish between such beliefs as people may choose to hold without regard
for scientific evidence—the Virgin Birth, for example—and those
held in stubborn defiance of scientific evidence: that capital punishment is a deterrent to crime, for example.

You will find in this book plenty of examples of the latter, none
of the former. No miracles are here demolished, no ghosts laid to
rest. For miracles (not to mention ghosts) are by definition sus-
pensions of natural law. We deal here, in other words, not with

matters of faith, but of reason. And—to paraphrase Josh Billings, the noted nineteenth-century humorist—I believe that when we stumble and fall, it's not because our reasoning faculties have tripped us; it's because of the things we know that just aren't so.

The Dictionary
of Misinformation

A

abacus. Many people—and not a few reference books—believe the abacus to be exclusively Oriental. This is not correct. The abacus was extensively used in ancient Greece and Rome. Nor is its use confined to the Orient in modern times. It is common in the U.S.S.R., where often in restaurants today the waitress will simply show the patron the abacus to indicate the cost of his luncheon, instead of bringing him a written slip. It is even used for money changing at the border, a process that is often accomplished elsewhere by a sophisticated little computer. Those who have watched the speed with which Soviet Union border personnel convert dozens of other currencies into rubles and kopeks using nothing but a small abacus will testify that in skillful hands it is just as fast as any modern device.

Absalom, caught by the hair. The story supported by most reference books is that when Absalom's mule went under that oak in the battle of Ephraim, Absalom's hair became entangled in the branches, and he hung there while the mule went on. That is not what the Bible says, however (2 Sam. 18:9). The text says that "his head caught hold of the oak." In other words his head could have become wedged among the "thick boughs." Probably the

idea of hanging by the hair has been encouraged by the statement
(2 Sam. 14:26) that Absalom cut his hair only once a year, and
the sheared hair weighed out at two hundred shekels, i.e., several
pounds.

acne. Acne, an unsightly disorder of the oil glands of the skin,
causes excruciating embarrassment to many adolescents who suffer
from it. The disease is much less frequent among people in their
twenties. No doubt this is why some people are convinced that acne
is alleviated by sexual intercourse and say, "It'll clear up when he
gets married." Acne has absolutely nothing to do with sexual
intercourse, nor is it caused by masturbation—another fallacy commonly held. Finally, it is not inherited.

advertisements, errors in. You cannot force a merchant to sell
you an item for a demonstrably wrong price—say, a $350 refrig-
erator for $35—as a result of a mistaken advertisement. An ad-
vertisement is not a contract; it's an offer. There are laws, of
course, against fraud, though they vary from state to state, even
city to city. But fraud has to involve intent—a deliberate effort to
mislead. (This is why fraud is so often difficult to prove.) All the
merchant need do is to prove that somebody somewhere—even in
his own advertising department—made the error without intent
to defraud. In the case of a $350 item offered at $35, that wouldn't
be so very difficult.

Because this mistaken belief is so common, many merchants now
carry a line in their advertisements saying, "Not responsible for
typographical errors."

adze marks. The owner of an old house will frequently point with
pride to the "adze" marks still visible on exposed beams. Nine
times out of ten he is actually talking about the marks left by the
hewing ax on a beam that was not smoothed with an adze. For the
adze was a *smoothing* tool, and was intended to remove the very
marks the modern owner may prize so highly.

air pocket. There isn't any such thing. When the airplane passenger says "We hit an air pocket and boy, did we ever drop in a
hurry!" he's really talking about a downdraft. A hole in the atmosphere is impossible.

air pollution. Without at least some air pollution, this planet would be in very poor shape. For raindrops will not form in a completely unpolluted atmosphere; there have to be what meteorologists call hygroscopic nuclei, or small particles in the air, around which the drops will take shape. No hygroscopic nuclei, no raindrops. And no rain.

Alas! poor Yorick. I knew him well. The correct quotation from Shakespeare's *Hamlet* (act 5, sc. 1, lines 202–3) is "Alas! poor Yorick! I knew him, Horatio."

alcohol consumption. Most of us have come to believe that in those sunny, "light-wine" countries like France and Italy, the total per capita consumption of alcohol is much *less* than in the "hard liquor" countries like the United States, England, and Sweden. This is not true. Reliable figures are scarce, but we have them for the decade of the sixties in the most populous countries of Europe —excluding the iron curtain countries other than Czechoslovakia —and, in addition, figures on Australia, New Zealand, Japan, and Israel.

These show that France was number one in per capita consumption of absolute alcohol, consuming nearly three times as much per person as the United States. Surprisingly, France was also number one in the consumption of absolute alcohol in the form of spirits.

Also surprisingly, Italy was number two in the total per capita consumption of absolute alcohol, 80 percent of it in the form of wine.

The United States was number eight on the list of twenty countries in its per capita consumption of absolute alcohol, but was second only to France in its use of spirits.

The United Kingdom, famous for scotch whiskey and commonly thought to be high on the list in the consumption of spirits, drank less spirits per capita than any country on the list.

Another fallacy, of course, is that "in Germany they just drink beer." It is true that Germany drank per capita the greatest number of liters of beer for any country on the list, but in its per capita alcoholic intake therefrom it was behind Australia. (Australian beers are heavier, obviously.) Also, West Germany was number four in its use of alcohol from spirits and number five in per capita consumption of absolute alcohol from wine. Switzerland was number three, and who was number four? Japan, with its sake.

The United States was ninth in its per capita consumption of absolute alcohol from beer. Eighth in wine.

Alexander the Great and his tears. Alexander the Great may or may not have wept, but if he did it wasn't because there were no other worlds left to conquer. Indeed, the exact reverse is the case. He wept because he hadn't even conquered one yet. Alexander was needled a bit by a Greek Sophist named Anaxarchus, who reminded Alexander that there were a great many other worlds besides the Eastern to mock his ambitions. To which Alexander said, "Do you not think it worthy of lamentation that when there is such a vast multitude of worlds, we have not yet conquered one?"

Alger, Horatio. A "Horatio Alger story" is a standard expression, especially among press agents, to describe a person who has risen from rags to great riches. Indeed, most people have taken it for granted that all Horatio Alger heroes became immensely rich. This is not true. Not one person in a Horatio Alger book ever got to be so much as a millionaire. Alger heroes were bootblacks and newsboys. They persevered with great virtue. They paid off mortgages, and they achieved respectability. But in monetary terms their successes were modest—with perhaps a raise from $5 to $10 per week.

Alice's Adventures in Wonderland. Almost everyone has heard of this charming book, and most readers assume that its author, Lewis Carroll, was primarily a writer of juveniles. Actually, Lewis Carroll is the pen name of Charles Lutwidge Dodgson (1832–1898), lecturer in mathematics at Oxford. He was shy and stammering, said to be a very boring lecturer. However, the world of little girls delighted him, and he liked to make up puzzles and games for them. For one of them, Alice Liddell, he wrote the book that accidentally made him famous.

An old story has it that Queen Victoria was so entranced with *Alice* that she asked its author to be sure to send her his next work. So he did: it was *An Elementary Treatise on Determinants*—or, in some versions, a bundle of abstruse mathematical pamphlets.

Like so many such charming stories, it's unfortunately completely apocryphal; Dodgson specifically denied it in the Advertisement to his *Symbolic Logic.*

A little knowledge is a dangerous thing. This is not what Alexander Pope actually said, though many think it is. Here, from part 2 of his famous *An Essay on Criticism,* published in 1711 though written somewhat earlier, when Pope was just twenty-one, are the lines containing his famous, if often misquoted, phrase.

> A little learning is a dangerous thing;
> Drink deep, or taste not the Pierian spring:
> There shallow draughts intoxicate the brain,
> And drinking largely sobers us again.

"alleged" as a defense against libel actions. The use of such words and phrases as *alleged* or *is said to* offers no defense whatever to a writer or publisher. A reporter who writes "Henry Brown is alleged to have received a bribe" and the newspaper or magazine that prints it are exactly as liable as if they had said "Henry Brown received a bribe." If this were not so, as a moment's thought will demonstrate, then the most vicious libels could go unpunished.

Allen, Ethan—and his Green Mountain Boys. Most people would aver that Ethan Allen organized the Green Mountain Boys to fight the British during the American Revolution. Not so. They were organized some years before the Revolution, and for the express purpose of fighting off the Yorkers, i.e., settlers from New York. This came about because the eastern boundary of New York and the western boundary of New Hampshire were ill-defined and both territories gave patents to the same land. So hot was the dispute and so effective was the gargantuan Ethan Allen that New York put a price on the heads of Allen and a couple of his associates.

After the American Revolution broke out, Allen and his Green Mountain Boys, still independent, fought the British and with Benedict Arnold and militiamen of Connecticut took Fort Ticonderoga. It was on this occasion that when asked by the commanding British officer by whose authority he acted, he is said to have replied, "In the name of the Great Jehovah and the Continental Congress."

It seems unlikely that Allen, a profane man, would have summoned up such dignity, along with the name of the Lord, on this occasion. In fact he was so much of an atheist that a book he wrote a few years later was destroyed by the printer, who was horrified by the "atheistic" contents.

Van de Water in *The Reluctant Republic* points out that there is no real reason to disbelieve Allen, who himself wrote these words down, and that there were other witnesses as well. This author also points out that Allen did commence with salty speech saying " 'you goddamned old rat' or 'skunk' or 'bastard.' " On this phraseology, however, there is no unanimity.

alligators killing people. There are only a very few authenticated cases of an alligator killing a person. Crocodiles, especially those along the Nile, are another matter; they are indeed dangerous to human beings, second, it is said, only to poisonous snakes as people-killers.

All men are born free and equal. Neither the United States Constitution nor the Declaration of Independence contains this statement.

American Revolution, modes of fighting. There is a widespread belief that the American colonists were able to beat the more experienced British armies in the American Revolution because they surprised the redcoats with Indian-type fighting that was totally unfamiliar to them. The history books portray our boys picking off the helpless soldiers of the king from behind stone walls and trees. Actually the British had had nearly seventy-five years of experience with this kind of tactics during the French and Indian Wars. Most battles of the war were fought in accordance with conventional eighteenth-century battle tactics. In fact, the Prussian von Steuben was hired to drill the Continental Army and teach it the methods that were employed by European armies of the period. While there was Indian fighting at various frontier points it was against Indians, hired by the British to harry the colonials.

Furthermore, the colonists did not—as is commonly supposed— have a special advantage in having developed the rifle, which had a longer range and greater accuracy than the smoothbore musket.

The rifle was virtually useless in warfare because it was so slow and difficult to reload. Both sides used muskets. The American muskets were not better than the British; in fact many of the muskets in American hands had been manufactured in the Old Country.

Nor is it correct to assume that the Revolution was a conflict of poor farmers against rich Tories. John Hancock, who signed the Declaration of Independence, was probably the richest man in America.

And the American Revolution was not, as some imagine, a war of the local populace struggling against the foreign overlords. Many colonials, of course, were fighting for the king. At times there were more Americans fighting for the king than against him.

anarchism. Entirely in contrast to the popular conception, anarchism is probably the most idealistic and peaceful of political theories. As a philosophy, it assumes a system in which the individual is free and living in peace; it looks forward to a time when human beings can coexist within a framework of voluntary associations. It is in no sense either Marxist or Leninist; anarchism in fact rejects the Marxist-Leninist theory of the dictatorship of the proletariat, as it rejects any theory involving control of one class or individual by another.

"And early though the laurel grows / It withers quicker than the rose." These lines from A. E. Housman's somber and beautiful poem "To an Athlete Dying Young" must be taken with a grain or two of poetic license. Laurel is, in point of fact, an extremely hardy perennial. It doesn't wither at all; and it grows neither early nor late; it grows all the time, as anyone knows who owns, or is owned by, a laurel hedge.

In all fairness, it should be added that Housman may have had in mind sprigs of laurels picked from the bush, or made into the sort of garland said to have been worn by Greek and Roman athletes and emperors. If so, then it must be submitted that in a personal experiment conducted by the writer, the laurel still wins leaves down. Or, rather, up.

A rose, cut fresh, and a sprig of laurel approximately ten inches (250 mm.) in length were both placed in a vase containing ordinary tap water. After twenty-four hours, the rose showed distinct signs of deterioration. After seventy-two hours, the issue was no longer in doubt; the laurel remained apparently fresh while the rose had clearly yielded up the ghost. It is, thus, clear that Mr. Housman, himself a scholar trained in the classics, sacrificed Truth on the altar of Art.

Angel Falls (Venezuela), name of. These falls, the highest in the world, are not so named for either "poetic" or quasi-religious reasons. Prosaically enough, they are named after Jimmy Angel, the explorer and bush pilot who first brought them to the attention of the outside world.

animal habitat. It is widely held that the deeper the woods, the more birds you will find; the deeper the woods, the more animals there will be. This is far from true.

Wild animals spend most of their time looking for food. Food supply is the chief factor in determining their population and distribution. For most birds there is less food in the deep dark woods than at the forest's edge, in fields, in wetlands, etc. In fact there are more than a hundred species of birds that cannot make their homes at all in a climax forest. One of these is the Kirtland's warbler, which needs young jackpine for its habitat. (Jackpine is systematically and intentionally burned off to provide new growth for them.)

Similarly the Virginia white-tailed deer do not thrive in forests of giant trees free of underbrush. Bambi would have starved to death in the kind of woods where he is commonly portrayed. Deer are browsing animals and they need young shoots that they can reach. Where the sun never reaches the ground there are not enough young trees and bushes to support a deer population.

"antelope" in American usage. There are no true antelopes native to North America. The graceful pronghorn of Wyoming and other western states where the deer and the antelope are said to play is so different from any other animal in the world that zoologists created a new family for it. The nearest relative of the antelope in America is actually the Rocky Mountain goat.

antifreeze, protection offered by. Anyone who believes that if a diluted form of ethylene glycol, commonest of the "permanent" antifreezes for automotive use, offers some protection, then an undiluted form must offer the maximum is quite mistaken. Pure antifreeze offers very little protection. Mixed half and half with water, it will protect to about thirty degrees below zero Fahrenheit. But used straight, it will become a useless slush at very little below the freezing point of water.

"Any man who hates dogs and babies can't be all bad." Commonly misquoted as "Anybody who hates children and dogs can't be all bad," this saying did not originate with W. C. Fields. It was, rather, said *about* W. C. Fields by Leo Rosten, who sired the unforgettable H*Y*M*A*N K*A*P*L*A*N. Rosten said this of Fields when introducing him at a dinner.

"Anything you say, I must warn you, will be taken down and . . ." ". . . may be used against you." Or so practically everyone would finish this famous sentence, immortalized by so many Scotland Yard inspectors in so many movies, books, and plays. But that's not what Scotland Yard operatives are told to say, as Agatha Christie, at least, knows. In her 1966 novel, *At Bertram's Hotel,* occurs the following brief exchange:

> "The famous policeman's warning! Anything you say will
> be taken down and used against you at your trial."
> "That's not quite the wording" [says the Inspector]. "Used,
> yes. Against, no . . . ."

The actual wording is "You are not obliged to say anything unless you wish to do so but what you say may be put into writing and given in evidence." There are various other wordings to fit other conditions (a written rather than oral statement by the suspect, for example), but none of them contains the words *against you.* The key phrase, *given in evidence,* is invariable.

aphrodisiac. Aphrodisiacs have been known for centuries as potions, pills, or other diet supplements that can be sneaked into food or drink to stimulate a loved one's passion. The fact, however, is that there is no such thing. There are, of course, countless substances believed to have aphrodisiac effect: peppers, hardboiled eggs, rhinoceros horn, and oysters. But they have no effect beyond the psychological. If, for instance, one is persuaded that oysters or truffles increase sexual desire, then they may well have such an effect. According to the *Encyclopaedia Britannica,* however, both oysters and truffles are, in fact, "singularly lacking in elements which might serve to bring on sexual stimulation." The same thing might be said of powdered rhinoceros horn, and it is one of the saddest ironies that the rhinoceri of Africa are being decimated by poachers for the sake of jaded, elderly Chinese gentlemen.

Spanish fly, in addition, is a highly dangerous substance to human beings. Although it can cause an erection, anyone so foolish as to administer it to a potential love-object, even in minute doses, will also bring on diarrhea, vomiting, great pain, severe depression, and blood in the vomit and excreta. Spanish fly is actually made not from flies but from the wing sheaths of beetles. Applied to the skin, it is a blistering agent. Given in large doses, it creates genito-urinary pain and causes the onset of menstruation.

Only if *aphrodisiac* is defined in the most general terms can it be said to have any meaning.

A poor thing but mine own. Although often attributed to Shakespeare, this saying is not to be found in his works. It is a popular rendering of "A poor virgin, sir, an ill-favour'd thing, sir, but mine own," in Shakespeare's *As You Like It* (act 5, sc. 4, lines 60–61).

archery, superiority of modern. It is widely said, and believed, that the frontier American Indian would stand little chance against a modern archer. It is widely forgotten that the only way to find out is to send a modern archer out to kill a buffalo. From horseback. With no saddle. Without a modern, fiber glass bow. It is fairly obvious that the Plains Indians were highly expert with bows, arrows, and spears; their lives depended on them.

armor, weight of. A persistent myth, aided and abetted by a scene from the Laurence Olivier film *Henry V* in which a warrior is hoisted by a derrick, is that medieval suits of armor were so heavy that an unhorsed knight could not move and needed help getting into the saddle. As a matter of fact, according to Dr. Helmut Nickel, Curator of Arms and Armor at the Metropolitan Museum of Art in New York, suits of armor were not only so well fitted that the wearer could move easily, but averaged in weight only some fifty to fifty-five pounds—no more than a modern fully equipped soldier's gear.

Other misconceptions involving warfare in the Middle Ages are that the large swords then used were two-handed, and that long-bowmen carried their arrows in quivers at their backs. The swords were actually balanced for use with one hand; and the English longbowman carried his arrows not after the fashion of Errol Flynn in *The Adventures of Robin Hood,* who evidently mistook American Indian practice for medieval custom, but rather in a sheaf tied loosely at the waist.

Aryan. This word no doubt suggests to many people the idea of "pure" blood. The Nazis tried to make Aryan denote a non-Jewish Caucasian, especially Nordic. This was a trumped-up meaning, of course.

Properly, Aryan has both an ethnic and a linguistic sense. In the ethnic sense Aryan refers to a people who inhabited the Iranian plateau, moved into north India, and merged with the peoples there. They spoke the Indo-European mother tongue. Strictly speaking, this group would include certain Indians and Iranians and their descendants, but would rule out most Germans, English, and Americans.

Used in the linguistic sense, though less commonly today, Aryan refers to the languages descended from the Indo-European mother tongue: such as Greek, the romance languages, Celtic, Germanic (including Scandinavian and English), Indic and Iranian languages, Armenian, Albanian, Slavic and Baltic languages, etc.

The idea of "pure" blood is fatuous and opprobrious. Man's ceaseless migrations have made certain that all of us are mixtures.

". . . ask not what your country can do for you; ask what you can do for your country." It is sometimes said that this most famous of the John F. Kennedy remarks was not original with him. But it depends on definition. The sentiment, as might be expected, is not particularly novel; both Oliver Wendell Holmes (". . . it is now the moment . . . to recall what our country has done for each of us, and to ask ourselves what we can do for our country in return") and Warren G. Harding (". . . we must have a citizenship less concerned about what the government can do for it and more anxious about what it can do for the nation"), unlikely as the pairing seems, expressed it, among others. But the catchy little inversion "ask not" appears to have been JFK's—and that is what, apparently, caught the public fancy and thus, in a sense, does make the remark original with him.

assault and battery. These terms do not at all mean the same thing; the expression is in no way tautological. *Assault* in legal terms is an attempt at, or threat of, force or violence and need not involve any actual physical contact; *battery* is the actual employment of force. It is a useful distinction; without it, the holdup man who does not touch his victim might go scot-free.

Shaking your fist at your neighbor is assault, if he wants to get sticky about it. But it's not battery unless you follow it up by punching him in the nose, at which point it becomes assault and battery.

assembly line in automobile factories. The technique was not introduced in the United States by Henry Ford. Instead, Ransom E. Olds, whose initials and name were to be immortalized in Reo and Oldsmobile, introduced the assembly-line technique to this country. In 1901, the Olds Motor Vehicle Company built 425 cars. The next year, after Olds introduced his revolutionary production method, the output of Oldsmobiles was over 2,500.

True, Ford improved on Olds's idea. Under the Olds plan, wooden platforms on casters passed between lines of workmen who added parts until the car was completed. Ford introduced the conveyor belt system, in which conveyors brought the various parts to the production line, itself kept in motion by a belt. Ford's method cut the time needed to produce a Model T from a day and a half to ninety-three minutes. Nevertheless, his contribution was a modification of another's idea, not an "original."

"Assume a virtue, if you have it not." This speech does not, as usually thought, represent in any sense a counsel to hypocrisy. When Hamlet says this to his mother (act 3, sc. 4, line 160), he is using *assume* in the sense of "take on"—a meaning still current, as in "He assumed the burdens of the presidency." Hamlet's actual words are as follows:

> Assume a virtue, if you have it not.
> That monster, custom, who all sense doth eat
> Of habits devil, is angel yet in this,

> That to the use of actions fair and good
> He likewise gives a frock or livery,
> That aptly is put on. . . .

In other words, custom, or habit, is two-edged; just as continuing to do the wrong thing makes a habit of badness, so may practicing the right thing make for goodness. Hamlet certainly does not mean that Gertrude should merely pretend goodness; that would defeat his whole intent and argument.

A straight line is the shortest distance between two points. This one is interesting in a kind of double-reverse way. No one questions its truth in Euclidean geometry. But then, geometry—like much of mathematics—is so neat and logical because it exists only in terms of its own definitions; it doesn't have to deal with that sweating, random, exasperating, shifting world all of us, including geometricians, actually inhabit. A line, to a geometrician, has only one dimension: length; it's what connects two points, and they don't have *any* dimension. Just location. Needless to say, neither line nor point exists physically; no matter how hard you try to spin out an incredibly fine filament, it's still going to have *some* width. (In a way, this is why certain mathematicians, or people with minds like certain mathematicians', have such an easy time of it discrediting historians and social workers, who do not have the privilege of working in a context which they create and control all by themselves.)

Those who know terrestrial navigation like to point out that a straight line is *not* the shortest distance between, say, New York and Liverpool. Rather, what is called the great circle route is really shortest. However, the line looks like a segment of a circle on a map only because a map is a flat representation of a round world. A string stretched across a globe between the locations of New York and Liverpool will be straight enough, if viewed from directly overhead. Yet it isn't really straight, in geometric terms; a truly straight line between New York and Liverpool would, of course, go right through under the ocean, as if carved out by an unimaginably powerful laser beam. So, like so many things, it all depends on definition.

None of the above involves Einsteinian theories of the universe, by the way. A straight line in Einsteinian terms would ultimately meet itself. But that's something else again.

autogiro vs. helicopter. The autogiro, invented in Spain by Juan de la Cierva in the 1920s, was not an early form of helicopter; it differed fundamentally from the helicopter in that its rotating blades were not engine-driven while the aircraft was in flight. They were, in effect, windmills. As a result, the autogiro was incapable of vertical ascent or descent and in order to remain aloft had to maintain forward air speed, just like a conventional fixed-wing aircraft. It was thus also incapable of hovering or flying backward or sideways. The helicopter's blades, on the other hand, are engine-driven and provide all the lift. Autogiros had wings and a conventional propeller in addition to the rotating blades, which provided much of the lift although not (as in a helicopter) all of it.

automobile, invention of. The first automobile was neither invented nor produced in the United States by the Duryeas, by Henry Ford, or by anybody else. Not even the *second* automobile, as a matter of fact, was invented or produced in America. Both honors go to Germany: The Benz Patent Motor Wagon was patented by Karl Benz in Mannheim in 1885; and the Daimler was patented the same year in Stuttgart, sixty miles away, by Gottlieb Daimler, working independently of Benz. By 1893, still a year before the Duryeas were to introduce America's first automobile, the Benz even had a named model, the Velo, ready for the general public, or such of it as could afford to buy one. It was water cooled, with a transmission, differential, carburetor, and top speed of twenty-five miles an hour.

AWOL (Absent Without Leave). Since *without* is one word, those who dislike the military sometimes assume that the expression reveals a woeful lack of literacy, or at least a minimal knowledge of spelling. But there's a reason for that *o;* without it, AWOL would become AWL, which means "absent *with* leave."

ax, for splitting rails. History books and encyclopedias for the young are forever showing Abraham Lincoln splitting rails with an ax. He split many rails, to be sure, but not with an ax. Rails were split with wedges, and these were hammered in with mauls. A good woodsman respected his ax too much to use it for this kind of work.

Azores, the southern. They are anything but "southern"; their latitude is approximately that of New York.

B

bagpipe. It is unfair to hold the Scots responsible for the bagpipe. It is a very ancient instrument—as old as ancient Persia—which was introduced into the British Isles by the Romans. While it is considered to be the national instrument of Scotland, historically it is hardly more Scottish than Irish. Surprisingly enough, some form of the bagpipe is found in Spain, Italy, France, the Balkans, and even Scandinavia.

Properly the name of the instrument is singular—not "bag-pipes." It is true that each bagpipe consists of five pipes: the intake pipe, through which the player's breath enters the bag; the pipe on which the performer plays the melody; and three drone pipes, to provide a bass background.

banana oil. It doesn't come from bananas, which produce no commercial oil of any kind. It's a synthetic compound which some think smells like bananas.

banana tree. There isn't any such thing; bananas do not grow on trees but rather develop on very large herbs; the banana "tree" does not, in fact, have roots but a rhizome. And what appears to be its trunk, or stalk, is actually made up of very large leaves in tubular configuration. Nor is the banana native to the Western

Hemisphere; its origin, according to most horticulturists, lies in Southeast Asia.

Contrary to popular opinion, bananas are not picked green merely for the convenience of the vendor. Oddly enough, bananas have better flavor and texture if they are allowed to ripen after picking.

bank checks, date, amount, and form. Many people continue to believe that a check drawn on a bank account must not be dated on a Sunday, cannot be drawn for any amount less than one dollar, and must be on a form specified by the bank. None of this is true. A check for one cent dated on a Sunday and written on a flat rock can be just as good as any other, at least in some states. An Oregon taxpayer, in fact, recently expressed his frustrations by sending the Internal Revenue Service a check cast in plaster of Paris weighing several pounds. It was duly cashed and returned to the bank, which processed it by hand.

Nor are so-called counter checks—that is, blank forms on which the name of the bank must be entered—illegal, although many retail establishments attempt to give this impression. The recent adoption by almost all banks of "personalized" checks designed for computerized operation has, it is true, discouraged the use of counter checks; and, of course, any establishment may refuse to accept any check, "counter" or not. But this is a matter of convenience—the bank's convenience, primarily—rather than a matter of law.

"Barbara Frietchie." John Greenleaf Whittier's famous poem with its often-quoted lines—" 'Shoot, if you must, this old gray head, / But spare your country's flag,' she said"—which purports to tell of an actual episode involving Stonewall Jackson during the Civil War, must be taken with more than a grain of salt. According to an eyewitness, Jackson's troops never got within three hundred yards of Barbara Frietchie's home. Even if they did, Ms. Frietchie could not have "[taken] up the flag the man hauled down" and set it in her attic window. Whittier gives her age as "fourscore years and ten," but she was actually even older: ninety-six. And she was bedridden and helpless, having lost the power of locomotion; she could move only with the help of attendants.

Bar Mitzvah. Among non-Jews, this event is often mistakenly assumed to involve the rite of circumcision. Of course it does not; it is, rather, the ceremony which symbolizes the step from boyhood to manhood at age thirteen and the assumption of adult responsibilities.

Barnes, Jake—and wound in Ernest Hemingway's *The Sun Also Rises*. Most people who have read Hemingway's classic novel of post–World War I expatriates in Paris assume that Jake Barnes, its narrator and protagonist, was emasculated by his wound, which is never specifically described in the book. But we have Hemingway's word that although Jake had lost his penis, his testicles were intact; he was capable, in other words, of normal sexual feelings but not of a normal sexual experience.

Because so much of the book is based on actual people and events, it sometimes has been assumed that Hemingway himself might have been wounded in an analogous fashion. An amusing, if possibly apocryphal, story has Hemingway, with a laugh, throwing aside his blankets and pulling down his pajamas during one of his fairly frequent hospitalizations in order to prove to some overly curious visitors that there was nothing wrong with him.

It might be added that had Jake suffered his wound during World War II, he might have been at least partially rehabilitated. The Russians, among others, achieved some success with the surgical creation of artificial penises for soldiers who had been similarly injured.

barrister, solicitor (British); attorney, lawyer (American). *Barrister* and *solicitor* are not synonymous terms in Great Britain; the former may plead cases in the superior courts, the latter may not. Both are lawyers, as Americans use the term. In the United States, *attorney* and *lawyer* are the same in practice, though in the strictest usage an attorney is one who acts for a client.

bar sinister. Romantic novelists to the contrary, there is no such term or symbol ("charge") in heraldry so far as the English are concerned. It is a popular error for *baton* sinister, which on a coat of arms is an indication of illegitimacy. It is not found in French heraldry.

The Old French word was *baston;* its similarity to the word *bastard* may have suggested, to the English, the *baston* (later, *baton*) *sinister.* The rules and vocabulary of heraldry are almost impossibly complicated; put as simply as possible, the baton, or "bar" sinister was created when an "ordinary," or conventional figure commonly placed or "charged" upon a shield—in this case, the bar—was "couped," or cut off before it reached the edges of the shield.

baseball, invention of. That Abner Doubleday invented baseball at Cooperstown, New York, in 1839, is so firmly enshrined in the American consciousness as to amount to an article of faith, an attack upon which verges on heresy. Yet this is far from historical fact; it was, rather, simply arbitrarily decided by a commission appointed by the president of a sporting-goods company, A. G. Spalding, and composed of three persons, each president at various times of the National League (one of them, Morgan G. Bulkeley, was later to be United States senator from Connecticut) ; an ex-Big League player who was connected with another sporting-goods firm; another ex-player, also head of a sporting-goods firm; the president of the Amateur Athletic Union; and a (then) senator, Arthur Gorman of Maryland. None of them had any qualifications as researchers or historians.

The commission determined, in 1908, that baseball is an American game owing nothing to "foreign" origins—indeed, many are convinced that reaching such a conclusion was the reason for its creation. Yet there are many references to baseball prior to 1839, including one in, of all places, a Jane Austen novel *(Northanger Abbey,* written about 1798) , whose heroine prefers both cricket and "baseball" to books.

Whether or not the game Jane Austen and many others refer to as "baseball" long before Doubleday was actually or even nearly the same as the American game is, of course, the crucial point. That there certainly was an English game very nearly identical even to baseball as played today is obvious from a description of "Rounders" in *The Boy's Own Book,* first published in London in 1828.

"Rounders" was played on a diamond with a base at each corner; the batter stood beside the fourth corner and could run when he hit the ball over or across the diamond; any other hit was a foul. If the batter missed the ball three times, or if he batted a fly which was caught, he was out. Running around the bases after a successful hit counted one point just as is true today. The only important difference between Rounders (which was probably also referred to as "baseball" in Jane Austen country) and the game Abner Doubleday certainly played, whether or not he "invented" it, is that in Rounders a fielded grounder could be thrown at the batter, who was out if hit by it. Such a rule would, of course, be unthinkable today—one shudders to think of the consequences—in either Big or Little League play. But within the memory of many, and perhaps still true in areas, if any, where Little Leagues have yet to penetrate, such a "rule" sometimes applies in the sandlots, particularly when because of limited space or resources a softer ball than regulation is used.

Important as this difference is, Rounders and American baseball would seem to resemble each other much more than American football and the Rugby from which no one denies it sprang.

None of the above information, incidentally, is particularly esoteric; most standard reference works (the *Encyclopaedia Britannica,* for example) include it as a matter of course. A recent book (Harold Peterson's *The Man Who Invented Baseball,* 1973) sets out to prove that Alexander Cartwright is the "real" father of baseball. And he may well have been, though there are still other candidates.

An interesting footnote to all of this is that the commission's own report (its notes, affidavits, etc., were unfortunately lost in a fire) includes a statement by one Abner Graves, an old man who testified that Doubleday's game as Graves learned it in Cooperstown included the provision that the runner could be put out if a fielder hit him with the ball. As the *Britannica* points out, this would lead one to suspect that Doubleday could scarcely, as claimed, have laid out the baseball diamond in its present dimensions; any ball hard enough to be knocked out of today's infield would surely be too dangerous a missile if thrown directly at a runner.

The founding of the Baseball Hall of Fame at Cooperstown in 1939 has, of course, tended to establish and maintain the Doubleday story as gospel. Or—and the word does not seem too strong—the Doubleday myth.

bathing caps and swimming pools. The notion, shared by many motel managers, that requiring women to wear bathing caps in swimming pools is somehow a "sanitary" measure has nothing to do with the realities. The use of bathing caps was originally intended to protect the pool, not its occupants; hair is a notorious clogger of filters and pumps. The American Public Health Association, as a matter of fact, no longer recommends the use of caps in pools; not because hair is cleaner than ever, but because modern recirculation systems are not likely to be bothered by it.

In a sense, of course, anything that interferes with proper filtering and recirculation of the water in a swimming pool does have secondary implications of the sort that might be called "sanitary." But this is hardly the same as the common assumption that bathers must wear caps so as not to dirty up the water around them.

bathtub hoax, the great. To this day, many people believe some or all of the following: the first bathtub in America was contrived by a Mr. Thompson of Cincinnati in 1842, following its introduction into England in 1828; there was bitter argument among medical authorities as to the hazards of bathing; in 1845 Boston made bathing unlawful; in 1851 Millard Fillmore was the first American president to order a bathtub installed in the White House; in 1862 bathing was introduced into the army by General McClellan; and, in 1870, the first prison bathtub was set up in Philadelphia. Not infrequently newspaper columnists will reprint some or all of the above "facts" in all seriousness.

But it's a pack of lies, and deliberate lies at that. On December 28, 1917, H. L. Mencken published in the New York *Evening Mail* a piece called "A Neglected Anniversary." It told the story summarized briefly above; in Mencken's own words, the whole thing was "a tissue of absurdities, all of them deliberate and most of them obvious."

"The article," said Mencken, "was planned as a piece of spoofing to relieve the strain of war days, and I confess that I regarded it, when it came out, with considerable satisfaction." But according to Mencken, he was astonished to discover that almost everyone took it seriously. And, apparently, some still do.

bats, flight of, in darkness. It is often said that bats can fly in the dark because they have a sort of built-in radar system. Since their ability to avoid obstacles has been proved to involve the bats' reactions to the echoes of their high-pitched squeaks, they do not have a radar, but rather a sonar system. Radar makes use of electronic rather than sound waves.

battles. See entries under BENNINGTON, BUNKER HILL, and LITTLE BIGHORN.

bears hibernating. Bears are not true hibernators; they may become torpid during much of the cold weather, but their body temperature, heart rate, and breathing do not drop to the levels characteristic of true hibernators. Bears can, in fact, be awakened quite easily from their "hibernation," and become fully active in a few minutes.

beaver. There are many fallacies about beavers.

1. That they carry cargoes of mud on their tails while swimming. They do transport quantities of mud and sticks, but by holding the material in their forepaws against their bodies. Nothing would ride very long on a swimming beaver's tail—least of all mud. This incidentally debunks the notion that beavers use their tails as trowels in mixing up the mud "mortar" they use in building their houses and dams. Rather they use their mouths and forepaws in their construction projects, the tail for help in swimming and, some say, to sound an alarm by slapping it down on the water.

2. That a beaver can fell a tree wherever he wants to. In fact, wherever beaver have cut trees, one sees many that fell the wrong way and were abandoned. Occasionally beavers are killed by trees they themselves cut down.

3. That beavers cut small to medium-sized trees, usually poplar. They prefer poplar for food, but will cut down trees at least eighteen inches in diameter of hard woods like beech, cherry, and even oak.

4. That beavers construct their dams with a curvature that withstands the thrust of the head of water. Sometimes beaver dams do embody this curvature, but there are many dams that are zigzag and of various patterns. There seems to be no consistency of design.

5. That there are curative qualities in a beaver's testicles. For example, the Ojibway Indians treat an ax cut in the foot with split beaver testicles. There seems to be no factual basis for this

belief, which may have resulted from a confusion with castor, produced from the perineal glands, and used in medicine and perfumery. The *Oxford English Dictionary* cites this confusion in 1693, which suggests the possibility that the seventeenth- and eighteenth-century beaver trappers brought it with them to North America.

6. That with the decimation of the beaver in the nineteenth century, the beaver trade became nonexistent. It is true that the beaver was slaughtered indiscriminately during the height of the fashion: the fashion, by the way, being men's beaver hats, not women's fur coats. That the fashion is very old is indicated in the Prologue to Geoffrey Chaucer's *Canterbury Tales,* written in the 1380s; Chaucer describes a prosperous merchant as wearing "Upon his heed a Flaundryssh [Flemish] bevere hat." Beaver hats continued to be popular in Europe until the midnineteenth century, when the beaver supply waned and silk came to be popular instead. Furthermore, beaver hair is particularly well adapted to making felt; vast quantities of it were used for this purpose.

Hundreds of thousands of beavers were slain each year between 1800 and 1850. By 1900 the catch had fallen off drastically. Now the beaver has come back, and the annual take is as great as it was during the height of the fur trade in the nineteenth century.

Becket, Thomas à. How that "à" got between the proper English names of the famous murdered archbishop of Canterbury is something of a mystery. He was born in England, son of Gilbert Becket; and there appears to be no contemporary authority whatsoever for referring to him other than as Thomas Becket. But somehow—possibly because his parents' origins were French—that little letter got stuck into his name, as if he were not himself as English as—well, as the archbishop of Canterbury.

T. S. Eliot knew better. In *Murder in the Cathedral* the name is properly given: Thomas Becket.

bees collecting honey. Bees do not collect honey; they collect nectar, which is changed to honey within the bee's body.

beet sugar vs. cane sugar. Those who manufacture or import sugar from areas where it is made from cane (Hawaii, for example) have long benefited from the popular belief that it is sweeter than sugar made from beets. It isn't. Beet sugar and cane sugar, if completely refined, are absolutely identical chemically and equally sweet.

belfry. Though today commonly meaning a bell tower, *belfry* has no etymological connection with the word *bell*. It is, rather, a variation of *berfry* or *berfrie,* words which in earlier times meant merely a tower, sometimes a movable tower used in warfare.

bellwether. It's not spelled *bellweather,* nor does it have anything to do with weather. A bellwether is a castrated male sheep (wether) which leads a flock while wearing a bell. Thus, metaphorically, a bellwether is a leader, though the word is often taken as a synonym for *harbinger.*

Ben-Gurion, David. Israel's first prime minister is known as David Ben-Gurion. That was not his real name, however. He was born David Green. In Jerusalem he adopted the pen name "Ben-Gurion," which he thought had a good Old Testament sound. It means "son of a lion cub." In the time of the Romans, the original Ben-Gurion was one of the last defenders of Jerusalem.

Bennington, battle of. The battle of Bennington was not fought at Bennington. It was not even fought in Vermont. The battle took place near Walloomsac, in New York; and the Bennington Battlefield there is now a state park of 171 acres. The battle came by its name by reason of the fact that two detachments of German dragoons were defeated by Stark on August 16, 1777, while they were on their way to capture supplies which were stored at Bennington.

between the devil and the deep blue sea. Most people believe that this means "between Satan and the bottom of the ocean." However, devil in this case has nothing to do with the ruler of the kingdom of evil. The "devil" was the seam in a wooden ship's hull right down next to the waterline, and it was called that because it was "the devil to get at" when caulking. Hence the distance between the devil and the deep blue sea was a very small margin indeed.

Big Ben. Not the clock and not the tower, but the bell that strikes the hour. *That's* Big Ben. It weighs thirteen tons and is named for

Sir Benjamin Hall, who was commissioner of works when it was installed.

birds listening for worms. A robin worm-hunting on the lawn and cocking his head as though he were listening is merely trying to bring his eye into position so that he can see where the worm is. Birds' eyes (with a few exceptions) are set in the sides of their heads, and they see out to the sides rather than straight ahead; they do not have bifocal vision as human beings do.

birdsong. Poets—and most of the rest of us—have always assumed that birds sing for the pure joy of it . . . or possibly as a part of the mating process. It is now thought that birds sing as a means of staking out their territories and announcing their domains. Evidently it has not been determined why birds sing so much more at some seasons of the year than others, and at some times of the day rather than others. One naturalist observed a bird that seemed to be staking out more territory in the morning than the evening —perhaps because he was less tired and more ambitious in the morning.

birth control. Persons who imagine that the advocacy of birth control emerged in the twentieth century and was "invented" by Margaret Sanger would do well to examine the endeavors of Frances Wright (1795–1852). More than a hundred and fifty years ago she was lecturing on birth control, equal rights for women, emancipation of the slaves, distribution of property, etc. Curiously enough, her doctrines were not resented as much as her unfitting, unfemale conduct in appearing on the lecture program. In fact, her own behavior produced more effect than her ideas.

black-eyed peas. They are not peas at all, but beans.

Black Hills of South Dakota. Those who have never visited them tend to underestimate their altitudes because of that word *hills*. The highest of these "hills" is 7,242 feet above sea level; several other peaks exceed 6,000 feet. They're really mountains, not hills. Harney Peak is, in fact, higher than any elevation in the Appalachian or the Ozark ranges.

Black Hole of Calcutta. A good deal of skepticism has been expressed about the grim tale of the Black Hole. (On June 20, 1756,

146 British prisoners were said to have been confined, after a losing battle with the forces of the nabob Siraj Uddaula, on a blistering hot night in a room just eighteen by fourteen feet, whose only means of ventilation was two small air-holes and a door. The next morning only twenty-three were found alive.) Some—including, not surprisingly, several Indian authorities— have maintained that the whole tale was a hoax inspired by the British to justify their repressive policies in eighteenth-century India.

It is usually said by detractors that the only account of the episode was told by one John Holwell, and that his reputation for veracity was questionable. But this is not true; there were two other witnesses who testified to the story, though Holwell's account is the most elaborate. And, as Ashley Montagu and Edward Darling point out in an excellent review of the circumstances of the Black Hole (*The Ignorance of Certainty,* 1970), none of the twenty-three survivors named by Holwell denied the story.

blacks in the American colonies. Not all blacks in colonial America were impoverished slaves. Some were not only both free and wealthy; they even owned slaves of their own, imported by them from their own homeland, Africa. Some imported servants from England until 1670, when the Virginia Assembly made it illegal for blacks to own white servants. Those blacks who were free, or slaveholders themselves, had been emancipated by their owners: some as a reward for faithful service, others as a result of religious convictions somewhat tardily come to by their white owners.

Bligh, Captain. Whether or not he was the tyrannical brute portrayed by Charles Laughton and others, it is certainly not true that Bligh's career ended with the famous mutiny. He later rose to considerable heights: promoted to rear admiral (later vice-admiral), he became governor of New South Wales in 1805. There, however, he faced another mutiny. According to his descendant Maurice Bligh, this was instigated because corrupt officers were mistreating prisoners; according to the *Encyclopaedia Britannica,* Bligh's "oppressive behavior" caused the revolt. He died in London in 1817. At the time of the first mutiny, moreover, Bligh was not the middle-aged man Laughton played. Instead he was a thirty-three-year-old lieutenant (called captain because he commanded a ship).

blimp. Perhaps because they resemble miniature editions of such famous airships as the *Akron,* the *Macon,* and the *Hindenburg,* the Goodyear blimps are sometimes reported to be zeppelins. But they are true blimps; that is, they do not have an internal structure to help them keep their shape. If the gas goes, so does the familiar cigarlike form.

Nor does the word *blimp* derive, as often reported, from the military designation of a supposed World War I British airship, "Balloon, Type B, limp." According to "Aerial Ambassadors," a booklet published by Goodyear, which has built more lighter-than-air craft than any other company, at no time during, before, or after World War I did the British have an airship with a "limp" designation, nor any referred to as a "Type B."

The *Oxford English Dictionary* rather avoids the etymological issue. Its *Supplement* includes a quotation under *blimp* referring to the word as onomatopoeic (that is, imitating a sound, like "buzz" or "plop"), but without saying why. The Goodyear booklet offers a possible explanation: a Lieutenant Cunningham of the British Royal Navy Air Service, while on a tour of inspection in 1915, flipped his thumb at one of His Majesty's airships and "an odd noise echoed off the taut fabric." Cunningham smiled and "orally imitated the sound his thumb had drummed out of the airship bag: 'BLIMP!' Those nearby saw and heard this unusual interlude in the inspection, and its account quickly spread."

It's possible. But, like the origin of *jeep,* the origin of *blimp* will probably continue to be argued, to no one's complete satisfaction.

"blood and iron." This is not what Bismarck said. Here is what he did say, in a speech to the Budget Commission of the Prussian House of Delegates on September 30, 1862: "It is desirable and it is necessary that the condition of affairs in Germany and of her constitutional relations should be improved; but this cannot be accomplished by speeches and resolutions of a majority, but only by iron and blood [Eisen und Blut]."

The words, moreover, were not original with Bismarck. Quintilian, the Roman orator of the first century A.D., uses the phrase "sanguinem et ferrum," or, translated exactly, "blood and iron."

"blood, sweat and tears." Actually when Winston Churchill took office as prime minister he said, "blood, toil, tears, and sweat."

Bloody Mary. Because of the adjective *bloody,* which history has bestowed upon her, Mary Tudor is thought by many to have subjected her country to a veritable bath of blood.

She did instigate religious persecutions, after having restored papal authority in England following the Protestant reign of her half-brother, Edward VI. Her methods are hardly to be condoned, to be sure, but what most people do not realize is that the total number of persons thus killed did not exceed 280. Some of her victims, like Thomas Cranmer, were famous and powerful, but most of them—probably 250—were of the working classes.

Also, Mary Tudor is frequently—though inexplicably—confused with Mary Queen of Scots. Both were ardent Roman Catholics. Mary Tudor reigned for five years; Mary Queen of Scots did not reign at all.

bloomers. It is ironic that bloomers, the baggy nether garments that girls used to wear for athletics, were not even worn by the lady who is supposed to have invented them. Nor did the "inventor" invent them.

Amelia Jenks Bloomer (1818–1894) was prominent in the women's liberation movement of 125 years ago. She advocated women's rights, dress reform, and temperance, three ideas that do not necessarily go together. In 1849 Mrs. Bloomer founded a vigorous magazine called the *Lily,* devoted to women's rights and temperance. In these matters she had considerable competition from a rival reformer, Mrs. Elizabeth Smith Miller, and it was Mrs. Miller, not Mrs. Bloomer, who was pushing the idea of reform in women's dress. It was Mrs. Miller, not Mrs. Bloomer, who had originated a style of loose trousers, descending from beneath a short skirt and gathered at the ankles. Mrs. Bloomer, like a good reformer, adopted the costume, wore it amid great ridicule, and sought to make it popular. Curious crowds came to see her, if not to listen to her, on the lecture platform.

The trousers she wore were the slacks of the midnineteenth century: not chic by today's standards, but far more practical and better looking than many of the things women wore then. Certainly they looked much better than the gymnasium variety of bloomers, to which poor Mrs. Bloomer unwittingly lent her name.

boiling water. Many cooks turn up the heat to make something "boil faster." Water boils at 212 degrees Fahrenheit (at sea level) and so long as it is in an open receptacle, its temperature cannot be raised any higher. Therefore furiously boiling water does not cook an egg, let's say, any faster than mildly boiling water. Proof of this is the fact that a three-minute egg (at sea level) is a three-minute egg no matter how hard it boils.

As neophytes in the mountains are forever learning, however, a "3-minute egg" takes a good deal longer at high altitudes, because water boils at a lower temperature there.

Of course a hot flame will cause more steam to form and pass off than a moderate flame, even though the temperature of the liquid remains the same. This has a bearing in the making of maple syrup, jelly, etc., where the purpose is evaporation.

booze, origin of word. Sometimes repeated (in the *Wall Street Journal* for September 13, 1973, for example) is the story that the word *booze* comes from one E. C. Booz of Philadelphia, who put his name on the first "booze" bottle. Not so; *booze* (which to an Englishman, by the way, means ale or beer rather than hard liquor) is a very old word going back at least to the fourteenth century and used both as noun and verb (meaning "to drink heavily or carouse") long before Mr. Booz arrived on the scene. The origin of *booze* is not entirely clear; it may be cognate with an old Dutch word, *buizen,* "to drink to excess." In any case, it has certainly been in the English language for many centuries.

Borgia, Lucrezia. "It has pleased Our Lord God at this hour to take to Himself the soul of Her Grace the Duchess, my most beloved consort . . . . I cannot write without tears, so heavy a burden is it to find myself deprived of so sweet and dear a companion, for such she was to me, both through her excellent conduct and that tender love there was between us . . . . And I would rather fain have my friends lament with me than offer me consolation . . . ."

Yes, that's Lucrezia. The words were written by her husband, Duke Alfonso, shortly after her death. If they seem inconsistent with a reputation so monstrous that "Borgia" is at once a proper and a common noun, then it is undoubtedly because Lucrezia Borgia is a much-maligned lady. More pawn than principal, and far from the murdering type, Lucrezia's reputation probably belongs not to her, but to Caterina Sforza, who really was a terror.

Boxing Day. As many people know, Boxing Day has nothing to do with pugilistics. What most people do not know is that it is not, by definition, the first day after Christmas, but rather the first *week-day* after Christmas. And for obvious reasons: on Boxing Day, which is a British legal holiday, one presents Christmas boxes to the postman and others.

brain trust. This term was not originated by FDR, as many suppose. James Kieran, writing in *The New York Times,* used the expression *brains trust* to describe Roosevelt's masterminds. FDR modified it to *brain trust* and thereafter used it himself.

branding. The branding of cattle did not originate in the West during the nineteenth century. In 1644, legislation was enacted by Connecticut providing that all cattle and swine be earmarked or branded and that the marks be registered. The West adopted this custom.

brandy. The number of stars on the label of a bottle of brandy has absolutely no significance whatever in terms of age, taste, quality, alcoholic content, or any other characteristic. The stars are decoration, pure and simple, in spite of the widely held belief that each star represents five years, or that "five-star" is the best brandy of all. Indeed, as one prominent importer of brandy has suggested, one might as well pick up his own stars at a variety store and paste them anywhere he wishes on any bottles of brandy he happens to have around.

The term "Napoleon brandy" has no special significance as a descriptive phrase, although many manufacturers would like you to think otherwise. Like the stars on the neck of the bottle, the terms "Napoleon" can be used by anyone who wants to add an air of class to his spirits. The same is true of the initials V.S.O.P., usually defined as standing for "Very Superior Old Pale."

The identification of brandy as cognac does mean something —if it's from France. Cognac must come from the area around the town called Cognac, in the Charente district.

brazilwood. Not named after the country; conversely, Brazil derives its name from the reddish tree the Spanish and Portuguese call *brasil.*

Breed's Hill. See BUNKER HILL, BATTLE OF.

"Brevity is the soul of wit." When Polonius says this in Shakespeare's *Hamlet* (act 2, sc. 2, line 90), he is not referring in any way to wit as we now define the word. *Wit* derives from the Old English verb *witan,* "to know." Not until long after Shakespeare's time did it acquire its present meaning; and its older meaning still survives in such expressions as "at wit's end."

Wit meant "wisdom" to Shakespeare and his audience. Polonius is thus saying that brevity is the soul of wisdom, that the wise know how to put things succinctly—a feat, by the way, far beyond the bumbling redundancy so characteristic of Polonius. His remark is a nice instance of dramatic irony.

briar pipes. Briar pipes are not made from the brier plant that we know (prickly stem, etc.) . The "briar" in pipes is really *bruyère* or in dialect *brière,* meaning "heath." It is grown in the south of France specifically for use in making pipes.

Britain and England. A surprising number of Americans use these words interchangeably. This is incorrect and frequently offensive to the British themselves.

England is one of the three countries that share the island of Great Britain. It is the southernmost and largest of the three.

Great Britain (frequently just called Britain) is the largest of the British Isles. It comprises England, Scotland, and Wales.

The British Isles comprise Great Britain, Ireland, the Isle of Man, and the Channel Islands.

The United Kingdom is the *kingdom* of the British Isles, and comprises Great Britain, Northern Ireland, the Isle of Man, and the Channel Islands. Officially the name is United Kingdom of Great Britain and Northern Ireland. (Between 1801 and 1922 it included all of Ireland.)

Thus English pertains to England and its people. British, on the other hand, pertains to Great Britain, and by extension to the United Kingdom and the British Commonwealth of Nations.

It is easy for Americans to forget that the English were relative latecomers to England. Long before the Angles, Saxons, and Jutes invaded what is now England in the fifth century, the Celts and the Picts (surviving as Scots, Welsh, and Irish) had lived there under Roman rule. Their languages (Gaelic, Welsh, Manx, etc.) were totally different from those of either their Roman or Germanic conquerors. Their separate cultural identities and their pride in them are still very real. Many a Scot has no hesitation in pointing out that England's greatest deeds were performed by Scots. See also SCOTCH, SCOTS.

British constitution. There is no such document as the British constitution. What might be regarded as a constitution for Great Britain is a collection of written documents and unwritten customs. The written sources include the Magna Carta, the Bill of Rights, the Reform Bill of 1832, etc. The unwritten sources of procedure include customs, precedents, and—not least—etiquette.

British Royal Family, predominantly German. It is sometimes remarked that in recent times the British Royal Family has been more German than British, but it is not always recognized to what degree this is true, and how long it has been true. From the death of Anne in 1714, the last of the Stuarts, to the crowning of George V British blood steadily diminished in Britain's reigning monarchs:

Monarch	Proportion of non-German blood
George I	$\frac{1}{4}$
George II	$\frac{1}{8}$
George III	$\frac{1}{32}$
George IV	$\frac{1}{64}$
William IV	$\frac{1}{64}$
Queen Victoria	$\frac{1}{128}$
Edward VII	$\frac{1}{256}$

George V married Mary, whose grandmother was Hungarian, with the result that George VI had presumably more than one quarter non-German blood. He married "all British," so that Elizabeth II (1952) is British indeed.

buffalo, American. It is sometimes pointed out that what Americans call a buffalo should more properly be called a bison, with the term *buffalo* reserved for the types found in Africa and Asia. Actually both the water buffalo and the American buffalo belong to the genus *bison; buffalo* applies with equal accuracy to either species, the qualifying adjectives serving to identify them. Originally, in fact, *buffalo* comes from the Greek word for an African gazelle.

Build a better mousetrap, and the world will beat a path to your door. Probably the most-quoted of remarks attributed to Emerson, this one does not appear in any of his published writings. In fact, he does not mention mousetraps at all in the 1855 selection from his *Journal,* which seems to have started it all:

> I trust a good deal to common fame, as we all must. If a man has good corn, or wood, or boards, or pigs, to sell, or can make better chairs or knives, crucibles or church organs, than anybody else, you will find a broad hard-beaten road to his house, though it be in the woods.

The common version, or at least one that comes closer to it, first appeared in a book published by Sarah Yule and Mary Keene in 1889, some seven years after Emerson's death. Mrs. Yule, apparently relying on memory, reported that Emerson said the following in an address:

> If a man can write a better book, preach a better sermon, or make a better mouse-trap than his neighbor, though he builds his house in the woods the world will make a beaten path to his door.

Note that the only words we know to have been actually Emerson's really do not mean quite what the popular expression is taken to signify. By "common fame" Emerson obviously intends something like "local reputation"; he was too wise to assume that "the world" would invariably seek out the best and most deserving, nor did he write any such thing.

bulldog. Not so named because of its appearance, but because bulldogs were especially bred during medieval times in England for the cruel sport of bullbaiting, which continued to be popular until the eighteenth century. (The practice was not actually outlawed until 1835, by act of Parliament.) In bullbaiting, the dogs were trained to fasten upon the bull's snout and hang on. Thus the particular attention paid to breeding animals with particularly strong neck and jaw muscles.

bulls seeing red. Many investigations have established that bulls cannot distinguish one color from another. The brightness of a flag or an object has a bearing, true; and if the flag or object is in motion, a bull is even more likely to take note. But the color is immaterial.

Bunker Hill, battle of. In the first place, the battle was not fought on Bunker (or Bunker's) Hill. The original battle report contained the error, never corrected. It was nearby Breed's Hill the Americans occupied when they heard that the British, who held Boston, were about to do so themselves. (Why they had not done so earlier is something of a mystery.) Moreover, the American revolutionary troops did not win the battle; on the contrary, they were driven off Breed's Hill with the loss of over 400 killed and wounded plus 30 taken prisoner. Estimates of the number of American troops engaged vary from some 1,500 to over 3,000; in either case, the casualty rate would have to be considered high. The British, however, lost almost half their men—about 1,000 of some 2,200 involved, an appalling number. Their victory was nothing if not Pyrrhic.

Most important, however, was that "Bunker Hill" became, for Americans, the sort of symbol that unites an opposition; it may have been a tactical loss, but its importance as a moral victory can scarcely be overemphasized. For the first time the colonials realized that regular British troops could be beaten—if not this time, then next time. Especially could they be beaten if they continued to display the monumental stupidity that cost them so dearly on the slopes of Breed's Hill. For the British troops, under Gage, three times advanced up a difficult slope straight into the muzzles of the colonists' guns—though it would have been easy to cut the Americans off from behind. Twice the Americans waited, with admirable discipline and restraint, until the British troops were in close range, then fired with devastating effect. The third British charge, which ended with bayonets, was successful.

A grimly interesting sidelight on the affair is that during the battle, residents of nearby Charlestown fired on the British. In reprisal, General Gage almost totally destroyed the village.

buoyancy of deep water. It is not true that the buoyancy of water increases with its depth. Shallow water and deep water are the same in terms of buoyancy.

buzzards. Buzzards in America have been accused of spreading disease, notably hog cholera. Not only has it been proven that they do not, but if anything they help by eating the carrion where disease could fester. The rumor was perhaps spread by people who like to shoot them for the fun of it.

BVD. One of the best-kept secrets for many years is just what "BVD" stands for; even H. L. Mencken was unable to pry loose from the corporate structure permission to print, in *The American Language,* the origin of this term.

It used to be said the initials stood for "Baby's Ventilated Diapers," or sometimes "Boys' Ventilated Drawers"—perhaps partly in jest. The truth is prosaic enough. "BVD" stands for the organizers of the company, three men named Bradley, Voorhies, and Day.

Byron, Lord—death of. The romantic notion that Lord Byron died while leading his troops in the battle for Greece's independence from Turkey is just that—a romantic notion. He was in Greece, yes; and he had hired some mercenaries to further the Greek cause. But the sad, even ugly, truth is that following a long walk and a horseback ride while already feverish, he was literally bled to death by his doctors. And much against his own better judgment. At one point he said, "Drawing blood from a nervous patient is like loosening the chords of a musical instrument, the tones of which are already defective for want of sufficient tension." No wonder that he referred to his doctors as "A d——d bunch of butchers."

As he grew worse, however, and steadily weaker, he finally succumbed to the "tearful protestations" of one of his physicians, a Dr. Bruno. Before it was all over, the various doctors in attendance were to remove *more than four pounds* of his blood—and to cap it all by "purging" him with a devilish concoction made up of senna, three ounces of Epsom salts, and three ounces of castor oil. The last blood to be drawn was taken while Byron was virtually unconscious and certainly powerless; leeches were applied to his temples, and left there all night. He was dead within twenty-four hours.

Another romantic notion is that Byron was basically an adherent to the Romantic school, like Wordsworth, Shelley, Keats, and

Coleridge. Byron's life was "romantic" enough, and certainly he wrote some remarkable lyrics. But his cast of mind was essentially eighteenth-century neoclassical.

C

cabal. The word has been considered an acrostic comprising the initials of Charles II's advisers:

Clifford
Ashley
Buckingham
Arlington
Lauderdale

Actually it was in use long before, having descended from the Hebrew.

cabinet (United States government). There is no provision in the United States Constitution for a cabinet; it has simply developed, over the years, as an unwritten adjunct to the American system of government. The accusation made against various presidents, particularly Andrew Jackson, that they somehow acted reprehensibly in consulting with friends and advisers in secret—the term *Kitchen Cabinet* is sometimes heard—has no real basis. Presidents of the United States are, and no doubt should be, free to consult with as few or as many advisers as they deem necessary. Certainly nothing in the Constitution either forbids or, as said, specifically sanctions, the giving of advice to the president either publicly or privately, by individuals or groups.

It is often said that the British government differs from the United States' in that the British often operate under an unwritten body of tradition which in practice has the force of statutory law. The acceptance of the cabinet as an integral part of the American system of government is an illustration that there is not so much difference between the two systems as Americans tend to believe.

Caesar, Julius—and his assassination. Almost everybody, including William Shakespeare, seems to think that Julius Caesar was killed in the Capitol. He wasn't. He was done in near the statue of Pompey, which was in the Senate House. The Capitol and Senate House were in quite different places in ancient Rome.

"C" after the clef sign in written music. A great many people, including some performers of music, think that the C after the clef sign stands for "common," that is 4/4 time. This is not correct.

In the early days of music the time most often used was "perfect" time, having three beats to the bar. In this respect it was considered analogous to the three aspects of the Trinity. Therefore a complete circle, suggesting the completeness and perfection of the Trinity, was used as its sign. When 4/4 time was employed, it was considered "imperfect" and an incomplete circle was used. So it is an incomplete circle rather than the letter C.

Cain, mark of. The mark of Cain was not designed to identify him as a murderer. Quite the contrary; a close reading of Gen. 4:13–15 reveals that it was placed upon Cain to protect him from those who, in his words, "shall slay me."

Calvin, John. So thoroughly Anglo-American does the name John Calvin sound that it is easy to forget that he was thoroughly French by birth, the son of Gerard Cauvin (spelled variously) and Jeanne le Franc, and named not John but Jean. His birthplace was Noyon, in Picardy; he moved to Switzerland when he was nearly thirty.

camel. It is well known that camels can go for long periods without drinking and then take in enormous quantities of water at one time; in fact, camels can refrain from drinking for as long as

eight days in summer and eight *weeks* in winter. After such ab-
stinence they have been known to imbibe as much as a hundred
quarts in ten minutes.

These facts have led many to believe that camels have special
storage areas in their bodies, like water tanks. Sometimes it is
thought that camels have a separate water-carrying stomach, or
that water is stored in the hump. These ideas are quite false.

There are no separate water tanks or stomachs, and it is fat the
hump contains, to be converted into energy when needed. The
water that the camel drinks enters its system; and it is its remarkable system that enables the camel to get along with so little.

Human beings perspire profusely in the heat because they must
keep body temperature near the "normal" 98.6 degrees by evapo-
rating water from the surface of the skin. The camel, on the other
hand, sweats very little; its body temperature can go all the way
up to 105 before it begins to sweat at all. Also the camel is very
sparing in its urination. It is believed that water which in other
animals would be passed off by the body is, by the camel, used
over again: in effect recycled, as if the camel had an almost closed
air conditioning system. In spite of the old joke that the camel
looks as if it had been made by a committee, it is in fact very
efficiently designed in terms of its environment.

camel's hair brushes. They are never made of camel's hair, but
usually from the tails of squirrels.

Fine fabrics are woven from the fleece of the two-humped or
Bactrian camel. The camels are not shorn but obligingly drop
their hair in clumps, which are retrieved by the caretakers. The
hair of the one-humped Arabian camel, or dromedary, is not
used for fabrics as it is too short.

Camille. In America, Alexandre Dumas's (fils) tragedy *La Dame
aux Camélias* is entitled *Camille* and its heroine is Camille. However, the name Camille does not appear anywhere in Dumas's
original story. The heroine is Marguerite Gauthier ("the Camellia
Lady") , not Camille. When the play was translated into English,
the translator simply changed the lady's name—and the play's
title—to Camille, probably thinking there was some connection
between that name and the name of the flower.

From the standpoint of derivation this conceit is incongruous. The French name *Camille* is derived from a Latin word meaning "attendant at a sacrifice." The word *camellia*, on the other hand, is derived from the name of a Jesuit botanist-priest, Kamel, who brought the lovely flower from the East.

Canute. King Canute (995?–1035) has the reputation of being an arrogant man who had his chair carried to the seaside and ordered the waves of the advancing tide to recede. This is just the opposite of what the story was intended to demonstrate. He got tired of the flattery of his courtiers, who even went so far as to tell him that he could halt the very waves of the sea. He took them down to the waterfront to show them this was not true, and to show them how foolish they were.

Our only source is the legend related by Henry of Huntington, (died 1155) who lived a hundred years later. It is probably partly oral tradition and partly the invention of the author.

Canute was a well-intentioned king, who sought peace for England and cooperation with the Holy Roman Empire.

capital punishment as deterrent. There are countless numbers of people who believe that the death penalty acts as a deterrent to crime.

The evidence of many studies proves otherwise. For example, in 1968 the United Nations published *Capital Punishment,* which comes to the conclusion that "Examination of the number of murders before and after the abolition of the death penalty does not support the theory that capital punishment has a unique deterrent effect. Nowhere has abolition been followed by an otherwise inexplicable rise in the murder rate; nowhere has reintroduction been followed by an otherwise inexplicable decline in the murder rate."

caste system. The caste system is inevitably associated with India, but actually it was not derived there. It was brought into India by the ARYANS when they invaded the Punjab and the valley of the Indus about 3,700 years ago.

catgut. Catgut is not made from the intestines of cats, and never has been; catgut comes from the intestines of sheep.

cats' eyes in the dark. No animal has eyes that can actually glow in the sense that a firefly can glow—that is, eyes that create rather than reflect light. There has to be some light, at least, to be reflected; if not, neither a cat's eyes, nor any other creature's, will be visible.

Cavaliers as "aristocrats." By derivation the cavalier is a horseman, especially an armed horseman, even a knight. By implication, therefore, he is aristocratic, and sometimes chivalrous.

Hence there is a popular myth that Virginia was "enriched" by an influx of English aristocracy, following the defeat of King Charles I by the Puritans, who established in our South an aristocratic society patterned after that which had supported the Crown in England.

The fact is, however, that *Cavalier* (with a capital *C*) was merely a *political* term, and the Cavaliers who went to Virginia were middle class—or lower. As Macaulay explained, "During some years they were designated as *Cavaliers* and Roundheads. They were subsequently called Tories and Whigs."

The development of the southern aristocracy and the cult of chivalry cannot be attributed to these emigrés.

"caviar(e) to the general." "I heard thee speak me a speech once," says Hamlet to one of the players (actors), "but it was never acted . . . for the play, I remember, pleased not the millions; 'twas caviare to the general" (act 2, sc. 2, lines 414ff). Those who know only the famous last phrase are likely to misunderstand what "general" meant to Shakespeare's audience. It means "general public." The remark is, in fact, somewhat on the intellectually snobbish side.

CCCP. None of the *C*'s stands for "Communist." *CCCP* is simply the Russian abbreviation for what is rendered in English as USSR, or Union of Soviet Socialist Republics. (In the Russian alphabet, *C* is equivalent to the English *S* and *P* to the English *R*.) Thus, put into the English alphabet, the phrase is Soîuz Sovetskiĥh Sotsialisticheskiĥh Respublik.

cellophane. Cellophane was neither invented nor given its name by anyone connected with du Pont, nor did it originate in the

United States. And it has been around for much longer than most people realize. Its origins go back to the turn of the century, when various British chemists developed a process for making a film from viscose, which is derived from cellulose. In 1911 a Swiss named Brandenberger devised machinery to make mass production of cellophane feasible—and also coined the name by combining elements of *cellulose* and *diaphane,* French for "transparent." Du Pont later bought United States rights to manufacture and sell the product.

Unlike Coca-Cola, Kodak, and Frigidaire, among many other examples, cellophane is not, in the United States, a registered trademark: the result of a court decision years ago. Thus, it need not be capitalized nor identified as a proprietary term; it is merely a common noun in the United States although this is not true in other countries.

century plant, frequency of blooms. Though they usually bloom infrequently, no members of the genus *agave,* the best known of which is *Agave americana,* or century plant, take as long as a hundred years. Nor does the plant die after blooming; the leaves do, but the roots remain alive to produce new growth. The actual time it takes for various members of the *agave* family to bloom varies considerably—from annually to as much as fifty years under certain circumstances. But none takes as long as a century.

chamois. Fortunately, the cleaning leather called chamois does not come from the rare Alpine animal of the same name. It's almost always sheepskin, especially treated.

chariots in ancient wars. The Romans used chariots for sport and transportation. They did not use chariots in war. The Britons sometimes did, and some ancient bas-reliefs show Assyrians and Egyptians driving what are apparently chariots in battle. But not the Romans.

Cheshire Cheese tavern frequented by Dr. Samuel Johnson. Although other taverns are mentioned by name in James Boswell's famous *Life of Samuel Johnson,* there nowhere appears the Cheshire Cheese in Fleet Street—or any other street. If the redoubtable Dr. Johnson did indeed frequent the Cheshire Cheese, as London visitors are often told, it must then have gone by some other name. Perhaps it was then called the Mitre tavern, which is identified by Boswell as Johnson's "place of frequent resort" (*Life,* Vol. 1, p. 399, as edited by Hill and published in 1934).

chief justice of the Supreme Court. There isn't any such person. There is a chief justice of the United States, yes. He is one of the nine members of the Supreme Court, appointed like all the others by the president with the advice and consent of the Senate. The chief justice is not elected by his peers, and though he does get paid a little more—not much—he has just one vote, the same as each of the eight associate justices.

children of Adam and Eve. Many people, if asked how many children Adam and Eve had, would answer, in some surprise, "Why, two, of course—Cain and Abel." Actually Adam and Eve also had Seth, and Adam (Eve isn't mentioned) sired an additional unspecified number of "sons and daughters."

Chinese grammar. Chinese may be a difficult language for Occidentals, but that is not because it has a complicated grammar. Indeed, Chinese has no grammar at all, as the term is used in discussions of Western languages. Chinese characters are indivisible units each standing for a sound and a root idea. Since they cannot be inflected, there is no means of indicating gender, number, case, voice, mood, tense, or person.

Counter to popular belief, the longer a language has been in use the simpler its grammar—not the reverse. Modern English is much simpler grammatically than Old English. The newest important literary language—that is, written as well as spoken, not just the latter—is Finnish, whose literary roots go back only to about the middle of the nineteenth century. Its grammar is very complicated; there are some fifteen cases, for example.

What makes Chinese difficult to learn is not the grammar, but the great number of characters/words that must be mastered. As in English, the simplification of grammar has been accompanied by a proliferation of vocabulary and/or idiom; a simple grammar does not necessarily make a language easy to learn.

It is often said that native speakers of English have special trouble with Chinese because it puts considerable dependence upon pitch, or tone, for meaning, and that this is not the case in English. But this is not entirely true; speakers of English utilize pitch to determine meaning more often than is, perhaps, realized. Compare the declaration "You are going" with the same words put as a question.

chop suey. Chop suey is not a native Chinese dish. It is said to have originated in a California mining camp when the Chinese cook simply threw together what he had left over and called it "chop suey," a phonetic transliteration of the Mandarin *tsa sui,* which means something like "various things." In other words, chop suey was simply a sort of Oriental mulligan stew. In any case, it did not originate in China.

Christ. Strictly speaking, not a name but a title derived from a Hebrew word for "the anointed one," though most people tend to think of "Jesus Christ" as a first and last name. His name, however, is Jesus; a correct rendition on historical-etymological grounds would be Jesus the Christ.

Christmas. In the minds of most American Christians, inextricably connected with the birth of Christ and its annual celebration are December 25, the Star of Bethlehem, Christmas trees, the Yule Log, mistletoe, and Santa Claus with his eight tiny reindeer. Actually, of course, the Christmas story is a blend of tales and beliefs generated in various countries from ancient times, many of them having nothing to do with Christ or Christianity.

The date itself is purely conjectural; there is no historical evidence that Christ was born on December 25. The date was not chosen until hundreds of years after the beginning of the Christian era. Meanwhile various dates had been used; finally, December 25 was officially adopted, in 354, by Bishop Liberius of Rome. It is not, however, universal even now among all Christians. Eastern Orthodox church members as well as those of the Ukrainian Catholic church, among others, still follow the old Julian calendar, established by Caesar in 45 B.C., rather than the Gregorian calendar instituted by Pope Gregory in the sixteenth century. For them, Christmas is thirteen days later.

It has been pointed out that December 25 comes during the rainy season in the Holy Land, at which time the shepherds would hardly be out in their pastures. Whether or not this conjecture is valid, it is interesting to note that the Hayden Planetarium in New York has ascertained, by re-creating the heavens as they were late in the year of Christ's birth (actually 6 B.C.), that there was a remarkable celestial phenomenon: three stars in proximity creating a spectacularly bright beacon in the sky. This might, of course, have been responsible for stories of the Star of Bethlehem.

It is quite possible that December 25 was picked because it is close to the winter solstice, the time when at last the days are becoming longer. Pagans of northern Europe had long celebrated it with numerous ceremonies of their own. So this festival day, coinciding with their own festival season, must certainly have smoothed the transition from paganism.

Pagan ceremonies included the Yule, from an old Norse word for a twelve-day celebration; the Christmas tree (trees were worshiped by primitive Scandinavians) ; mistletoe, prominent in the traditions of the Druids and the lore of northern Europe; the wassail bowl of Scandinavia; the holly. The Twelve Days of Christmas are a carry-over from Roman times: festivities of the Saturnalia were followed by twelve holy days which ended on January 1. The Christmas tree did not come into the English tradition until Queen Victoria married Prince Albert, who brought this now indispensable feature from his native Germany about 1840.

Many children will be relieved to learn that there really was a Santa Claus. The actual person was quite different from the idol of American youngsters. He was Saint Nicholas, a very kind bishop who became patron saint of schoolboys in the Middle Ages. (The feast day in his honor was December 6.) In the Netherlands he is said to bring gifts to good children and switches to bad children. When the Dutch emigrated to America, they brought this tradition with them. In 1809 Washington Irving, under the pen name Diedrich Knickerbocker, embroidered upon it somewhat in *A History of New York,* wherein Saint Nicholas, a jolly personage smoking a Dutch pipe, skimmed over the treetops in a wagon and dropped presents down the chimneys.

A few years later, in 1822, Clement C. Moore wrote a poem for his own children which is most often called "The Night Before Christmas." Its correct title, however, is "A Visit from St. Nicholas." Many are unaware that Moore never once uses the term

Santa Claus, although the reindeer are there, a part of the legend undoubtedly developed in America, probably by Scandinavians in the United States. At last, in 1863, Thomas Nast, the cartoonist, drew a picture of Santa Claus pretty much as he is known today. Also by this time the name Santa Claus, the result of English-speaking children's attempts to pronounce the Dutch San Nicolaas, had become established.

churches out of line to correspond with the drooping head of Christ. In a few European churches the portion east of the transept is on a slightly different axis from that of the nave. That is, the chancel is *crooked* with respect to the nave. Guides love to explain that this was done to represent the head of Christ on the cross, drooping to one side as depicted in paintings. Actually there is no evidence whatsoever of such intention. Usually such a deviation came about because the church—like so many ancient Christian edifices—was built and rebuilt over the centuries. The reason was structural rather than symbolic. Furthermore, the church is intended to represent the cross as a Christian symbol, not the arrangement of the body of Christ on the cross.

Cinderella's slipper. Only in versions of the Cinderella story deriving from French tradition do her famous slippers turn out to be glass; almost certainly in the original versions of the Cinderella tales as told and retold orally they were made out of a much likelier, more comfortable material: fur. *Vair* is an old French word for "ermine." "Glass," in French, is *verre:* same pronunciation but of course an entirely different word. Many believe that when Charles Perrault wrote down the Cinderella story in 1697, he mistook *vair* for *verre.*

There are hundreds of versions, in many languages throughout the world, of the Cinderella story. (In one of them Cinderella and her governess cooked up a plot to kill the grandmother.) In all but those that can be traced to French sources the slippers are made out of something else—never glass. It does seem more than likely that the *vair/verre* confusion put Cinderella into those glass slippers.

circumcision. It is not, as widely believed, an operation exclusive to males. Both the penis and the clitoris have a prepuce, or foreskin; circumcision can, thus, be performed on females. Among other common misconceptions involving circumcision is that it may prevent cancer of the cervix or of the penis or prostate gland; that it prevents venereal disease; that it increases the pleasure of sexual performance; and that it is a generally approved surgical procedure. Indeed, the American Academy of Pediatrics Committee on the Fetus and Newborn said in 1971 that there are no valid medical indications for circumcision. (Neither this, nor other medical groups, has any quarrel with religious ritual circumcision.)

Among the Jews at least, the idea of circumcision was associated with purification and as a sign of a covenant between God and them.

circumstantial evidence. Few legal concepts are more widely misunderstood than "circumstantial evidence," which is commonly taken to mean suspicion without proof. As a matter of fact, all evidence except that given by witnesses is "circumstantial." Without it, no legal system could possibly work. And, as a matter of fact, erroneous convictions are much more likely to result from false testimony than from false inferences, as Bergen Evans reminds us in *The Natural History of Nonsense* (1968).

There can really be only two kinds of evidence: that resulting from personal observation either by witnesses or victims, and circumstantial. That witnesses are only too frequently unreliable has been established so often that it belabors the point to emphasize it. And, since in the Anglo-American legal tradition the accused is considered innocent until proved guilty, in the absence of a confession a conviction must be secured either on the basis of testimony—as said, only too often unreliable—or circumstances. The murderer who is caught with smoking gun or bloody knife bending over a dying victim *must* be convicted on the basis of circumstantial evidence.

As a matter of fact, even confession is not enough for conviction; there has to be something to confess *to* (that is, a "circumstance") ; and as only too often reported in the newspapers, any major murder case is likely to inspire a rash of false confessions by the unstable or publicity-seeking—or both. The evidence provided by circumstances remains, on the whole, the best of all, the most useful, and the least likely to result in an unjust conviction.

classical sculpture, white and pure. Much has been written about the chaste and pure whiteness of Greek statues. Actually the Greeks loved to paint their statues colorfully, and many were not white at all to the contemporary beholders, but only to us. They even covered some with gold and ivory—which no doubt disappeared long before painted colors.

"Cleanliness is next to godliness." This phrase is not from the Bible. John Wesley, who, together with his brother Charles, founded Methodism, said it in one of his sermons. Wesley's precise words, moreover, were "Cleanliness is indeed next to godliness." Wesley put the words in quotation marks, perhaps as an admission that he was borrowing, with some changes, a phrase from one of the Hebrew fathers.

Cleopatra. There were actually seven women who reigned under the name "Cleopatra," although only one—the seventh and last —made a considerable dent in history. And none of them was Egyptian; the Ptolemys who ruled Egypt for some 250 years were Macedonians. The first Ptolemy was son of Lagos, a Macedonian general under Alexander the Great who seized Egypt and installed himself as king.

Nor was Alexandria really an Egyptian city, except for its location; its architecture, customs, language, dress, and art were Greek. It is likely that none of the Ptolemys, including the most famous of the Cleopatras, ever wore Egyptian costume except, perhaps, on rare ceremonial occasions. Ironically, thus, neither the person nor the city most often associated with ancient Egypt was actually Egyptian at all.

Cleopatra's Needles. These two famous obelisks, one in London and the other in New York City, were not commissioned by, nor made during the reign of, any of the Cleopatras including the most famous (or notorious). Made about 1500 B.C., long before any of the Ptolemys had reached Egypt, they were brought from Heliopolis to Alexandria in 12 B.C. by the Roman emperor Augustus. Both obelisks were removed to their respective present locations in the nineteenth century.

clocks and watches, turning their hands back. It is often said that to turn the hands of a clock or watch backward will cause harm to the works. That is true only of *some* old timepieces. Turning back the hands of a modern clock or watch does not harm it. In the case of alarm clocks and striking clocks, of course, provision must be made for the setting.

Coca-Cola. There is a wonderful old story about the secret message that enabled Coca-Cola to grow from a tiny little business to a multimillion-dollar beverage corporation. For many years, of course, Coca-Cola was sold to the soda fountain as a syrup and the counterman squirted some syrup into a glass, then added plain soda water, handed you the mixture, and put your nickel in the cash register. It seems that an unknown person went to the Coca-Cola Company and told those in charge that for $50,000 he would give them a secret that would make the company prosper beyond their dreams. The secret was simply, "Bottle it." The only trouble is that the story is not true.

In 1886 an obscure druggist named Pemberton was selling drinks made out of a syrup he had concocted. That year he spent $73.96 in advertising; it brought him about $160.00 in sales. Around 1890 an Asa Candler, pharmacist, of Atlanta acquired the business from Pemberton's heirs. Soon afterward two men came to him with a proposition. They were Benjamin F. Thomas and Joseph Whitehead of Chattanooga. They tried to persuade Mr. Candler to go into the business of bottling Coca-Cola. He did not think much of the idea. Finally, however, he gave in, and a contract was signed on July 1, 1899, whereby Thomas and Whitehead would set up bottling plants. An advertising agency was engaged and it produced this line among others: "Sold at all founts and carbonated in bottles, 5¢."

coffee and inebriation. Often forced upon the intoxicated on the premise that it aids in sobering up, coffee is of help only in that it takes some time to drink it. And time is the only remedy for too much alcohol in the bloodstream. What is sometimes called, particularly by those who must deal with drunken drivers, "the great coffee myth" is actually a dangerous bit of folklore; many a driver with a half-dozen cups of coffee forced upon him has gone out to die on the highway.

The human body burns alcohol at the rate of about one-half ounce an hour. And there is no way to speed up this rate.

coffee beans. Actually, they are the pits of a red, cherrylike fruit rather than beans.

Colossus of Rhodes. Counter to what almost everyone thinks, this wonder of the ancient world did not stand astride the harbor of Rhodes, a belief which is a medieval invention. The statue, done by Chares, was of the patron of Rhodes, Helios, the sun god. It stood near the harbor, not across it, and was some 70 cubits (about 105 feet) high.

The Colossus was not the most lasting of the Seven Wonders. It stood for only fifty-six years after its completion in 292 B.C. before being toppled by an earthquake.

A thousand years later the remains were recycled. The junkman is said to have needed more than a hundred camels to carry them away.

colts' legs, growth of. It is often said that the legs of a colt are as long as they will ever get. Not so. Although they are disproportionately long, they do increase in length as the colt becomes a horse.

Columbus, Christopher—and a flat world. The notion that most people in Columbus's day believed that the world was flat is quite nonsensical. Not since the days of ancient Greece had anyone of consequence proposed that the earth is not a sphere.

First advanced by the Pythagoreans in the sixth century B.C., the theory that the world is round was proved by Ptolemy in the second century A.D.; he pointed out that the shadow of the earth on the moon during an eclipse is invariably rounded. He further adduced what today remains a convincing enough argument; that the mast of a ship approaching from the sea is visible before the hull.

Medieval theologians were happy to accept the classic theory. The sphere was regarded as the most nearly perfect form; therefore, God would most certainly have made the world in this shape.

Early guesses as to the size of the earth's circumference varied, although one, proposed by Hipparchus about 150 B.C., came surprisingly close to the some 25,000 miles we now accept. According to him, the circumference of the earth is 21,420 miles. This was not bad for an inferential estimate made without benefit of modern technology.

Other estimates, notably Ptolemy's, were not so accurate. Somewhat ironically, Ptolemy's mistaken calculations—he thought the earth to be considerably smaller than it actually is—probably encouraged Columbus in his ambitions, for they made it appear that his voyage would be shorter than it was—or would have been if he had actually completed it instead of stumbling upon his completely unsuspected landfall. Columbus calculated the distance between the Canaries and Japan at only 2,400 miles, whereas the court authorities in Spain and Portugal knew that the ocean was much larger and the continents of Europe and Asia much smaller than Columbus figured. Although no one knew of the existence of America, those who opposed Columbus's plans really had more sense on their side than we give them credit for.

common cold, cure for. There is no cure for the common cold. Some proprietary preparations, the advertising for which certainly often leaves the impression that they are "cures," can only relieve certain symptoms. Whether or not the common cold can be *prevented* is still controversial. Dr. Linus Pauling's theory that massive doses of vitamin C can help prevent colds was greeted with considerable skepticism by many medical researchers. (Pauling, a Nobel laureate, is a chemist, not a physician.) However, the rejection of his findings is not universal; two researchers at the University of Strathclyde in Scotland, Mary Clegg and Sheila Charleston, decided that Pauling is right after a controlled experiment involving large doses of ascorbic acid, which is heavy in vitamin C. Those who took the ascorbic acid daily had almost 50 percent fewer colds than those given a placebo, or dummy pill containing no ascorbic acid. Their one-time research, which they apparently found conclusive, involved, however, fewer than one hundred subjects.

Whether or not undesirable side effects or toxicity may result from large doses of vitamin C is a question raised in some medical circles, as is the possibility that vitamin C pills kept for too long a time on the shelf may undergo undesirable chemical changes.

compass, indicated direction at North Pole. Most people know that a compass points to the north *magnetic* pole, which is far from the North Pole. And though it's often said that all directions are south if one is standing at the North Pole, it is certainly not true, obviously, that this is what a magnetic compass would tell one; a compass with nothing but "South" on its card, or dial, would be a fairly obvious absurdity. As a matter of fact, conventional compasses do not even actually point toward the magnetic pole. Rather, they align themselves with the earth's magnetic field at a given location. And the variation of the compass may change from year to year. If one were to follow the indications of a magnetic compass until he reached either of the magnetic poles, north or south, his path would not be the most direct possible; it would be a somewhat irregular course which would, true enough, end at the magnetic pole, but would certainly not represent the course a navigator would plot.

Another way of putting it is that compasses are not actually influenced by, nor do they really "point to," either of the magnetic poles. They indicate magnetic north or south; but if this is actually the geographical direction of the magnetic pole it's an accident. Magnetic north and south, in other words, are simply the direction indicated by a compass needle when it is aligned with the magnetic lines of force at any given location. The magnetic lines of force of the earth are not straight, like the artificial meridians on a globe; nature cares nothing for neatness. The magnetic poles might be described as simply the places where the earth's magnetic lines of force all come together after their more or less wandering journey and, in a sense, dive beneath the ground. A compass needle free to assume any angle would, at either of the magnetic poles, point downward.

***Compleat Angler, The,* plagiarized.** Periodically there surfaces the story that Izaak Walton stole his famous work from the anonymous author of a treatise published in 1577—Walton was born in 1593—and called *The Arte of Angling* (not to be confused with *The Art of Angling* by Thomas Barker, published in 1653, from which Walton quotes with full credit). It all started with the discovery in 1954, and publication by the Princeton University Library in 1956, of *The Arte of Angling*.

Newspaper accounts following the discovery and publication of the earlier work gave rise to the impression that Walton was a plagiarist. But it is a tempest in a fishing creel. Professor Marcus Selden Goldman of the University of Illinois first discussed the relationship between Walton's work and the earlier treatise in 1958; * it is further explored in John R. Cooper's definitive *The Art of "The Compleat Angler"* (1968).

And it is true enough that a comparison of parallel passages leads to the conclusion that Walton did some borrowing from *The Arte of Angling.* But it is most unlikely, thinks Cooper, that Walton had a copy of *The Arte* before him. In any case—and perhaps most persuasive—Walton never pretended *not* to borrow from other sources; indeed, in the fifth (1676) edition of his work, the last to be published in his lifetime—Walton died in 1683 at the age of ninety, a statistic many a fisherman's wife must know by heart—Walton specifically credits almost seventy sources upon which he drew. One would not suppose that a man with plagiarism in mind would be quite so open in acknowledging indebtedness.

True, Walton does not mention *The Arte of Angling.* But, very much within the mainstream of earlier English literary tradition —Chaucer borrows heavily from Boccaccio in his *Troilus and Criseyde,* and Shakespeare rarely used a plot of his own contriving —Izaak Walton thought of the past work of others as a resource freely available to him, to be used as needed. As Cooper points out, the structural integrity of *The Compleat Angler* is what matters; and no one has successfully challenged that, nor is likely to do so in the future.

Walton did not, incidentally, say of the worm, "Use him as though you loved him, that is, harm him as little as you may possibly, that he may live the longer." He was, rather, talking about the frog. Nor is he properly referred to as "Sir" Izaak, a misnomer perhaps arising from confusion with Isaac Newton, who was knighted. Walton was not.

condemned men freed as a result of mechanical failure. It is widely believed that if an electric chair or gas chamber should fail to operate, or the rope break during a hanging, the prisoner must go free because he cannot twice be put in jeopardy for the same offense. But this is a confusion between the *trial* and the *sentence.* A man cannot, under the Constitution, be *tried* twice

* "Izaak Walton and *The Arte of Angling,* 1577," in *Studies in Honor of T. W. Baldwin* (Urbana, Ill., 1958), pp. 185–204, as cited in Cooper.

for the same offense. But once he has been convicted and sentenced, then the sentence must be carried out, malfunctioning equipment or no, if the law is to be followed.

Congressional Medal of Honor. Strictly, no such thing exists; it's officially just the Medal of Honor. But since it is presented "in the name of the Congress of the United States," the popular appellation has come to include the term *Congressional*.

Consistency is the hobgoblin of little minds. This is not what Emerson said. He said, "A *foolish* consistency," etc., which makes a considerable difference in meaning.

Cooper, D. B. The first and most famous, or notorious, of the aircraft hijackers-for-cash was never known as D. B. Cooper except in the public mind. Imprinted sweatshirts and hastily thrown together ballads to the contrary, the man who took over a 727 jet in the Pacific northwest and later parachuted with $200,000 called himself simply Dan Cooper when he bought his ticket and boarded the plane at Portland, Oregon, en route to Seattle, where he commandeered the jet and got his parachutes and money. And it is as Dan Cooper that the FBI is still looking for him as of this printing.

The D. B. Cooper misapprehension arose because there really was a D. B. Cooper; the FBI checked him out after uncovering, by a process of elimination, the name Dan Cooper. (Dan Cooper was the only name left on the passenger list after the others on the plane were released in Seattle.) But the real D. B. Cooper was in jail at the time of the skyjacking and thus was eliminated as a suspect. There had been a man named Cooper on the plane, but he got off at Portland and in any case his first name and initials were neither Dan nor D. B.

It does not seem likely that the hijacker used his real name. But D. B. Cooper was never the name under which he flew; rather, it was as Dan Cooper that he bought his ticket.

copper bracelets as antidotes to arthritis. There is no scientific evidence that copper or any such metal worn on the wrists or ankles has an effect on arthritis. The belief is an old one. Even the great seventeenth-century physician, Paracelsus, said that a ring

made of electrum would protect the wearer from epilepsy, apo-
plexy, palsy, or any pain. More recently in Canada there spread
the belief that a copper wire bound tightly around the waist would
ward off rheumatism.

copyright. There is much misinformation about copyright.

Many people think that copyright is a commercial right that can
be bought and sold. That commercial right is the license to publish. The copyright on the other hand is a legal right which gives
the creator of a work the means of protection from infringement
by others.

There are two kinds of copyright. Common-law copyright is
automatic protection on an unpublished work, and endures until
the work is published—with or without copyright. After publication, if in accordance with certain formalities, statutory copyright
takes over.

However, contrary to common opinion, the Copyright Office
does not grant copyright protection. It simply registers the claims
to copyright. If a dispute ensues, it is the law, not the Copyright
Office which decides the issue.

Another misconception is that titles may be copyrighted, and
people often rush to do so. They cannot be, and a number of book
titles have been used over and over again (e.g., *Swift Waters, The
Art of Thinking, Out of This Nettle*). Some of the confusion on
this point doubtless comes from the law covering trademarks.
Under proper circumstances a trademark can be registered,
thereby giving exclusivity to its owner.

corn. In America we use the word *corn* to mean only the kind of
grain that grows on the cob. Originally, however, the word meant
all the grains that are used as food for men or horses, which is what
it still means in England. The English refer to our "corn" as
maize, using the name adapted from the Spanish. Originally corn
in America was "Indian corn," but over the years the qualifying
word *Indian* was dropped.

Generations of American schoolchildren who haven't known
the basic meaning of the word have been puzzled by the English
corn laws. Similarly, Missouri rather than Moab is suggested when
in his "Ode to a Nightingale" John Keats speaks of ". . . the sad
heart of Ruth, when, sick for home, / She stood in tears amid the

alien corn . . ." Incidentally, that setting is entirely Keats's own creation. The Book of Ruth in the King James Bible does not contain the phrase "alien corn."

corpus delicti. Contrary to widespread popular belief, the *corpus delicti* is not the corpse in a murder case. True, *corpus* here means "body," but the body of the crime, not of the victim; that is, the essential evidence, or body of evidence, necessary for conviction. Obviously the corpse in a murder case may also constitute the *corpus delicti,* or the major part of it. But the terms are not synonymous.

Cortes, Balboa, and the Pacific Ocean. Although John Keats thought so, Hernando Cortes did not "discover" the Pacific. (*Discover* is in quotation marks as a reminder of an implicit cultural bias perhaps so obvious as to be almost universally overlooked: countless generations had known the Pacific thousands of years before the first *European* happened to find it.)

One of Keats's most famous and often-quoted sonnets, "On First Looking into Chapman's Homer," ends as follows:

> Then felt I like some watcher of the skies
> When a new planet swims into his ken;
> Or like stout Cortez when with eagle eyes
> He stared at the Pacific—and all his men
> Look'd at each other with a wild surmise—
> Silent, upon a peak in Darien.

But Keats was, of course, mistaken. It is Balboa who is generally given the credit for first sighting the Pacific with European eyes after crossing the Isthmus of Panama, known in Keats's day as the Isthmus of Darien. Interestingly enough, however, and an instance of error compounded, it was not Balboa, actually, who first saw the Pacific. Two years before him, in 1511, the Portuguese had sailed into the Pacific from the other direction, by way of the Indian Ocean. If one may say that there was a "discoverer" of the Pacific, it was one Antonio d' Abreu: *neither* Cortes nor Balboa. (See KEATS, JOHN.)

covered bridges. In spite of the many rather romantic theories about them, it appears most probable that covered bridges were covered for an entirely practical reason: to help protect the structural members from the weather. It is much easier and cheaper to keep the roof in repair than to replace rotten bridge timbers. That would amount to building the bridge all over again, which would be difficult, costly, and often dangerous.

Covered bridges are not confined, as some people think, to New England. There are said to be more covered bridges in Ohio than in Vermont, and they are to be found as far west as Oregon.

crap, crapper. Those inclined to dismiss these words as common vulgarisms should be aware that they are not Cockney slang or the like but rather come directly from a most respectable source, and by the same established linguistic process that gives us *sandwich* (from the Earl of Sandwich), *bowdlerize* (from Thomas Bowdler, a nineteenth-century editor of prudish inclinations), *macadam* (after John McAdam), and—by the way—*Birdseye* as the proprietary name for certain frozen foods, from Clarence Birdseye. (It might also be pointed out that the Polaroid Land camera, for those unaware of this fact, is not specifically designed for terrestrial rather than aerial use; its name comes from that of its inventor, Dr. Edwin Herbert Land.)

The valve-and-siphon arrangement which made the modern flush toilet possible was, in fact, invented by Thomas Crapper (1837–1910), a sanitary engineer and inventor of such eminence and respectability that his firm achieved not one, but four royal warrants, allowing the use in advertising of the magic words "By Appointment to Her Majesty the Queen." Crapper did not invent the flush toilet per se; even the Romans had various systems of plumbing in which running water carried away human waste. He did, however, contrive the mechanism, basically unchanged since his time, which automatically shuts off the water after its job has been done—not a small matter when one considers the waste of water implicit in either a constantly running system or one in which it is up to the user to time the operation.

The Crapper story, and a fascinating one it is, is told with style and grace by Wallace Reyburn in *Flushed with Pride: The Story of Thomas Crapper*, published in 1969 in London. It's a work well worth adding to one's library, in bathroom or elsewhere.

Creole. Some people think that the word *Creole* is intended to designate only a person of mixed white and black blood. This is neither the original nor the basic meaning of the word.

In Louisiana it originally meant anyone born there whose ancestors were French and had come to Louisiana to settle. American use broadened this to include also the descendants of Spanish and Portuguese settlers in all the Gulf States.

In the West Indies and Spanish America it meant a native descended from European (most usually Spanish) stock, as distinguished from European immigrants, Negroes, aborigines, and natives of mixed blood. Napoleon's wife, Josephine, was a Creole. Her parents were French and emigrated to Martinique, where Josephine was born. She had no Negro blood.

Eventually the meaning was broadened to include persons born in the New World, but of some race not indigenous, regardless of color.

Later the term came also to mean a Negro born in the Americas, as distinguished from a Negro brought from Africa, and any person with both Negro and Creole blood who spoke Creole. In New Orleans, for instance, there is an ethnic group known as "Creoles of color." They do not consider themselves to be in the same class with blacks or whites (though many pass into white society). Thus they have remained aloof from both groups and have maintained an enclave below Canal Street.

Plainly the term *Creole* has many meanings in many places. In Brazil it is applied to blacks, and in Alaska it was once used to designate persons of mixed Russian and Indian ancestry.

crocodile tears. Since crocodiles have no tear glands, they are unable to shed tears. However, crocodiles do have secretions to keep their eyes moist. The belief that crocodiles shed (hypocritical) tears while eating their victims is not, apparently, something else to blame on Pliny; first reference to this myth seems to go no farther back than the fourteenth century, and then to have been picked up, for whatever reason, by many Elizabethan authors.

crossword puzzle, origin of. Usually thought to have made its appearance on the scene in 1924 with the publication of the first crossword-puzzle book by Simon and Schuster, Inc., the crossword puzzle had actually been presented to the public years earlier; in 1913, in a supplement to the New York *World* on December 21. It was prepared by Arthur Wynn.

crucifixion, the. The Romans used various types of crosses for crucifixion, which was a usual form of punishment reserved for common criminals. There is no positive evidence that Christ was crucified on the *crux imissa,* or so-called Latin cross; it may have been the "Tau," or T-shaped cross. That it was the former may be inferred from Matt. 27:37 ("And set up *over his head* [italics added] his accusation written, THIS IS JESUS THE KING OF THE JEWS").

cyclone. A cyclone is neither a tornado nor a hurricane. Indeed, it isn't even a wind. A *cyclone,* as meteorologists use the term, may be as wide as a thousand miles, and is simply the *pattern* of winds circulating around a low-pressure area, clockwise in the Southern Hemisphere and counterclockwise in the Northern.

Kansas cyclone as a term for *tornado* may have originated as a sort of grim meteorological joke based on reverse analogy, like calling a cantaloupe a Texas grape.

D

daddy longlegs. The creatures usually called daddy longlegs are not spiders. They have the right number of legs, eight; but their legs are far longer and thinner than those of true spiders. In addition, the daddy longlegs lacks the constriction which, in spiders, divides the body into two segments.

The long legs are, in fact, a useful accessory. Like certain automobiles which can jack themselves up by means of a central hydraulic system, the daddy longlegs can, without benefit of hydraulics, raise his one-piece body high enough above the ground to avoid ants or other small enemies.

damned Yankee. Not originally a term applied by Southerners to Northerners; actually, it first arose during the Revolutionary War and was used against northern "provincials" by "Yorkers" who were members of General Schuyler's northern army.

"Damn the torpedoes—full speed ahead!" This remark, attributed to Admiral David Glasgow Farragut at the battle of Mobile Bay on August 5, 1864, has no reference to torpedoes as we understand the term today. The first self-propelled torpedo in the modern sense was not perfected until after the Civil War, by an English engineer named Robert Whitehead. Before that, *torpedo* was used for what we today call mines. The "torpedoes" Admiral Farragut referred to were actually beer kegs filled with powder.

dandelion. Really does have something to do with lions, although not how dandy they may be. The word is the English version of the medieval French *dent de lion,* "lion's tooth." (Modern French for dandelion is *pissenlit.*)

darkening the room to avoid injury to eyes of children who have measles. This is an old wives' tale. Children may have trouble with vision after they have had measles, but it is the measles that caused the problem, not the fact that the room was lighted.

"Dark Eyes" ("Otchi tchernye"). Customarily taken to be the very quintessence of Old Russian romanticism, "Dark Eyes" was actually written by Florian Hofmann, a "Russianized German," in the words of Nicolas Slonimsky. And it was not originally a song (the words were added later by someone else), but a piece for violin and piano entitled "Valse Hommage," about as Russian as the *Marseillaise.*

Darwin, Charles Robert. The idea of evolution was not original with Darwin (1809–1882), nor did he ever claim it was. *Origin of Species* does not deal with the evolution of man, nor did Darwin ever try to prove that men are descended from apes. Darwin did not originate the expression "survival of the fittest," nor does "fittest" mean "best," or "most powerful," or—most certainly—"most deserving."

Darwin himself, in the third edition of his *Origin of Species* (1861), credits Aristotle with having "shadowed forth" the principle of natural selection. Indeed, throughout the whole of what he called "An Historical Sketch of the Progress of Opinion on the Origin of Species, previously to the Publication of This Work," Darwin gives full credit to the many others who had, one way or another, anticipated him. Like Sir Isaac Newton (1642–1727), who is said to have remarked that if he saw farther than others it was because he stood on the shoulders of giants, Darwin did not fail to acknowledge his debt to his predecessors.

Nor did he fail to acknowledge his debt to his somewhat younger contemporary, Alfred Russel Wallace (1823–1913). It is sometimes said that Wallace deserves equal credit with Darwin for presenting to the world the theory of evolution. But Wallace himself made no such claim; although scientists link his name with Darwin's, Wallace maintained, with commendable modesty, that his contribution was as two weeks are to twenty years.

In a classic case of simultaneous research leading to a common conclusion, Wallace had written, quite without Darwin's knowledge (not so surprising in view of the fact that Wallace was living in the Malay Archipelago, Darwin in England), a paper entitled "On the Tendency of Varieties to Depart Indefinitely from the Original Type." According to Sir Charles Lyell (1797–1875), whose own *Principles of Geology* (1830–1833) had proposed a kind of evolutionary theory in terms of the earth itself, Wallace in February 1858 sent Darwin a copy of his paper with the request that Darwin show it to Lyell should he think it, in Lyell's words, "sufficiently novel and interesting."

For the past eighteen years Darwin had been collecting data in support of his theory; one can only imagine the shattering effect of Wallace's paper. Fortunately, Darwin had, as early as 1844, allowed others to read from his yet unpublished work; it was clear that he had anticipated Wallace. Still, Darwin was quite willing to waive any claim to priority. As a matter of fact, on the same evening—July 1, 1858—both Wallace's paper and a chapter from Darwin's manuscript entitled "On the Tendency of Species to Form Varieties, and On the Perpetuation of Species and Varieties by Natural Means of Selection" were read to the Linnaean Society in London. (Some, including Lyell himself, have wondered whether Darwin would ever have got around to publishing his work if Wallace had not independently come to much the same conclusions as he.)

Great discoveries do not spring forth like Minerva from the brain of Jupiter. It is the peculiar characteristic of genius to recognize what others have seen but not grasped, have observed but not fully understood, and then to put everything together so that it makes a new kind of sense. George Buffon (1707–1788), Jean Lamarck (1744–1829), Darwin's own grandfather Erasmus (1731–1802)—all these had dealt, one way or another, with the idea that some forms must have evolved from some others. Even Alexander Pope's eighteenth-century notion, expressed entirely in literary rather than scientific terms and itself deriving from

John Dryden, of a "great chain of being," or orderly universe in which there is a place for everything and everything has its place, must have stirred speculation that some of the complicated forms had, so to speak, worked their way up the chain: that is, have evolved from the simpler.

Even "survival of the fittest" (the phrase is Herbert Spencer's; but Darwin liked it and came to adopt it) had been suggested, according to Darwin himself, by William C. Wells in 1813 and Patrick Mathew in 1831. Still, it was indeed Darwin who did put it all together; and to him properly belongs the same kind of credit that belongs, for example, to Albert Einstein, who could not himself have proposed, at the turn of the century, his own revolutionary theory were it not for the work of the American physicists Michelson and Morley in the 1880s.

There continue to exist many misconceptions both of Darwin's actual theory and its implications. *Origin of Species* is often confused with Darwin's decade-later *Descent of Man;* it is the latter, not the former, that deals with man's origin. Darwin never proposed that humankind is descended from monkeys, though this remains the commonest basis for attack upon his theories. He postulated, rather, that human beings and monkeys have a common ancestor. It suited certain nineteenth-century (and certain twentieth-century) political, social, and economic theories to assume that "survival of the fittest" means "survival of the strongest." It does not, nor did Darwin—who was, after all, a naturalist, not an economist—ever maintain any such thing. That organism survives, in Darwinian terms, which is best suited to its environment; were "strongest" truly the term, obviously dinosaurs would still walk the earth.

And, most certainly, "survival of the fittest" has no implications whatever to give a racist comfort. Far from being a rationale for developing a superior breed or an elite corps, it says, rather, that adaptability matters: not brute strength, not power nor the arrogance of power, but rather that adjustment to circumstance which is, in effect, its opposite.

dead reckoning. It is often said that *dead reckoning* represents a corruption of *ded.* (for *deduced*) *reckoning.* There is no evidence for such a belief. Most likely the "ded. reckoning" explanation is what linguists call folk-etymology, or contriving an explanation for the origin of a word or phrase not because it is true, but because it sounds as if it ought to be, or could be.

Dead reckoning simply means deriving one's position by putting together speed, direction, and distance, with due allowance for drift if any. The position established by this process is, thus, an inferential one, and applies, strictly, only to a ship which in seafaring terms is dead (that is, motionless) in the water. A motorist using dead reckoning would establish his or her location by "deducing" it from the fact that he has travelled due north for one hour at sixty miles an hour. But this location is valid only as long as the car is not moving; at a dead standstill. It is easy to see why the "deduced" explanation persists, even in some dictionaries.

"Dear hearts and gentle people." Despite a widespread belief to the contrary, these are not the words found on a scrap of paper in the possession of Stephen Foster when he died. They are, rather, from a popular song of the 1950s. What Foster had written was "Dear friends and gentle hearts." Nobody has ever figured out why he wrote it. Some speculate that it was a title or a phrase he meant to use in a song.

Declaration of Independence. This historic document is dated July 4, 1776, and it is generally supposed that on that day it was first adopted by the Continental Congress and unanimously signed by the members. Actually July 4 was the day on which the last draft was voted on, and on that day not all delegates had approved it and there were no signers at all.

This is what really happened. On June 7, 1776, Richard Henry Lee of Virginia introduced a motion for a declaration of independence. A committee of five was selected to produce the document, including Thomas Jefferson, who performed the actual writing. His version was revised by Benjamin Franklin, John Adams, and Jefferson himself, before it went to Congress. Congress did some editing of its own. A resolution of independence was adopted by Congress on July 2, 1776. That was the day the action was taken, and the statement itself was terse. The committee's declaration, in the wonderful language of Jefferson, is a much fuller statement which sets forth the theory of this new country's government and the justification for the break in the light of the specific grievances that its people had endured.

The final draft was not approved unanimously by July 4. New York did not even vote on it until July 9.

The signing was even more gradual, and it is quite misleading to speak of the "fifty-six original signers of the Declaration of Independence." By August 6 most of those whose names are on the document had signed, but at least six signatures were attached later. One signer, Thomas McKean (abbreviated to Tho. M:Kean) did not attach his name until 1781! Some of those who signed were not even in Congress when the Declaration was adopted, and some who voted for it in Congress never did get around to signing it. Robert R. Livingston was one of the committee of five; he helped to frame it; he voted for it; and he never signed it.

deepest gorge in the United States. It is often pointed out that the deepest gorge in the United States, if not the world, is not the Grand Canyon, but Hells Canyon of the Snake River between Idaho and Oregon, which at some 7,900 feet apparently has the Grand Canyon beaten by about a half-mile. (It is also called Grand Canyon of the Snake.) It should, however, be pointed out also that there is really no direct comparison possible. The Grand Canyon is a great hole in the surrounding plateau; Hells Canyon is in mountainous country.

deer, and what they eat. Deer have a hard time finding enough to eat if there are deep snows covering their browse all winter. Consequently kindhearted people will put out hay for them. The deer cannot eat it. They are not grazing animals, but browsing animals. When there are such relief measures taken in our national parks, they are usually for elk, which do graze. In New England forests winter deer will browse on pine, hemlock, mountain maple, swamp maple—and will chew up ash twigs the thickness of a pencil.

democracy, early American settlers' attitude toward. Often appearing in newspapers or magazines on or near Thanksgiving Day are advertisements of the type sometimes called public service or institutional. Shown will be a group of tall-hatted Puritans, muskets on shoulders, going to or coming from church. Underneath, a caption proclaims something like, "To these we owe our fundamental liberties."

But such a concept could scarcely be farther from the truth. John Winthrop, first governor of the Massachusetts Bay Colony, one of the most famous and influential of the early Puritan leaders, once said of democracy that it is "accounted the meanest and worst of all forms of government." As the treatment of Roger Williams and Anne Hutchinson indicates,* the Puritans in colonial America were anything but tolerant of dissent; the religious freedom they sought in the New World was for themselves only; it did not extend to those who disagreed with them. It was the Massachusetts Bay Colony which, in its somewhat ironically titled "Body of Liberties" in 1641, made blasphemy a crime punishable by death.

When in 1691 Massachusetts lost its independence and became a royal province under a royal governor, Samuel Sewall, rich and influential, also one of the most prominent seventeenth-century Puritan leaders, did not protest; he wrote, in fact, that it was intolerable for "private persons to print reflections and censures on the highest acts of government."

Not even during the American Revolution was the word *democracy* much used; it does not appear in the Declaration of Independence, any of the first state constitutions, nor indeed in the Constitution of the United States. Thomas Jefferson himself did not publicly call himself a democrat or use the term in any of his public addresses. He believed that government by a simple majority could be as despotic as one-man rule and did not trust "the mobs of the great cities." Nor did the word *republic* find any great favor among those who seemed fearful of democracy; the Constitution does not officially declare the new nation a republic.

In any case, the concepts on which the new nation was founded certainly did not derive from those seventeenth-century Calvinist-Separatist Puritan doctrines which inspired our earliest New England forebears. They sprang, rather, from the *eighteenth*-century Anglo-European religious, philosophical, and political climate of resistance to monarchy and its underlying basis, the divine right of kings. It was the Age of Enlightenment, so called, whose philosophy derived from such as Locke, Berkeley, and Hume, not

---

* Because of their refusal to conform to Puritan theory and practice, both were expelled from Massachusetts—Williams in 1636, Hutchinson two years later. Both went to Rhode Island which, unique among the colonies, did accept the principle of tolerance.

such as Calvin and Knox, from which sprang the American Revolution and the notion that all are born equal and entitled to life, liberty, and the pursuit of happiness.

Franklin even thought of himself as a Deist, a religion (or a philosophy) which would certainly have led to his own expulsion from Massachusetts Bay had he been born a few generations earlier. It is quite impossible to imagine that the Declaration of Independence or the Constitution of the United States could ever have emerged from the royalist, theocratic, and authoritarian climate in which lived the actual Puritans ostensibly depicted in those Thanksgiving Day advertisements.

dentists and anesthetic. "I don't want an anesthetic because then the dentist won't be able to tell when he is near the nerve." In fact, the dentist doesn't need the patient's responses to know where he is anatomically within the mouth. If he were to use the patient's responses as a guide, he would think that the nerve of the tooth is quite close to the surface because the actual area that is most sensitive is the junction of the enamel and the dentin, a level far from the nerve.

Desiderata. The poster, or wall-hanging, that goes by this name (desiderata, from Latin, can be roughly translated as "those things to be considered desirable") and opens "Go placidly amid the noise and haste, and remember what peace there may be in silence" is still sometimes thought to have been "found" at Old St. Paul's Church in Baltimore and to date back to 1692.

Actually it was written by Max Ehrmann and copyrighted by him in 1927; the copyright was renewed in 1954 by Bertha K. Ehrmann. First versions of the poster, which swept the country a few years ago and is still a standard item in gift shops, erroneously claimed that it dated to the seventeenth century and had been discovered during some remodeling at Old St. Paul's.

Old St. Paul's was actually founded in 1692, which perhaps accounts for the early confusion. Current versions of the poster carry a proper copyright notice, thus restoring to Mr. Ehrmann the credit he was entitled to all along.

destroying United States coins. Nothing in the law forbids anyone from destroying coins, in spite of a belief to the contrary.

Defacing or mutilating a coin and then passing it as currency is another matter.

destruction of surplus crops. The notion that it was Franklin D. Roosevelt's New Dealers who first thought of plowing under crops in order to create an artificial scarcity and thus raise prices is quite false. In 1639, tobacco prices were so low in Virginia that half the crop was burned on order of the general assembly.

de Valera, Eamon. De Valera, the symbol of Irish independence to so many, was born not in Ireland but in New York City, at Fifty-first Street and Lexington Avenue. He was taken to Ireland at the age of three.

Devil's Island. It is natural to assume that the famous Devil's Island off the coast of French Guiana is so called because of its lethal climate. Most people do. Actually the name came from the turbulence of the waters surrounding it.

There are a group of three islands off this coast, called the Safety Islands, of which Devil's Island is only one. The islands themselves were a part of the French convict colony, the rest of the colony—and worst—being on the mainland. Perhaps because of the notoriety resulting from Alfred Dreyfus's imprisonment there for several years, Devil's Island became associated in the public mind with the penal colony as a whole.

Devil's Island is by no means the hellhole it has been made out to be. Later prisoners were political rather than criminal, and never numbered more than a dozen at a time. They lived in cabins with books and other personal effects.

Quite in contrast to the popular notion, the climate is not at all bad. There are many groves of tall coconut trees cooled by the sea breezes. In fact there has recently been talk of turning Devil's Island into a tourist resort.

diet pills and diet fads. Contrary to widespread belief, there is no pill or medicine which will cause a person to lose weight. Similarly there is no diet that will reduce weight unless it means reducing total food consumption or reducing the consumption of fat-producing foods.

In other words, the only way to reduce weight is to eat less: to eat less of weight-producing food, to eat less of all food, or both.

dirigible. A dirigible is not distinguished from other lighter-than-air craft because it has a rigid frame. A dirigible is any lighter-than-air craft *which can be steered.* (The word comes from the Latin *derigo,* "to turn," "to aim," or "to direct"; or possibly Latin *dirigo,* "to put in line" or "to arrange.") The Goodyear blimps, thus, may also quite properly be referred to as dirigibles.

discretion is the better part of valor. This is not quite the way Shakespeare put it. In *Henry IV, Part I* (act 5, sc. 4, line 120) he wrote, "The better part of valor is discretion."

Dixie. The term did not originally apply to the Confederate South, but only to New Orleans. The usual explanation is that a New Orleans bank, soon after Louisiana became a part of the United States, issued bilingual ten-dollar bills identified as to denomination, on one side, by the French word *dix* ("ten") . The bills came to be called dixies, and the term, or its Anglicized singular form, dixie, came to be applied to New Orleans. It was Daniel Decatur Emmett's song, written in 1859 and almost at once adopted as the informal anthem of the South, that was responsible for the extension of *Dixie* to all the Confederacy.

doctor, as title. Medical doctors and dentists invariably refer to themselves and to others holding the M.D., D.M.D., or D.D.S. degree as "Doctor." As everyone knows, it is incorrect to refer to the holders of these degrees as "Mr.," "Mrs.," or "Ms."

Contrary to popular belief, however, it is entirely proper to address holders of the Ph.D. as "Mr.," "Mrs.," or "Ms." In fact, in America it is regarded as rather pretentious for the holder of a Ph.D. to put "Dr." on his office door or calling card.

Similarly we look somewhat askance at military officers who retain their titles in daily life after they were but briefly in the service.

European custom differs. A German professor, for example, may well carry cards which list full name, the title of professor, and degrees. In England lay persons do not hesitate to list their titles, degrees, and honors on the passenger list of a cruise ship, for instance. (In our country a person who put B.A. after his name would be laughed at.)

Perhaps the extreme was reached by certain students in India who went to Oxford, failed, and still wanted credit for having tried. They put on their calling cards "Oxon—failed." (Oxon is, of course, the abbreviation for Oxonia, the medieval Latin name which Oxonians prefer.)

Dodgers, Brooklyn. Now, of course, merely the "Dodgers," this most famous or—according to the point of view—notorious of baseball teams did not acquire its name because of agility on the playing field. Rather, it is a shortened form of "Trolley Dodgers," indicating agility in the street rather than the infield. The term was first applied to Brooklynites many years ago, at the height of the trolley-car era, because of the maze of trolley lines crisscrossing the borough.

dogs sweating through their tongues. Dogs do not "sweat with their tongues," as is often said. There are some sweat glands in dogs, but the only ones of any significance are on the soles of their feet. There are no sweat glands anywhere near a dog's muzzle. Dogs cool themselves primarily by rapid breathing, which is why they pant after running. But when a canine sticks his tongue out, he does so because it is moist and evaporation helps to cool it, not because he is sweating.

dollar across the Potomac, George Washington's throwing a. If, indeed, Washington ever did it, then the river was the Rappahannock, not the Potomac. It was on the Rappahannock that George Washington spent his boyhood. Anyway, there weren't any dollars during Washington's youth; the currency was, naturally, British.

"Don't fire until you see the whites of their eyes." If William Prescott said this during the battle of BUNKER HILL, he was not the first to make such a remark. Both Prince Charles of Prussia in 1745 ("Silent until you see the whites of their eyes") and Frederick the Great in 1757 (". . . no firing till you see the whites of their eyes") are credited with similar statements. This need not, of course, take any credit away from Prescott nor the other American troops, whose bravery in waiting under fire for the right moment is a matter of history.

Doom, Day of. This phrase does not mean the day on which everyone will be doomed. *Doom* here derives from the Old English noun *dōm,* which meant "judgment." The Day of Doom, thus, is the Day of Judgment.

double-jointed persons. Nobody is truly double-jointed. Some people simply have looser ligaments than others.

double negative. Parents and teachers sometimes tell their charges, "If you say 'I haven't got none,' then you are *really* saying 'I *do* have *some.*' You should be more logical." Double negatives once held, in fact, an honorable place in our language; as witness Chaucer's immortal lines describing the Knight in the Prologue to the *Canterbury Tales:* "He never yet no vileynye ne sayde / In al his lyf unto no maner wight." Or, in modern English, paraphrased freely but quite accurately: "He never said nothing bad in all his life to nobody."

The argument that a double negative "cancels itself out" is borrowed, apparently, from elementary algebra, the rules of which have nothing to do with grammar.

dove as symbol of peace. If those who selected the dove as a symbol of peace knew what Konrad Z. Lorenz knows about them, they might have made a different choice. Lorenz, an expert on animal behavior, put a male turtledove and a female ringdove in a cage together and left for Vienna. On his return he was horrified to find the turtledove prostrate on the floor of the cage, his featherless back a dripping bloody mass. The female "harbinger of peace" was methodically pecking away at what was left of her mate's back.

When observing two adversary wolves, on the other hand, Dr. Lorenz noticed that they stopped short of hostile action that might prove fatal.

He concluded that animals that are well equipped to kill their food possess a built-in reluctance to use their killing power on each other; but creatures that are equipped to flee have no such inhibitions and take no such precautions.

dragonflies stinging. Among the rather mean little myths so often inflicted upon children is that dragonflies may "sew your eyelids together." As a matter of fact, dragonflies don't even have stingers and are quite harmless, except to the mosquitoes and gnats they catch and consume on the wing.

dreams in color. It is often said that dreams are never in color, but rather always in monochrome. This is simply not so.

drink like a fish. Fish don't drink. The water they take in passes through their gills, where oxygen is extracted. While they are "breathing," their gullets are so tightly constricted that little if any water gets into the stomach. The water they do need is largely supplied by the moisture content of their food.

Drop the gun, Louis. A staple of comics who specialize in impersonations of the late Humphrey Bogart, this is not what Bogart said in *Casablanca*. His actual remark is "Not so fast, Louis."

drowning persons always rising three times. This is absolute and utter balderdash. Persons who are drowning may sink at once or may struggle their way to the surface. How many times depends on how much they struggle.

dry-cell battery. These batteries, used, for example, in flashlights and those motorized toys which, at Christmas time, are the bane of parents everywhere, aren't dry, really. They're moist inside, and must be. Otherwise they won't work.

Dying Gladiator, The. This well-known statue does not represent a dying gladiator, in spite of its popular title. It is rather a representation of a dying Gaul, wounded in battle, not the arena.

dynamite, detonation of. There is a common belief that if you put dynamite in the fire, it will explode. Actually dynamite requires detonation by spark or percussion. Warming up dynamite will make it more responsive to the detonator, but not explode it. Years ago in the lumber camps of Maine dynamite was heated up in a frying pan on cold mornings. (The practice is not recommended.) Incidentally, dynamite was invented by Alfred B. Nobel, who established the famous peace prize.

E

education as a major factor in assuring higher income. For many years it has been an article of American faith that the better one's education, the better the chance of increasing one's income. Various charts and tables purport to illustrate the "value" of a high school or college education in purely monetary terms. However, the implication that the best way, thus, to equalize economic opportunity is to improve the education of the poor turns out to have little basis, at least according to a three-year study by a Harvard research team, which concluded that cognitive skills are only weakly related to earning power.

Indeed, even such factors as heredity, home background, intelligence quotient, and quality of schools attended turned out to account for only about one fourth of the variation in American incomes. The other three fourths, apparently, is determined by such imponderables as luck, personality, and whatever it is that enables some to make a lot of money regardless of background or the presumed advantages of a better education.

The study would make it appear, thus, that attempts to ensure equal economic opportunity solely through improvement in schools, no matter how laudable these improvements may be from other points of view, are not likely to succeed.

efficiency of loudspeakers. This is not used as a term of praise by audio buffs—nor of dispraise, either. The efficiency of a loudspeaker has nothing to do with its quality or the way it sounds. It merely relates to how loud it "speaks" for a given amount of electrical energy fed into it—that is, how well it transforms electrical energy into acoustic energy. Since almost all contemporary amplifiers, barring those so cheap as to amount merely to toys, can put out more energy than even the most inefficient conventional loudspeaker can handle, efficiency is an irrelevant consideration when comparing speakers. As a matter of fact, two kinds of speakers are, broadly speaking, the most efficient: very small and cheap ones, and the very large and astronomically priced "horn" systems.

eggs, color of shell. There is no difference either in nutritional value or flavor between brown-shelled eggs and white-shelled eggs. Popular prejudice is responsible for variations in price between different-colored eggs, so that brown eggs have been known to command higher prices in Boston than in New York, white eggs higher prices in New York than in Boston.

Egyptian secret art of embalming. According to Jessica Mitford, author of *The American Way of Death,* the Egyptians had no special embalming secrets; it was the unusually dry climate and relative absence of bacteria in the air and sand that account for the remarkable state of preservation of Egyptian mummies.

Eighteenth (Prohibition) Amendment. Nothing in the Eighteenth Amendment prohibited the *consumption* of liquor, but rather only its manufacture, sale, or transportation, including import or export of course.

Thus, under prohibition it was not a crime to drink intoxicating liquor, to possess it, or even to buy it.

Furthermore the Eighteenth Amendment did not define what an intoxicating beverage is. This was accomplished by the VOLSTEAD ACT, a law which preceded and supplemented the Eighteenth Amendment. Many people thought the Volstead Act was simply another name for the amendment.

It may be a matter of some surprise that the vote by various state legislatures for ratification of the Prohibition Amendment was more than 80 percent in favor, with only two states failing to ratify it: Connecticut and Rhode Island.

elective system of college study. Usually Charles Eliot (1834–1926), president of Harvard from 1869 to 1909, is given credit for inaugurating the elective system in colleges and universities—that is, allowing students to choose the courses they wish to take rather than imposing the same curriculum or curricula upon them. In fact, the College of William and Mary in Williamsburg, Virginia, instituted such a system as early as 1779.

electric fans as cooling agents. No fan, electric or otherwise, cools the air. In fact, strictly speaking, an electric fan increases the temperature of the air in a room because of the heat given off by the motor (and—though it's very slight—even the heat resulting from friction of air against the blades). What creates the cooling *effect* of a fan is the increased evaporation of moisture from the skin resulting from increased air circulation.

electricity, direction of the flow of. Although conventional wiring diagrams always show the direction of current as being from positive to negative, it has been known for many years that the exact opposite is true: the electrons flow from negative to positive. Whether the diagram shows current flow from plus to minus, or minus to plus, however, makes no difference whatsoever in any practical terms. Thus, rather than change all the thousands of diagrams in all the thousands of books and articles about electricity and its applications, the original indications of current flow are maintained even though they are as wrong as they can possibly be.

electric self-starter for automobiles. The automobile self-starter was not originated by Charles Kettering, although he is usually given the credit. Clyde Jay Coleman of New York invented a self-starter in 1899. The Delco Company, later taken over by General Motors, purchased Coleman's rights; and in 1911 the first commercially practicable self-starter was offered by Cadillac. Later, in 1915, Kettering was issued a patent on an "engine starting device." But his was not the first patent for a self-starter.

elephant graveyard. One of the most enduring beliefs is that elephants in Africa and Asia all go to die at some common place which has never been discovered. Many a fantasy has been spun out of the wealth of ivory such a "graveyard" would contain. But it just isn't so. The quick disappearance of bodies—even elephant bodies—in the jungle through decay, scavengers, and rapid growth of vegetation perhaps helps to keep the myth alive.

elephants and tobacco. Elephants like tobacco, apparently, in spite of the tales about the elephant who never forgets the rustic who offers him a chaw. (Chewing tobacco usually contains licorice, sugar, or other flavoring.)

Emancipation Proclamation. Lincoln's Emancipation Proclamation had no legal force, did not free any slaves, and was not inspired by altruism—though this is not to say that Lincoln's dislike of slavery was any the less genuine. It specifically applied to slaves *only* in the Confederate States, not to those (and there were many) in the slave-holding states (Kentucky and Maryland, for instance) which had chosen to stay with the Union. Since it applied only to an enemy with which the United States was at war, obviously it could have no legal force, any more than a proclamation by President Roosevelt ordering Hitler to free all Jews could have had such force in 1943.

Needless to say, the proclamation was ignored by the Confederacy; and since it applied only to the Confederate states, the net effect was that no slave was freed. Its motivation appears to have been almost entirely military-political; in 1862 Lincoln told the South that any state which did not return to the Union by the end of the year would have its slaves declared free men. No state accepted the offer, so on January 1 the proclamation was issued. As a matter of fact, its international impact was greater than its domestic significance. By making it appear that the Civil War was a crusade against slavery, the proclamation made it less likely that England and France would, as the South hoped and expected, join forces with the Confederate States in order to save their major source of cotton.

engine, location of, in automobiles. It is often said that the reason automobile engines are usually located at the front is that early inventors and manufacturers could not break with tradition. Horses pull carts; so why should not the engine "pull" the car? However, with a single exception every one of the earliest auto-mobiles—Benz, Daimler, Serpollet, Duryea, Ford, Stanley, Fiat, Packard, to name a representative pre-1900 list from various countries—had its engine at the rear.

The exception is the French Panhard Levassor, of 1895. And the reason, according to Jack Brabham's introduction to Piet Olyslager's *Illustrated Motor Cars of the World* (1967), was so that the automobile would not "look like a carriage."

Epicureanism. That the modest, kindly, and moderate Epicurus should have inspired the name for a way of life the paradigm of which is usually taken to be "Eat, drink, and be merry" is a considerable irony. Epicurus—who was, incidentally, as much a kind of early atomic physicist as anything else—neither believed in nor practiced the immoderate pursuit of pleasure at all cost. It is true that he propounded a pleasure-pain theory; but he was no more a gross sensualist than the man who some twenty-two centuries later was also to propose such a principle, Sigmund Freud.

Nor were his followers. Indeed, so large a part do prudence and moderation play in historical Epicureanism that some of Epicu-rus's followers came to believe more in suffering pain with indif-ference than seeking out its opposite. Actually, Epicureanism calls for peace of mind, freedom from pain through pursuit of cultural interests, development of inner serenity, and temperance in sen-sual pleasure. It does not reject but accepts Aristotle's "Golden Mean."

What most people seem to think *Epicurean* means is better ex-pressed as *hedonism* (from the Greek word for "pleasure"). But even hedonism itself does not have to mean the immoderate pur-suit of sensual pleasure. Many hedonists believed in the rule of reason.

equal pay for everyone under Communism. Probably the most widespread layman's assumption about what is loosely called Communism is that under such a system everybody gets, or is sup-posed to get, the same income. But there is nothing in Marxist-Leninist theory that assumes or implies equal pay for everybody. "From each according to his abilities, to each according to his needs" (said by Marx, but not in either the *Communist Manifesto* or *Das Kapital*) quite clearly evades the issue; it all depends on how "needs" is defined. And in any case it does not say "To all the same."

The most famous proponent of equal pay for everybody was actually George Bernard Shaw, in his *The Intelligent Woman's Guide to Socialism and Capitalism* (1928). Shaw was no Marxist; indeed, he remarks (p. 441) that Marxism "is not only useless but disastrous as a guide to the practice of government."

Eroica (Third) Symphony, dedication by Beethoven. Few myths about music and musicians are more persistent than that Beethoven, after first dedicating his great Third Symphony, the *Eroica,* or "Heroic," to Napoleon in the belief that he was a champion of liberty, tore up the dedication page in wrath after Napoleon declared himself emperor. He did not; the page still exists, though it is true that Napoleon's name is deleted. Long after Napoleon's proclamation, however, Beethoven referred to the work as "eigentlich Bonaparte gennant"—or, freely translated, "really named for Bonaparte."

escalator, walking up. Many have the impression that an escalator "works harder" if one walks to its top as it moves. Quite the contrary; the lesser time spent upon it under this circumstance *lessens* its load.

Estes Park, Colorado. Often taken to be the same as Rocky Mountain National Park, which it is not. Estes Park, or Estes Park Village as some old-timers still call it, is some miles from Rocky Mountain National Park. In Colorado usage, an open area in the mountains was called a "park" in the old days, and often enough still is. Estes Park, then, is the name both of the valleylike plain in which Estes Park, the village, stands, and of the village itself. You can visit Estes Park without ever getting inside Rocky Mountain National Park.

Ethelred (or Aethelred) the Unready. Few epithets have done less justice to their bearers than "the unready" as applied to Ethelred, king of England from 978 to 1016. Far from being "unready," Ethelred, the father of Edward the Confessor, was in fact only too "ready." The epithet derives not from any word meaning "pre-pared," but rather from the ancient word "rede," meaning "coun-sel." (Ophelia, in *Hamlet* [act 1, sc. 3, line 50], speaks of one who "recks not his own rede;" that is, does not follow his own advice.) Ethelred was called the "unready" because he was prone to ignore the advice of the Old English council of wise men with the jaw-breaking title of the Witenagemot. In other words Ethelred, far from being too hesitant, was thought to be too rash.

eunuchs and erections. They can have them, all right, if castra-tion involves removal only of the testicles and takes place after puberty. It has, in fact, been said that some ancient Roman ladies —or, perhaps more accurately, certain ladies of ancient Rome— preferred eunuchs as lovers not only because of the freedom from risk of pregnancy but because they were actually able to maintain an erection longer than the uncastrated, although the method of establishing the statistical basis is a bit difficult to reconstruct.

Everest as world's highest mountain. This is a fact that depends entirely on a convention: measuring the height of mountains from sea level. If they were measured in terms of how far they stick out into space from the center of the earth, Chimborazo, a peak in the Ecuadorian Andes, at 20,561 feet, against Everest's 29,028, would be the "highest"; the earth is not round, but rather bulges out at the equator so that sea level there is some fourteen miles farther from the center of the earth than at the North Pole. As Robert L. Birch, a *Scientific American* reader, points out, Chimborazo is within two degrees of the equator; Everest is nearly twenty-eight degrees from it. On this basis, Chimborazo is some two miles higher than Everest.

"Everybody talks about the weather, but nobody does anything about it." Attributed to Mark Twain by practically everybody, this famous and funny remark first appeared in an editorial in the Hartford *Courant* for August 24, 1897. The editorial was not written by Twain; Bartlett attributes it to Charles Dudley Warner, Twain's friend and collaborator on the novel *The Gilded Age,* who was then associate editor of the *Courant.* Twain himself gave credit to Warner for the remark. As so often happens, how-ever, it became firmly attached to the more famous of the two men.

Every man has his price. This is not what Sir Robert Walpole either said, or, obviously, meant to imply. He had specific reference to a particular group of political enemies; his remark was *"All those men* [italics added] have their price." Had he actually said or meant what is so universally attributed to him, the words he really spoke would have been pointless.

evolution as "progress." It is generally assumed that in Darwinian terms, the "higher" forms have evolved from "lower" ones, which in turn implies that evolution is Nature's way of implementing what man calls "progress." But Darwin thought no such thing; in his *On the Origin of Species by Means of Natural Selection, or the Preservation of Favoured Races in the Struggle for Life,* usually simply if somewhat inaccurately called *Origin of Species,* Darwin remarks that "Natural Selection includes no necessary and universal law of advancement or development—it only takes advantage of such variations as arise and are beneficial to each creature under its complex relations of life . . . ." (See DARWIN, CHARLES ROBERT.)

exception proves the rule, the. This is one of the most fatuous of proverbs, as usually applied. Quite clearly an exception cannot prove a rule; quite the opposite; it *dis*proves it. Originally the expression made sense, because *prove* was used in its old-fashioned meaning: "test." (Latin *probo,* "I test," from which both *probe* and *probate* derive.) And, true enough, an exception certainly does test a rule.

"Proves," in "the exception proves the rule," is what scholars call a linguistic fossil—that is, the survival of an older meaning or form because it is preserved, like a fly in amber, by the surrounding context. "Proving ground" is another example; strictly, it's the place not where an automobile proves how good it is, but where it's tested to see if it *is* any good. "The proof of the pudding is in the eating" is another obvious example of "proves" as a linguistic fossil. Here, however, the older meaning survives at least enough so that the expression does make some sense.

Sir Arthur Conan Doyle was not taken in: In *The Sign of Four* he has Sherlock Holmes say to Dr. Watson, "I never make exceptions. An exception disproves the rule."

exchange of weapons, duel scene in Shakespeare's *Hamlet*. In modern productions of *Hamlet,* the exchange of weapons between Hamlet and Laertes—who carries a weapon both "envenom'd and unbated," or poisoned and sharpened—is commonly played as if it were accidental. To "change rapiers" involved a definite technique in Shakespeare's day, deliberately employed as a means of disarming an opponent. Any Elizabethan fencer would be taught how to perform the maneuver by getting inside the opponent's point, grasping the hilt of his weapon with the left hand, and twisting outward. Because of the leverage employed, the opponent cannot prevent having his rapier torn from his grasp. His only defense is to employ the same disarm; that is, he also moves in, seizes the attacker's rapier hilt with *his* left hand, and rips it outward. Thus both fencers would be disarmed. More importantly, they would also have exchanged weapons, both fencers stepping back, shifting the weapon taken from the opponent from left hand to right, and continuing the match. This disarm-and-seizure by left-hand exchange, a method well known in Shakespeare's time, would have been exactly appropriate for the dueling scene in *Hamlet,* allowing Hamlet to force an exchange in order to obtain the sharp weapon for himself.

Turning the exchange in Hamlet into the inadvertent result of a scuffle not only makes Laertes seem uncharacteristically stupid in accepting a weapon he knows to be harmless while allowing Hamlet to pick up the deadly rapier; it also makes the final, climactic scene turn upon a mere accident, surely less than we expect from England's greatest playwright. In the words of Professor James L. Jackson, Chairman of the Department of English at George Mason University, ". . . in *Hamlet* the [forced] exchange is crucial, of course, since one weapon is sharpened to a point and the other is not. . . . This exchange would have shown Hamlet in a dignified light, trying to control his fate—instead of Hamlet's being the lucky one to catch up the sharp rapier after a vulgar scrum. Even worse is the idiotic idea that Hamlet steps on the sharp weapon which has been knocked from Laertes' hand and presents his own blunt [weapon] to Laertes, who is then supposed to be dumb enough to take it."

F

Far from the Madding Crowd. This is the title of Thomas Hardy's novel as correctly rendered; the word is not *maddening*, which is often said and which means something else. *Madding* means "frenzied"; *maddening* means "annoying." Hardy did not originate the phrase, but borrowed it from Thomas Gray's "Elegy Written in a Country Churchyard."

fasting as beneficial. The belief that doing without food and/or water somehow purifies, preserves, strengthens, or "cleanses" is a superstition analogous with the old concept that "bleeding" is beneficial. (See BYRON, LORD—DEATH OF.)

As the science author Martin Gardner puts it, "Actually a prolonged fast by a healthy person can cause nothing but harm. There is such a general weakening by the entire body, and lowering of resistance to disease, that only an extremely vigorous and healthy person can stand a lengthy fast."

fire department, first in the United States. The first American fire department was not started by Benjamin Franklin, though he is usually given the credit. (Franklin did organize the first fire department in Philadelphia.) In 1659, almost a half century before Franklin's birth in 1706, Peter Stuyvesant saw to the distribution of 250 buckets, plus ladders and hooks, in New Amsterdam; a tax for maintaining the equipment was levied. Ten years later a "brentmaster" was appointed: probably the first fire chief.

first American "ace" in World War I. Captain Eddie Ricken-backer was not the first World War I American pilot to become an "ace" by shooting down five enemy planes. In his autobiography, *Rickenbacker* (1967), he mentions several who were already aces when he started combat flying in France in the spring of 1918, among them Raoul Lufbery (described by Ricken-backer as "the American ace of aces"; Lufbery, though French born, had emigrated to the United States as a young man). Rickenbacker was ultimately to shoot down more enemy aircraft than any other American pilot: twenty-five, four of which were balloons. But he was not the first to become an American ace.

According to his account in his autobiography, "Rickenbacker" was originally "Rickenbacher"; Rickenbacker changed the "h" to a "k," he says, in order to minimize its Germanic origin.

first day of the twentieth century. January 1, 1900, was *not* the first day of the twentieth century; the first day of the twentieth century was, in fact, January 1, 1901. (From January 1, year 1, to December 31, 99, was obviously only ninety-nine years. And so on.)

First heavier-than-air craft to make a sustained flight under its own power. The airplane was not invented by the Wright Broth-ers; in 1896 Samuel Pierpont Langley's "Model No. 5" flew about three quarters of a mile along the shores of the Potomac, remain-ing aloft some one and one half minutes. It descended gently, was refueled and relaunched the same afternoon. Langley's plane did not carry a passenger; it weighed only twenty-six pounds and was only sixteen feet long. It was driven by a one horsepower steam engine.

To the Wright Brothers does go the honor of achieving the first flight to carry a human passenger, at Kitty Hawk, North Carolina, on December 17, 1903. But to Langley must go the credit for proving that powered flight is possible—although when he prophesied that one day the airplane would be used to carry men and women he was laughed at.

first nonstop transatlantic flight. The first person to fly the Atlantic nonstop was most certainly not Charles A. Lindbergh. Perhaps the most famous of the Robert Ripley "Believe It or Not" cartoons pointed out in 1927 that, in fact, Lindbergh was the sixty-seventh man to make a nonstop flight across the Atlantic. Following the appearance of the item, Ripley received some two hundred thousand indignant letters and telegrams. But Ripley was right; Lindbergh was merely the first to make a nonstop *solo* flight across the ocean.

However, long before Lindbergh, in June 1919, John William Alcock and Arthur Whitten Brown in a two-engined Vickers had flown nonstop from St. Johns, Newfoundland, to Ireland. The other sixty-four who crossed the Atlantic nonstop before Lindbergh were thirty-one in a British dirigible, the R-34, in July 1919, and the thirty-three aboard the German dirigible LX-126, built as a war reparations payment and later christened the *Los Angeles,* which was delivered to the United States by a transatlantic flight in October 1924.

The flight of the R-34 was a round trip, not surprising in view of the fact that it was based in Britain and getting it back home by surface mail would have been, to say the least, a bit on the awkward side. Ripley might, thus, have said that ninety-seven passengers on four separate flights had crossed the Atlantic nonstop before Lindbergh, and still have been correct.

first settlement in New England. Plymouth was not the first settlement in New England. In 1607, long before the famous 1620 landing, a colony numbering 120 persons was established at the mouth of the Kennebec River in Maine under the leadership of George Popham. It did not, however, last; a combination of circumstances, including the hard winter and the death of two of the colony's chief sponsors, resulted in its abandonment the next year. But it remains the first New England colony to be established, short-lived though it was.

fish, as "brain food." Perhaps the myth that fish is "good for the brain" arose from the fact that the nerve tissue which forms a part of the brain is rich in phosphorus, and fish do provide phosphorus-containing compounds. But so do meat, poultry, eggs, and milk. Sometimes celery is thought to be a "brain food."

But there does not seem to be even a tenuous basis for this one; celery contains only a little phosphorous.

fish, as Christian symbol. Although it might seem to have, the fish as a symbol for Christ and, by extension, for Christians or Christianity, has nothing to do with the miracle of the loaves and fishes. The fish symbol, found in the catacombs and many other ancient monuments, started as a Greek rebus. The letters in the Greek word for "fish" form the first letters of the Greek words "Jesus Christ, Son of God, Savior."

fleas, according to Jonathan Swift.

> For dogs have fleas upon their backs,
> Upon their backs to bite 'em;
> The fleas themselves have lesser fleas,
> And so *ad infinitum*.

Often regarded as anonymous, the quatrain above is actually a rather loose rendition of what Jonathan Swift had to say in *On Poetry. A Rhapsody:*

> So, naturalists observe, a flea
> Hath smaller fleas that on him prey;
> And these have smaller still to bite 'em;
> And so proceed *ad infinitum.*
> Thus every poet, in his kind,
> Is bit by him that comes behind.

flying fish. In spite of the implication of their name, these fish don't really fly, of course, in the sense that birds and some insects do. Instead, they glide. However, they can make as much as a quarter of a mile in one glide at speeds up to thirty miles an hour.

Similarly, flying squirrels do not fly but glide and only downward. A flying squirrel climbs up one tree, glides to the foot of the next, and repeats this process.

Fogg, Phineas. In fact, it's Fogg, Phileas, if you are referring to the hero of Jules Verne's *Around the World in Eighty Days.*

forest fires, cause of. Most forest fires are not caused by careless campers or tourists, but by lightning. Of the others, many are, it is true, "man-caused." But the man responsible is not so likely to be a weekend visitor to the woods as to be loggers or even the United States Forest Service itself. The Forest Service supervises slash-burning, which is the cheapest (though by no means the only) way of getting rid of the cut or broken limbs, uprooted shrubs, and other residue of logging operations. Only too often, slash-burning gets out of hand, and a forest fire results.

forgotten man. So much a part of Franklin D. Roosevelt's campaign vocabulary was this expression that he was thought to have invented it. He adopted it, for William Graham Sumner, famous sociologist of Yale University, used the phrase in a speech in 1883.

forks. Perhaps encouraged by the memorable film performance of the late Charles Laughton as a finger-licking Henry VIII, the belief that forks were unknown until quite recently is widespread. This is not so; there is a reference to a "silvir forke" for table use in the *Oxford English Dictionary.* The quotation is dated 1463, almost thirty years before Henry VIII was born.

forlorn hope. Apparently this expression derives from the Dutch *verloren hoop* which does not, however, mean forlorn hope (the assumption that it does is folk etymology) , but rather "lost [*verloren*] band or group [*hoop*]." Neither forlorn nor hope in this expression, in other words, originally meant either "forlorn" or "hope." But since the Dutch expression, like the French *enfants perdus* and the German *verloren Kinder,* refers to soldiers embarking on a desperate mission, it is easy to see how the common meaning became established.

Fourscore and seven years ago our forefathers brought forth upon this continent a new nation. . . . . This is not what Lincoln said, although many people say it today. What he did say was, "Fourscore and seven years ago our *fathers* brought forth *on* this continent a new nation. . . ." (Italics, of course, are added.)

Frankenstein. A common misconception is that the name of the monster in Mary Shelley's book, *Frankenstein, or The Modern Prometheus,* is Frankenstein. Frankenstein was not the name of the monster but the name of the person who created the monster.

Thus, to use the word as an equivalent of *monster,* as is often done, is historically incorrect. However, common usage has effected a curious transfer of the name from the creator to the thing created.

Even those who are aware that the creator of the monster was Frankenstein are still likely, however, to think of him as "Doctor" Frankenstein, another common but mistaken belief. He was not a doctor; he wasn't even a medical student. A young man with a love of science, Frankenstein turned to natural history and mathematics as a seventeen-year-old student at the University of Ingolstadt, where he created his monster. There really was—and is—an Ingolstadt; it is a city in Bavaria, and it had a university. There is also a city in Germany called Frankenstein, and while it is not, of course, the locale of the story, it may have provided Mrs. Shelley with the name of her young student, so overshadowed by his creation.

Mrs. Shelley, who was the famous poet's second wife, wrote *Frankenstein* in 1818, when she could not have been more than twenty-one. She was one of a party of three in Switzerland when it was proposed that each should write a tale of the supernatural. Only hers became immortal. To have done so well so young she was obviously in fairly fast literary company: the other two in the party were Percy Bysshe Shelley himself, and George Gordon, Lord Byron.

Franklin, Benjamin—and the *Saturday Evening Post*. Two phrases have been identified with the *Saturday Evening Post* from time very nearly immemorial: "An American Institution," and "Founded A.D. 1728 by Benjamin Franklin." Both phrases continue to appear on the "new" *Post.*

An American institution the *Post* no doubt was; its death as a weekly magazine was mourned by millions.

But it does not, did not, in fact never did have any connection whatsoever with Benjamin Franklin. The story that he "founded" the magazine, or any magazine which could be regarded as being even remotely an ancestor of the *Post,* was simply invented out of whole cloth in 1897. A magazine so sternly dedicated for so many years to the old-fashioned American virtues should not have been, one cannot help feeling, so cavalier with the truth.

It is true enough that in 1729 (not 1728), when Franklin was in his early twenties, he bought a mediocre newspaper, the

Pennsylvania Gazette, which he then, with his characteristic genius, turned into a flourishing success. It survived Franklin's death in 1790 by some twenty-five years, disappearing in 1815. The *Post* was born August 4, 1821, some six years later.

The story of the false "genealogy," as told by Ralph S. Combs in his unpublished paper, "The Saturday Evening Post: A Condensed, Nostalgic History," is as follows. The *Saturday Evening Post* was the brainchild of Charles Alexander and Samuel Atkinson, printers, who took over the printshop that had been used by the *Gazette* some years before. Combs reports that the only relationship between the *Gazette* and the *Post* is that "both publications were printed in the same shop at different times."

When Cyrus H. K. Curtis bought the *Post* in 1897, its masthead announced that it had been founded "A.D. 1821." On the cover of the January 29, 1898, issue, however, printed while the magazine was under the guidance of its first editor, William George Jordan, mysteriously sprouted the phrase "Founded A.D. 1728." Shortly thereafter, in September of 1899, when George Horace Lorimer was starting the long editorial career with the *Post* which was to identify him with "his" magazine, the cover of the *Post* first carried the magic phrase: "Founded A.D. 1728 by Benjamin Franklin." It was a phrase never to be abandoned, though many were aware that the claim (which was never made by the original founders in 1821) was patently false.

free lance. Although it sounds as if it came right out of the Middle Ages, the phrase *free lance* is a comparatively modern invention, having been coined by Sir Walter Scott in 1820.

French fried potatoes. Belgians claim that "French" fried potatoes originated not in France but in Belgium. A gentleman of Liège named Rodolphe de Warsage (born 1876) writes of bringing home this delicacy from the little shops where they were prepared, tasting them on the way. (In those days Belgian "French" fries were not prepared in the home.) Their popularity spread to the north of France, especially Lille. And now—*voilà.* They are everywhere, especially America.

French generals "kissing" soldiers when presenting awards. It is not done, although that appears to take place. What the French officer does is to give the soldier an accolade: that is, he touches each cheek in turn with his own, the medieval ritual for the new-made knight.

Freud, Sigmund—and sexual license. Somehow Sigmund Freud has been espoused as an advocate of sexual laissez-faire. Dr. Freud was a very moral—even severe—person, who would probably be horrified at what has been wrought in his name.

fuller's earth. Neither invented, discovered, nor popularized by someone named Fuller. "Fuller" in "fuller's earth" is not a proper name and thus should not be capitalized, although it often enough is. To "full" cloth is to treat it so as to give it more body (i.e., make it fuller). One John Olson discovered fuller's earth at Benson, Ark., in 1891; it's a kind of clay. Since it turned out to be most useful when employed by a "fuller" of cloth, fur, etc., the name "fuller's earth" came to be applied to it.

Fulton, Robert, inventor of the steamboat. Not only did Robert Fulton not invent the steamboat but he does not even come close to deserving the credit. In fact, it was only after observing the successes of others that in 1807 Fulton built his own, twenty years after James Rumsey and John Fitch had each run steamboats, on the Potomac and Delaware rivers respectively. Nor was it, incidentally, either registered as or ever referred to as the *Clermont* either by Fulton or his associate, Robert R. Livingston.

How the name *Clermont* came to be so firmly fixed to Fulton's boat is told by Ashley Montagu and Edward Darling in *The Prevalence of Nonsense* (1967). As they remark, in effect, it is a fascinating if somewhat discouraging illustration of how popular error survives in the face of plain evidence to the contrary. Fulton's boat was registered simply, if prosaically, as *North River Steam Boat*. Its first hailing port was the *town* called Clermont. But the boat itself was never so referred to by anyone—until a biography by one Cadwallader D. Colden, *The Life of Robert Fulton*, was published in 1817, two years after Fulton's death. Nobody knows why Colden chose to call the boat by a name it never had. But he did; and from then on the error was fixed, to be eternally repeated in textbooks, reference works, and encyclopedias—including the *Encyclopaedia Britannica*.

But grosser by far, of course, is the mistaken attribution of the invention of the steamboat to Fulton. Particularly sad is the case of John Fitch; few have so obviously pioneered and been so obviously overlooked by succeeding generations. He got the idea in 1785; the next year his steamboat was operating on the Delaware River. In 1787 he built a larger boat, and by 1790 he was operating regularly scheduled and advertised trips carrying both passengers and freight between Philadelphia and Trenton. Several states granted him exclusive rights for boats propelled by steam.

But, unfortunately, he was ahead of his time. He could neither survive financially nor persuade anyone to back him. He died both broke and broken at Bardstown, Kentucky, in 1798.

Fitch died in obscurity because he could not put his idea across. Fulton achieved fame because he implemented and promoted the ideas of others. (So did Elias Howe.) But when Fulton offered the steamboat idea to the great Napoleon, he turned it down as impractical. If Napoleon had recognized its value, perhaps he could have invaded England.

G

Galileo. There are many fallacies connected with this famous Italian astronomer and physicist:

1. Galileo did not invent the telescope; it was invented in 1608 in Holland. He did, however, make his own telescope in 1609 and pioneered its use as an astronomical instrument.

2. Although *tried* by the Inquisition he was never tortured.

3. He never uttered under his breath "E pur si mouve" ("Nevertheless it does move"). The story that after his "recantation" or "abjuration"—and there does seem to be some question as to whether Galileo admitted he was wrong or simply agreed to keep quiet—Galileo rose from his knees and added this remark under his breath did not surface until 1761, some 130 years after the trial.

4. He never spent so much as a day in prison; his punishment was a kind of "house arrest," in the phrase of Montagu and Darling. He was never actually put into a prison cell.

5. He did not come to any theories about the pendulum as a result of observing a swinging lamp in the cathedral of Pisa, nor did he drop anything from the Leaning Tower to show that objects of differing weights would fall to earth at the same velocity. Neither of these "facts" was mentioned by Galileo or his contemporaries; they were attributed to him years later.

6. Otherwise, what most people think they know about Galileo is quite correct, except that his name was Galileo only in the same sense that Lincoln's name was Abraham. His father was Vincenzio Galilei, who named his son Galileo Galilei.

Gandhi, Mahatma—and civil disobedience, and Henry David Thoreau. Henry Seidel Canby, among other distinguished scholars, gives Henry David Thoreau's famous essay "Civil Disobedience" credit for introducing to Mohandas K. Gandhi (his actual name; *Mahatma* is a title of respect) the concept of passive resistance; indeed, this is almost an article of faith among scholars in American literature. But Gandhi did not read "Civil Disobedience" until 1907. It was in 1906 that Gandhi and his followers first employed passive resistance, in a protest against the Indian Registration Ordinance of South Africa.

Gandhi himself did not particularly like the negative implications of the phrase "passive resistance." He preferred to call it *satyagraha,* variously translated as "soul force" or "truth force," a manifestation of *Ahimsa,* or a positive state of love.

Although so thoroughly identified with the struggles of India for independence, Gandhi did not arrive at his philosophy on native ground. His intellectually formative years were spent not in India but in South Africa, where he went in 1893 as a young lawyer for an Indian firm. He lived in South Africa for more than twenty years, and it was against Boer repressions of the Indian population of South Africa that he directed his early efforts and came to stand as a symbol of resistance without violence. He did not, in fact, oppose the British during his early days in South Africa; he even received a decoration from the British government for his work in connection with an ambulance corps during the Boer War. Later, of course, it was to be another story; and the 1906 resistance was directed against the government of the Transvaal, at least nominally British since the end of the war.

Gandhi himself gave credit to the New Testament for first influencing him in the direction of satyagraha, though later he said he found his philosophy reflected also in the Hindu scripture, Bhagavad Gita. Those who have read *Resurrection* by Leo Tolstoi should not be surprised that Gandhi also was under his influence, again before he encountered Thoreau. Certainly Gandhi found in Thoreau a kindred soul. But he did not originally derive his principal ideas or philosophy from him. The most he would admit was that Thoreau's ideas "paralleled" his own.

Garbo, Greta—feet and penchant for solitude. Everybody knows two things about Greta Garbo: she has big feet, and she once said, "I vant to be alone." Neither is true. Her shoes are 7AA, about right for her size. And what she really said—but let her put it in her own words: "I never said, 'I want to be alone' . . . I only said, 'I want to be *let* alone.' "

gasoline tanks, "empty." An empty gasoline tank is far more dangerous than a full one. Gasoline burns only when mixed with air; as every mechanic knows, allowing a spark near a gasoline tank which has been emptied of fluid—in order to make a repair by welding, for example—risks setting off the highly explosive vapor inside. Welders always fill the "empty" tank with water, to drive out the gasoline-air mixture remaining, before starting to work.

gendarmes. *Gendarmes* is not a generic term for policemen in France, even though it is often used that way by Americans. Gendarmes are soldiers on police duty; they belong to the military. The word for the police in France is simply *police*. The French even pronounce it correctly.

Geneva Conference of 1954 on Vietnam. It is widely believed that the United States was alone in failing to sign or to ratify what is loosely called the Geneva agreement, or the Geneva accords, of 1954. The fact is that none of the powers involved—Cambodia, the Democratic Republic of Vietnam, France, Laos, the People's Republic of China, the Republic of Vietnam, the Union of Soviet Socialist Republics, the United Kingdom, and the United States of America—signed what was officially called the "Final Declaration of the Geneva Conference on the problem of restoring peace in Indochina." It is possible that the attitude of the United States influenced the decision of all the powers not to require signatures. Nor did a single one of the various delegates ever even submit the declaration to his government for ratification.

In fact, the agreements are vague, incomplete, and legally defective. As a result, complete and satisfactory answers to the question of what violated what, or whom, or in what order, or why, are impossible.

Nor is it true that the Geneva Conference met only to consider the problems of Indochina. Perhaps because it ended in a deadlock which amounted to failure, few recall that the Korean question was also a part of the conference, but it was.

German silver. German silver is made from copper, zinc, and nickel. There is no silver in it.

"Get thee to a nunnery!" The ever-widening gap between Shakespeare's meaning and what audiences now take to be his meaning is well illustrated in this famous injunction by Hamlet to Ophelia. *Nunnery* to Shakespeare's audience was recognized at once as Elizabethan slang for "whorehouse." When Hamlet, in this famous rejection scene (act 3, sc. 1, lines 90 ff.) , spurns Ophelia's advances, he is being a good deal more frankly brutal than most of those in today's audience realize.

Gettysburg Address. The popular notion that Lincoln wrote his most famous speech on the back of an envelope while en route by train to Gettysburg is wholly false. As William E. Barton says in *Lincoln at Gettysburg* (1950) , "It would have been an incredible thing that [Lincoln] should have made no preparation for an address to be delivered on such an occasion as the Gettysburg dedication."

The address was delivered on November 19, 1863. Lincoln, whose intent from the beginning was to keep his remarks very brief, nevertheless started work on the first draft on Sunday, November 8, almost two weeks before the event. He wrote, rewrote, fussed over it; in all, there were to be five written drafts. It is possible—no one knows for sure—that he may, indeed, have continued the process of revision on the train. But he most certainly did not write it there, nor did he use an "envelope" or any kind of paper he might have picked up on a train; the speech was written on the kind of paper Lincoln regularly used in the White House.

Nor is it true that Lincoln "mumbled" his remarks, or failed to be heard for any other reason. True, he spoke after a master orator at a time when oratory was an established art (Walt Whitman had trained for it) ; and his style was different from that of the preceding speaker, Edward Everett. But Lincoln was himself a highly skilled and experienced speaker; he knew how to address an audience. And it is plain that he was both heard and understood, even though his remarks did not immediately become enshrined as classic. (There were still plenty who recognized their merit; Edward Everett was one of them. And it is worth noting that the Associated Press report of the speech carried in the New York *Tribune* has Lincoln interrupted no fewer than five times by applause and adds that following the address there was "long-continued applause.") It should be noted, however, that Ashley Montagu and Edward Darling in their excellent sequel to *The Prevalence of Nonsense* (1967), *The Ignorance of Certainty,* point out that the Associated Press had been given an advance copy of Lincoln's speech and the references to applause might have been inserted out of deference to the president when the speech was printed. (Montagu and Darling, taking their cue from the reporter who took down the president's remarks as he spoke them, are inclined to skepticism about the applause.)

Interestingly enough, the story that Lincoln wrote his address on the train owes its currency, at least in part, to a letter written by his son Robert long after the event—in 1885. But as Barton points out, Robert's letter "only shows that Robert T. Lincoln . . . had no very exact knowledge of the origin . . . of the address."

ghost-writer. Many people are not aware that there is a difference between a ghost-writer and a collaborator. A book by a celebrity, with "as told to" and the name of some writer under the celebrity's own name, is not ghost-written. It's a collaboration, and as such both legitimate and honest.

A truly ghost-written book is, in a sense, a lie: that is, the celebrity's name appears alone as the author, whether or not he or she contributed so much as a line.

The late Charles Lindbergh's *We* is sometimes incorrectly cited as an example of a ghost-written book. This misconception may be based on the fact that the original manuscript of *We,* by Carlisle MacDonald, was actually a ghost job. However, Lindbergh, when he learned that the manuscript was done in the first person (he had been extensively interviewed by MacDonald), refused to permit its publication and sat down and wrote his own version.

gin, origin of. *Gin* does not derive from the city Geneva, which is neither the birthplace of gin nor the source of its name. The word comes instead from *geneva* (no capital) , a corruption of the French word *genièvre,* or "juniper," the source of gin's characteristic flavor. A Dutch physician invented gin in the seventeenth century as a medicinal.

Git thar fustest with the mostest. This is certainly *not* what Nathan Bedford Forrest, the Confederate general, said, according to the two other generals who quoted him; their testimony is that Forrest said, simply, "Get there first with the most men." How the vulgate version came into being is hard to determine; it may involve a certain amount of snobbism, since Forrest was self-educated. But he was neither ignorant nor illiterate.

goats eating tin cans. Even goats draw the line somewhere; they will nibble at practically anything, but they don't eat tin cans.

God is always on the side of the big battalions. Napoleon is most often credited with having made this remark first. However, it can be traced back to Tacitus, who wrote in his *History* (Book IV, 17) during the first century ". . . the gods are with the stronger (side) ," and thence through a half dozen writers of the seventeenth and eighteenth centuries, including Voltaire, Frederick the Great, and Madame de Sévigné.

God rest you, merry gentlemen. This Yuletide phrase is often printed—and sung—with this punctuation and the pause it implies. But that's not the way the charming old carol has it. Properly, it's "God rest you merry, gentlemen." The phrase "rest you merry," which is older than Shakespeare, who uses it in *Romeo and Juliet,* dates to the beginning of the fifteenth century.

Incidentally, the Old English word for "merry" did not mean gay and lively, but merely pleasant or agreeable. By the fourteenth century, however, it had acquired its present meaning.

"God tempers the wind to the shorn lamb." This quotation is not from the Bible, to which it is frequently attributed, but from

Laurence Sterne's novel *A Sentimental Journey*. It is not, moreover, original with Sterne—as perhaps he indicates by having one of the characters in the novel speak it. One Henri Estienne, 1531–1598, is credited with having said it first. Of course, he did say it in French. ("Dieu mesure le froid à la brebis tondue.") *Froid* doesn't quite mean the same as "wind," however, and there's more sheep than lamb (*agneau*) in *brebis*.

Golden Rule. "Do unto others as you would have others do unto you" is found nowhere in the King James Bible, but is rather a paraphrase of various statements from both Old and New Testaments, among them Christ's words as reported in Matt. 7:12, "Therefore all things whatsoever ye would that men should do to you, do ye even so to them: for this is the law and the prophets"; and as reported in Luke 6:31, "And as ye would that men should do to you, do ye also to them likewise." Lev. 19:18, from the Old Testament, offers ". . . thou shalt love thy neighbour as thyself . . . ." (Incidentally, this is often taken to be a New Testament utterance.)

golf, origin of. There is no firm evidence that golf originated in Scotland, as many people think. It may well have started in Holland, where a game much like golf, with a name (*kolven*) from which *golf* may be derived, was played on ice. It has even been suggested that the Romans, who occupied Britain until A.D. 410, brought the game with them; it may be that a sport of theirs called *paganica*, apparently played with a leather ball stuffed with feathers and a bent stick, was the ancestor of golf. True or not, the image of Cicero trying to talk his way out of a sand trap does have some charm.

gorilla. The gorilla is not the fierce, belligerent animal that is commonly portrayed. Actually it is rather moody, slow, and limited in initiative. Its diet is vegetables, birds' eggs, and small mammals.

got, gotten. Contrary to common American belief, "gotten" is not the English way to say "got." Quite the reverse; "gotten" is considered by the English, who do not hesitate to say "I have got my pay," as something of an American barbarism. How "gotten" came into American English is hard to determine. An educated guess might be the old-fashioned schoolteacher notion that it is somehow improper, even vulgar, to say "I have got a pencil." However, those Americans who say "have got" may be hoist on either of two petards; some will think the expression illiterate, which it is not; others will, paradoxically, see in it an attempt to imitate upper-class English usage, which it is.

Gothic. In a manner of speaking this word is a phony, for it has nothing to do with the Goths. The word was coined in the Renaissance, and used by painters like Raphael and writers like Giorgio Vasari to describe the glorious architecture of the twelfth-to-sixteenth centuries, which to their classic taste seemed rude and barbarous.

Gothic arch as result of observing interlacing tree branches. It is sometimes sentimentally observed that the Gothic arch must have resulted from some unknown genius's observation of the interlacing branches of trees above a path or roadway. There may be a fancied resemblance; but the Gothic arch developed out of Byzantine and Romanesque architecture for solid engineering reasons.

The original Roman arch was well suited to the kind of massive engineering projects characteristic of the Roman Empire; but (as in the famous aqueduct at Nîmes, or the Colosseum) in order to achieve height the arches had to be, in effect, stacked one atop the other because too large a Roman arch puts too much thrust upon the sides or walls, which unless impossibly thick could not continue to stand. The genius of the Gothic arch is that it directs more of the thrust of its weight downward (though not so much so that the flying buttress was still not essential, in many cases, to shore up the walls against outward collapse).

Thus, when the seeds of the Renaissance were sprouting and the aspirations of builders and architects were literally aimed toward the skies, the Gothic arch, which is in a sense the Roman arch squeezed together, made possible the soaring interiors which today continue to impress worshipers and tourists alike. And though it is always dangerous to generalize overmuch about cultural differences, it may be that an enlightening look at the contrast between the Roman and the Renaissance spirit is implicit in the difference between the Pantheon and the cathedral at Chartres: the one squatly huge, round, sturdy, symmetrical; the other—well, Chartres.

gout. It used to be thought that gout was caused by eating too much rich food and drinking too much of alcoholic beverages. To this day gout sufferers receive too much advice along these lines. Actually the cause is not known. We do know that it results from the accumulation of purines $(C_5H_4N_4)$ in the affected part. An attack can be precipitated by such an innocent thing as too much exercise with too little water intake.

Another mistaken belief is that gout is visited mostly upon elderly gentlemen. This is far from true, for vigorous young men can succumb to attacks of gout which they successfully resist in later years.

"Government of the people, by the people, and for the people." This famous remark, identified with Lincoln's Gettysburg Address of 1863, was probably inspired by Theodore Parker (died 1860), a Unitarian minister better known in his day than ours. He said "government becomes more and more of all, by all and for all."

"Go west, young man . . . ." This phrase is not original with Horace Greeley, to whom it is usually attributed, but first appeared in an article in the Terre Haute *Express* in 1851, written by a John Soule or, as sometimes spelled, Soulé. In an attempt to give credit where it was due, Greeley even reprinted Soule's article in his newspaper, the New York *Tribune*. But to no avail; the phrase stuck to Greeley.

Grant's whiskey and Lincoln. The oft-told, oft-believed tale that Abraham Lincoln, when told that Gen. Ulysses S. Grant drank too much, said "Tell me what brand it is, and I'll send a barrel to the other generals," is a fabrication pure and simple. One Charles G. Halpine, writing under the name Miles O'Reilly, put the words into Lincoln's mouth in a burlesque report of an imaginary banquet. Unlike some of the other remarks falsely attributed to Lincoln, this one does seem to have the stamp of the authentic Abe upon it. For that reason, no doubt, it has continued to be attributed to him.

Lincoln himself repeatedly denied that he had ever made the remark about Grant and the other generals. According to W. E. Woodward, Lincoln traced the story's origins to George II of England, who, when somebody complained that Gen. James Wolfe was mad, said, "If General Wolfe is mad I hope he bites some of my other generals."

As a matter of fact, the whole issue of Grant's drunkenness looks most dubious when examined. In a recent biography, *Grant Takes Command* (1969), the respected historian Bruce Catton maintains that the whole thing is a myth started by a John Rawlins, who misunderstood the nature of Grant's participation on a rather wet evening—but one involving some of Grant's aides, not Grant himself. In fact, says Catton, it was Grant who broke up the party, when he found out about it, with a few words that "raised blisters." There is little doubt that Catton believes Grant to have been "as abstemious as any man needs to be . . . ."

greatest good for the greatest number. First, although the phrase is often cited as his, that's not how Jeremy Bentham put it. Second, he neither originated this nor any analogous statement, nor pretended to. Third, Bentham attributed the statement to the wrong person or persons. Said Bentham in volume 10 of his *Works,* "Priestley was the first (unless it was Beccaria) who taught my lips to pronounce this sacred truth,—that the greatest happiness of the greatest number is the foundation of morals and legislation."

But earlier than Joseph Priestley or the Marchese di Beccaria came one Francis Hutcheson, who in 1720 wrote, "That action is best which procures the greatest happiness for the greatest numbers."

Great Society, the. Although used by President Lyndon B. Johnson to describe his objective for America, this expression was not coined by him. It was the title of a book by the famous liberal writer Graham Wallas and it appeared in 1914, nearly a half a century before LBJ became president.

greyhound. Somewhat surprisingly, the first syllable has no reference to color. The "grey" in "greyhound" derives from a very ancient word of uncertain origin, but one that does not have any connection with the other "grey" as used by interior decorators or painters. The *Oxford English Dictionary* suggests *grøy*, an Old Norse term for "bitch," although it soon came to mean, apparently, simply "dog" without reference to sex. Incidentally, the modern racing greyhound, product of centuries of breeding, probably does not much resemble the animal to which the term was originally applied.

ground glass in food. Sneaking ground glass into an enemy's food, in spite of the popular belief, would not likely cause him very much if any discomfort—if, that is, it was ground finely enough to be undetectable. Glass is not per se a poison.

Bits and pieces of glass are quite another story. Anything big enough and sharp enough to cut the walls of the stomach or intestines is going to cause plenty of trouble.

growing pains. In years gone by young people who complained of pain in their legs or other parts of their bodies were frequently dismissed with the advice, "Oh, you just have growing pains." But growth of itself does not cause pain. All persistent pain has some important reason.

guillotine. This instrument of execution was not named for its inventor. Nor, in fact, was it even called the guillotine when it was first introduced in France. Nor was the inventor himself the first victim, though all of this is widely believed. Indeed, the guillotine is not even French; it was adapted by a Dr. Louis from a similar device that had been used in Italy for centuries. As a result, it was first called a "Louison" in France. It took its present name from Dr. Joseph Ignace Guillotin, who, because he was opposed for humanitarian reasons to the cruel eighteenth-century devices of torture and execution, devoted much time to persuading the National Assembly to adopt the guillotine officially as the state means of execution. This was done on March 25, 1792.

The first victim of the guillotine was no political figure, but a certain M. Pelissier, a bandit. During the Reign of Terror, however, the original guillotine alone cut off the heads of some eight thousand Frenchmen. So strongly did Dr. Guillotin and his family feel at having their name attached to what had become so infamous an agent of terror that in 1814, when the doctor died, his children officially changed the family name.

The guillotine is still the official means of execution in France.

guilt, presumption of in French law. Most Americans think that in French law, as contrasted with Anglo-Saxon jurisprudence, the accused is considered guilty until he or she is proved innocent. But this is not true. Perhaps the misconception arises because in French law the plea "not guilty" does not exist; rather, the prisoner must prove that the examining magistrate has no basis for an indictment, which is to say that the magistrate has no case. Indeed, French law is in some respects more forgiving than Anglo-American; it is possible for a murderer to escape punishment if the jury finds extenuating circumstances even though a murder is actually proved.

guns of Singapore (World War II). Often repeated is the story, apparently given currency by Winston Churchill himself, that the guns of the Singapore fortifications were installed so that they could fire only toward the sea, since the British assumed that attack from the land, or "impenetrable-jungle" side, was quite impossible. Of course, that was the side from which the Japanese actually attacked.

But there isn't a word of truth in the tale, according to Richard Miers, writing in *A Law unto Themselves: Twelve Portraits* by C. Northcote Parkinson (Houghton Mifflin, 1966). (Miers was commanding officer of the First Battalion, South Wales Borderers, Singapore, in the early 1950s.) Says Miers:

> The oddest feature of the Singapore forts is the legend attached to them that their guns would not bear on the side from which the Japanese actually attacked . . . . Most of the guns had, in fact, a 360-degree traverse, the exception being those originally mounted in a battleship, which retained the dead arc of their naval mounting—the arc representing the ship's own super-structure. Not only would they bear, but some of them were in action for two days, firing until the gunners were exhausted and their ammunition spent. Whoever was responsible for the fall of Singapore, it was not the officer who sited its fixed defenses nor even the officer who allocated them (sensibly enough) a high proportion of armor-piercing shell.

gyrocompass. The persistent notion to the contrary, notwithstanding, a magnetic compass whose platform has been stabilized gyroscopically is not a gyrocompass. It's just a compass whose platform has been stabilized by gyroscopic means; and while it may be easier to read because it doesn't jiggle around quite so much, it will still be subject to all the faults magnetic compasses are heir to.

A true gyrocompass is not a magnetic device at all; instead, it exploits the unique characteristic of a rapidly spinning wheel, or gyroscope, to maintain a constant position *in space*. Gyrocompasses have their limitations, too: bearing friction, for example, and the fact that since a gyroscope ideally spins in the same plane forever, the turning of the inconstant earth beneath means that constant correction must be applied to the gyrocompass's indications of direction, or heading.

All kinds of compasses are, in a sense, much less important to navigation today than they have been in the past, particularly to aerial navigation. The only "perfect" navigational system for aircraft is one which enables the navigator to check his location directly against known points on earth, either visually—unlikely at six hundred miles an hour and thirty thousand feet—or by means of electronic signals from known locations on the surface of the earth.

habanera from Bizet's *Carmen*. The song from grand opera perhaps most likely to be recognized, the habanera from *Carmen* was not original with Georges Bizet; he "borrowed" the melody from Sebastian Yradier. Nor is "Habanera" or "The Habanera" its title; a habanera is simply a slow dance in 2/4 time. What Carmen sings in the opera, to this beat, is customarily referred to by opera buffs as "L'amour est un oiseau rebelle." Finally, the habanera is not native to Spain; it's Cuban in origin.

habeas corpus; freedom from bills of attainder; prohibition against ex post facto laws. These three fundamental rights, guaranteeing, respectively, against imprisonment without cause shown, the confiscation of property, and the passage of any law which, after the fact, declares to be illegal an act which was legal when committed, are not to be found in the Bill of Rights, or first ten amendments to the United States Constitution. (The term *Bill of Rights*, it might be mentioned in passing, is nowhere mentioned in the Constitution.) They are, however, among our Constitutional guarantees, being incorporated in Section 9, Article 1, of the original document itself. But a part of the so-called Bill of Rights they are not.

hair growing on a corpse. The macabre belief that hair continues to grow after death is no doubt based on the fact that there is some tissue shrinkage in a corpse; the hair, thus, may seem to have "grown" because the skin around each hair has receded somewhat. In fact, though, the hair has not grown at all.

hair on the chest as an indication of virility. There is no basis whatever for the common belief that hair on the chest indicates masculinity or virility. Hair on the chest means just one thing: hair on the chest.

Hale, Nathan—and his dying words. Nathan Hale is best remembered for saying on the gallows, "I only regret that I have but one life to lose [not "give"] for my country." However, that is not what he said. Recently discovered is the diary of Capt. Frederick Mackenzie, a British officer who was there. He praises Hale for his courage but records his last words as, "It is the duty of every good officer to obey any orders given him by his commander-in-chief."

In Joseph Addison's *Cato* (act 1, sc. 4) are the words, "What pity is it that we can die but once to serve our country!"

halo, nimbus. Strictly speaking, the radiance surrounding the head or figure of saints, etc., in paintings is not a *halo,* which is a general term for any disc or luminosity (like that seen around the sun during an eclipse), but a nimbus. *Nimbus* since pagan times has had specific application to the radiance said to surround godlike figures when they appear on earth.

Hamlet's madness, the question of. There certainly was never any question in Shakespeare's mind as to whether or not Hamlet is "really" mad. In the first act (sc. 5, l. 172), Hamlet tells his friends Marcellus, Bernardo, and Horatio that he may "put an antic disposition on," which is to say *pretend* to madness, and that if and when he does, they are to keep their mouths shut and not give away his ploy. He later (act 3, sc. 4, lines 140 ff.) tells Queen Gertrude, his mother, the same thing in most forceful terms. Nor was there ever any question of madness in earlier versions of the Hamlet story upon which Shakespeare obviously drew; in them Hamlet's madness is deliberately put on, a protective device giving

Hamlet greater freedom of action in a situation most dangerous to him—after all, he is facing a hostile, murderous king who has already killed Hamlet's father.

handiwork. This word does not have any form of the word *handy* in it, but rather is simply the modern English for the Old English *hand-geweorc,* or "handwork." It is the now-missing middle syllable of the Old English term that is indicated by that vestigial *i,* which does not, thus, stand for *y.*

hangnail. A hangnail is not so called because it, or anything about it, hangs. It just hurts. *Ang,* in Old English, meant "pain."

harem. Contrary to the common notion, *harem* does not necessarily mean the place where all those wives are kept. *Harem* is simply the word adapted from Arabic which means, approximately, "secluded (or forbidden) sanctuary." This is the part of the house set aside for *all* the women of a Muslim household. It can be—sometimes is—made up of mother, sisters, servants, female in-laws, etc., and just one wife.

Ha(w)thorne, "judge" at Salem witch trials. It is almost universally believed, even among scholars, that one of Nathaniel Hawthorne's ancestors was a judge at the Salem witch trials, a misapprehension illustrated in the classic American short story "The Devil and Daniel Webster" by Stephen Vincent Benét. (" 'Justice Hathorne * is a jurist of experience,' said the stranger. 'He presided at certain witch trials once held in Salem.' ") Randall Stewart's biography of Nathaniel Hawthorne repeats the error, as do numberless textbooks and essays.

The fact is that no ancestor of Hawthorne's ever was at any time a judge of the Special Court of Oyer and Terminer appointed by Governor Phips in 1692, the only court which sat on the witchcraft cases. Its members were William Stoughton, the chief justice; Samuel Sewall, Bartholomew Gedney, Wait Winthrop, Nathaniel Saltonstall, John Richards, and William Sergeant. Saltonstall later resigned, being replaced by Jonathan Corwin.

---

* Benét is right about the spelling; the "w" was added later, by Nathaniel himself, as a matter of fact.

An ancestor of Nathaniel's, John Ha (w) thorne, was involved in the Salem witch trials, true; but only as an examiner of accused persons prior to their indictment, rather like a staff investigator on a "subversive activities" investigating committee. David Levin, the colonial historian—and one of the few who have long been aware of the misapplication of the title "Judge" to Nathaniel's ancestor —says that John Hathorne's "questioning was sufficiently sharp to form an important part of the record at the actual trial. It is therefore easy to see why people have called him a judge on the court—and the more easy because Jonathan Corwin, his fellow magistrate and examiner, did sit on the Special Court of Oyer and Terminer." But a judge John Hathorne was not.

headcheese. Of course headcheese is not cheese at all, but rather portions of the head and feet and other parts of a pig pressed together. It is not called "cheese" because it tastes like cheese or is cheeselike (as some dictionaries say), but because it used to be molded in the *form* of a cheese.

heartburn. It has nothing whatever to do with the heart despite its name. Insofar as the term has any medical meaning, the symptoms it purports to describe arise solely from difficulties in the esophagus or stomach.

"heavy air." Baseball fans and golfers often assume that in damp weather the air is "heavy"; a three-bagger might be a home-run if the day were clear and sunny; a three-wood short of the green would have made it except for the drag of the heavy air.

But the fact is that water vapor is lighter than air, not heavier. And when the weather is bad, the barometer reads low, not high. A barometer is simply a device for weighing air, just as the scales in the supermarket are a device for weighing oranges and bananas. And air does have weight, obviously; otherwise, the earth could not retain its atmosphere, held in place, as of course it is, by gravity.

There may be reasons why a ball does not travel quite so far on a wet day: the grip on the bat or club may not be so secure if not perfectly dry; the slight added weight of the ball if even a minute amount of moisture has condensed on it may have some effect; or the increased drag of wet grounds or grass may inhibit the amount of roll. But "heavy air" is not one of the reasons.

Hebrew and Yiddish. Widely confused by those not acquainted with Jewish culture and history, Hebrew and Yiddish are not only entirely separate languages; they do not even spring from the same roots. *Yiddish* is simply an Anglicized form of the German word *jüdisch,* or "Jewish"—or, somewhat more accurately, the Anglicized and shortened form of the German phrase *jüdisch Deutsch,* "Jewish German." It is a part of the Indo-European language family to which both English and German belong. Hebrew is not; it belongs to another family entirely, the Semitic—of which Arabic, incidentally, is also a member.

Nor is it proper to think of Yiddish as being only a kind of inferior dialect. It is a dialect, yes—as linguists use the term. That is, Yiddish is Middle High German as modified by many cultural-linguistic-historical elements. But Yiddish is no late-comer; its sources go back to the tenth century. And its literature, especially in recent years, is varied and rich; for example, the works of both Sholem Asch and Sholem Aleichem are in Yiddish, not Hebrew. As a literary language, Yiddish is much older than Finnish, for example. Yiddish literature emerged in the thirteenth century, Finnish as a written language not until the nineteenth.

Hebrew is, of course, very ancient. It is true, too, that its "prestige" among educated Jews is higher than that of Yiddish, perhaps because Hebrew is the Jewish "classical" language. The reestablishment of Hebrew as a living language with the rise of Israel as a state, moreover, does tend to put Yiddish somewhat on the defensive. But it thrives, and no doubt will continue to do so.

One reason, perhaps, for the Yiddish-Hebrew confusion is that Yiddish commonly uses the Hebrew *alphabet.* But this no more makes it Hebrew than an identical alphabet makes English the same as French, or modern German the same as Spanish.

Heinz's 57 Varieties. Although the Heinz company advertises "57 Varieties," this is hardly an accurate figure. In fact there were more than sixty varieties by 1892.

There is a prevailing notion that the number was simply picked out of the air by the original Mr. Heinz. This is not true either. Mr. Heinz was a good copywriter with an eye for a slogan. While riding the elevated trains in New York one day, he noticed an advertisement that featured "21 Styles of Shoes." It occurred to him that an adaptation of this would serve his own line, and that is how the expression "57 Varieties" was born.

heir presumptive. This term carries no implications whatever of pushiness or fraud, although it appears to. If a reigning monarch has no children, then the heir presumptive is the one who, according to the custom of the country, is next in line of succession. He is called "presumptive" because his chance of succession is lost if the monarch should happen to have a legitimate child; he is "presumed" to be the heir, but it's not a sure thing until the monarch dies without issue.

The heir *apparent* to a throne will—in fact, must—succeed the reigning monarch if the heir apparent lives long enough. The Prince of Wales in England is always the heir apparent. He cannot also be the heir presumptive; the two terms are mutually exclusive.

Hell Gate (East River, New York). Hell Gate is not named for the nether regions, but is rather an English rendering of the original Dutch *Die Helle Gat,* or "beautiful passage," a term originally applied to the East River. Later the term was applied only to the then-dangerous passage between the river and Long Island Sound.

helpmeet, helpmate. An interesting example of folk-etymology (see SIRLOIN, ORIGIN OF). No such word as *helpmeet* (later to become *helpmate* through the kind of misconception which folk-etymology by definition involves) originally existed. When the King James Bible was being put together, in Shakespeare's day, one meaning of *meet* was "suitable, fitting, or proper." Hamlet, it may be recalled, says at one point (act 1, sc. 5, lines 108–9) "Meet it is I set it down / That one may smile and smile, and be a villain." (Somewhat more accurately, there were *two* words, both spelled identically but coming from different sources: *meet* meaning "to come together" from Old English *mētan,* and *meet,* meaning "fitting," derived by extension from the quite separate Old English verb *metan* [no mark over the first vowel], "to measure.")

In Gen. 2:18, the Lord God says, "It is not good that the man should be alone; I will make him an help meet for him"—*help* being here used, as it still often is, as a noun ("She was a great help to me") . But nobody apparently noticed that the King James scholars (quite properly) put down *help meet*—two words meaning "a help suitable (or fit) ." Somehow the noun and the adjective got turned into one word. Thus, *helpmeet* and *helpmate* are words which in a manner of speaking don't really exist.

Hemingway, Ernest—and war experience. At no time in his life was Ernest Hemingway either a soldier or an officer in anybody's army anywhere. His World War I service was entirely as a Red Cross worker; he was wounded while engaged in the unromantic task of delivering cigarettes, chocolate, and postcards to Italian military personnel. Though he did do some ambulance driving, this was not his assignment at the time of his wounding; he was in charge of a bicycle then.

During the Spanish Civil War and World War II, Hemingway served entirely as a civilian correspondent. Indeed, near the end of World War II, he was in some danger of losing his accreditation and being sent back to the United States for, in effect, playing soldier while a civilian, an obvious violation of the rules for re-porters.

None of this reflects in any way upon Hemingway's courage, which was unquestionable; nor his experience of war, which was more than considerable. He was, in fact, the first American to be wounded in Italy in World War I. But he was not the first American *soldier* to be wounded in Italy, or anywhere else. (See also BARNES, JAKE—AND WOUND IN ERNEST HEMINGWAY'S THE SUN ALSO RISES.)

hemlock. In the United States hemlock is an evergreen tree having nothing to do with the poison that killed Socrates. In Europe, however there is a plant belonging to the carrot family called poison hemlock (*Conium maculatum*). All parts of it are deadly. It was from this plant that came the poison Socrates drank. Another plant, the water hemlock, also of the carrot family (*Cicuta maculata*), grows in swampy places in the temperate zone. All portions of it are dangerous, especially the roots.

hereditary disease. A disease which one contracts during his life-time from contagion or infection does not affect the genes and cannot be passed on to the offspring. Thus, hereditary disease, as commonly understood, does not exist. Even SYPHILIS, which used to be considered hereditary, is now known to be congenital (as well as infectious). (The syphilis spirochetes in the blood-stream of the mother can enter the fetus.) Also, tuberculosis was once thought to be "hereditary," for it was observed to persist in some families, but the disease was not transferred from parent to child. However, the physique can embrace special tendencies that persist in certain families generation after generation: a tendency to pulmonary weakness, a tendency to weakness of the heart, etc. This has been a source of confusion to the layman, who may conclude that a disease like tuberculosis itself is, for instance, inherited.

An example of a so-called hereditary disease (of which there are few) is hemophilia, with which the Russian Tsarevich Alexis was afflicted. This is actually a defect in the blood plasma. It may not be contracted from another person but is carried from one generation to the next by the females.

"He that complies against his will / Is of his own opinion still." Often misquoted as "A man convinced against his will / Is of the same opinion still," Samuel Butler's words (from *Hudibras*) actually do not mean quite the same thing.

hippopotamus sweating blood. It does look very much like blood. But it's not. The hippopotamus exudes an oily reddish fluid from various large pores in its thick skin. Apparently the fluid is a kind of skin-conditioner which the hippopotamus needs to prevent dried and cracking skin when he is out of the water. That this secretion becomes both more copious and redder than usual when the hippopotamus is excited or wounded has obviously further perpetuated the notion that it must be blood.

Hitler, Adolf. Hitler's name was never Schicklgruber. He was never either a house painter or a paperhanger. His birth was quite legitimate. Adolf's father, Alois Hitler, had been born out of wedlock, true; but whether Alois was illegitimate depends on definition; his mother, Adolf Hitler's grandmother, married the putative father (Adolf's grandfather) when Alois was five years old. That Hitler's father preferred to go by his mother's name, which was indeed Schicklgruber, until he was in his middle thirties no doubt accounts for the belief that Adolf Hitler's name was "really" Schicklgruber. But, of course, it was not; he was born Adolf Hitler, son of Alois Hitler and his third wife (the first two had died).

Hitler painted pictures, not houses. As a youth he wanted to study art at the academy in Vienna, but failed the entrance examinations. That he was not, however, entirely without talent is indicated by the recommendation of the academy that he undertake the study of architecture; but he lacked enough formal education to qualify as a student. Some of his pictures, done when he was a youth, have survived. They appear to be at least as good as some done by such celebrated amateurs as Winston Churchill and the late President Eisenhower.

How Hitler came to be identified as a paperhanger is hard to determine. The fact which spawned the myth may have been his temporary work, in his late teens or early twenties, as a laborer in the building trades.

Hobson's choice. This phrase does not really mean "no choice at all," as is commonly thought, but rather a choice between what is offered and nothing. The term is said to derive from the custom of one Thomas Hobson, a seventeenth-century English liveryman who required that customers take the first horse in line. That this is obviously the fairest method of renting out merchandise that is bound to vary in quality seems to have been forgotten.

holidays, national. "National holiday" is a widespread phrase, but there aren't any, not even Independence Day. The president and Congress can legally designate holidays only for federal employees and the District of Columbia. It's up to each state to determine whether or not it wants to observe a given holiday. There are, as a matter of fact, very few "legal holidays" which are actually observed on the same date by every state in the union. They are New Year's Day, Independence Day, Labor Day, Thanksgiving Day, and Christmas Day. Veterans, or Armistice, Day is observed by all the states, but not on the same date; a few still stick to the old November 11 rather than the new fourth Monday in November.

Neither Washington's nor Lincoln's birthday is a legal holiday in every state, nor are Good Friday, Memorial Day, Columbus Day, or General Election Day. Except for Christmas, no Christian, Jewish, or other religious holy day is a country-wide legal holiday, although religious holidays are often observed, some of them very widely (Easter) .

homosexual. *Homo* is a Latin word for "man," as in *homo sapiens,* for example. No doubt it is for this reason that there is a widespread belief that our word *homosexual* describes men only. However, the *homo* in *homosexual, homogeneous,* etc., is from a Greek word meaning "the same." Thus, *homosexual* means "partial to the same sex," not "partial to the male sex." It is correct to use it in describing females.

hot bread. Go ahead and eat bread or biscuits fresh from the oven, if you are lucky enough to have the opportunity. Notwithstanding old wives' tales to the contrary, hot bread is just as good for you as yesterday's stone-cold loaf. On the other hand, it is no better, nor is a "good hot meal" any more nutritious than a good cold one. (A hot lunch for every schoolchild certainly is a laudable objective on many grounds. But it has nothing to do with nutritional values.)

hot water and cold water, time to freeze. One of the most enduring folk myths is that a bucket of hot water will freeze faster than a bucket of cold water. It won't. True, water that *has been* heated or boiled before cooling may freeze faster, because heating or boiling drives out some air bubbles that otherwise inhibit freezing because they cut down on thermal conductivity. It is for this reason that hot-water pipes may be the ones to burst: the water they carry will turn into somewhat denser ice. It is not the thawing of the pipes that makes them burst, by the way; they are first burst by the freezing, but, obviously, frozen water is going to stay where it is. The break becomes apparent only when the thaw sets in.

Howe, Elias. Elias Howe is customarily credited with inventing the sewing machine. He did not. Using the inventions of others, he produced a workable machine, patented it, manufactured it, and died a millionaire. The real inventors of the machine died with little fame and less fortune.

Even in the eighteenth century the eye-pointed needle and a horizontal support for the fabric had been developed. By 1830 in France, a tailor named Barthélemy Thimonnier had patented a machine that worked so well other tailors suppressed it for fear of losing their jobs.

However, the really forgotton man of the story is Walter Hunt, who by 1834 had produced a machine with all three basic elements: the eye-pointed needle, a shuttle carrying the thread, and the lock stitch.

He was twelve years ahead of Howe; no one knows why Hunt did not seek patent protection. Some think that he may have been afraid of throwing seamstresses out of work.

Howe's story is one of relentless determination and difficulties.

Employed in a machine shop, he happened to hear a superior say that anyone who could produce a sewing machine that worked would be rich. From that point on he never rested. It is not exactly clear where he got the inspiration for some of the ideas he used. He said the notion of the eye-pointed needle came to him "in a dream."

He got his exclusive patent in 1846, but then had to fight against all kinds of opposition, indifference, and sharp practices. He organized the Howe Sewing Machine Company of Bridgeport, Connecticut. His patent was infringed, but he won in the courts and received royalties from the infringers, sometimes amounting to $4,000 a week. He deserves great credit, but like Robert FULTON he was not the first man with the idea, nor even the man with the first machine.

Hudson, Hendrick. There was no such person. Or at least if there was, he wasn't a Dutch explorer. The man whose real name was Henry—not Hendrick—was born, lived, and died an Englishman. True, he was working for the Dutch East India Company when he sailed up the river named for him. But, as a matter of fact, the English felt so strongly about his working for the Dutch that when his ship, the *Half-Moon,* put in at Dartmouth in 1609, it was seized and Hudson, along with the other Englishmen of the crew, was commanded to stay home and serve his own country.

Hudson seal. Hudson seal does not come from seals; it is one of many such terms, like GERMAN SILVER, that are designed with persuasion rather than accuracy in mind. Hudson seal is actually muskrat.

humble pie. *Humble* in the expression "humble pie" is not even indirectly related, historically or linguistically, to the word *humble* as in "He is a humble person."

Humble in "humble pie" was originally *umble,* a term cognate with *umbilical,* as in "umbilical cord." The "umble pie" eaten by the poor often included the umbilical cords of animals, scorned as food by those better off. Thus, to eat umble, or humble, pie originally signified poverty, not humiliation. (The word *humble* in its usual sense comes ultimately from Latin *humus,* "earth," which you are close to if you are humble.)

I

"I am Eagle!" When the Russian cosmonaut Titov shouted this into his microphone, he was neither engaging in Russian rhapsodicals nor displaying Soviet arrogance. He was merely identifying himself; the name of his spacecraft was *Eagle* (in Russian as transliterated, *oryol*).

ice cream as a "cooler." Ice cream may have a psychologically cooling effect for the moment. But calories are a unit for measurement of heat. Ice cream is loaded with calories. Thus its ultimate effect is to make one hotter, not cooler.

icing of aircraft wings and carburetors. Although common sense suggests otherwise it doesn't have to be cold outside for carburetors to ice up; ice can form in an aircraft (or any other conventional) carburetor at air temperatures well above freezing, as student pilots are invariably warned early in their training. The reason is the so-called Venturi effect. G. B. Venturi, an Italian physicist of the early nineteenth century, gave his name to a tube with a constricted middle section. When a fluid (air is a fluid) flows through this smaller midsection, its velocity increases. Increasing the velocity of air lowers its temperature. Conventional carburetors contain a form of Venturi tube, or simply a Venturi, as it is usually called. Hence, air, especially moist air, which is "sucked" through the carburetor may easily have its temperature decreased from well above to well below freezing; ice will form; it will clog the carburetor and result in loss of power.

Ice on an aircraft's wing is, of course, dangerous partly because of its weight. But more important and less known is the fact that it destroys the *shape* of the wing, or "airfoil," as it builds up. It is this loss of the wing's efficiency, obviously causing a loss of lift, which is the more important danger. An airplane loaded below its rated capacity might be able to support the added weight of ice on its wings; but if, at the same time, the shape of the wing is so altered that it no longer can provide enough lift, there is trouble.

id, the. Although identified with him, this term was not invented by Freud, nor did he pretend it was. Actually, the original word was *das Es, Es* being the indefinite pronoun *it* in German. A physician named Georg Groddeck, who had become interested in psychoanalysis and with whose ideas Freud was in sympathy, had apparently taken the term *das Es* from a physician-teacher of his, Ernst Schweninger. Freud, in turn, adopted the term, giving the expression its special Freudian meaning as the primal reservoir of psychic energy, the "unorganized chaotic mentality," in A. A. Brill's phrase, that the child brings into the world.

There was apparently some argument among translators as to just how *das Es* ought to be rendered into English. A direct translation, "the it," did not seem altogether satisfactory, for fairly obvious reasons. Putting *it* into Latin appeared to be the best solution. Thus *id.*

It would not, however, be accurate to say that *id* as used in a psychological context is "Latin." The word has become thoroughly Anglicized. More precisely, it became Anglicized the moment it was adopted—with a meaning obviously different from the Latin.

"I disapprove of what you say, but I will defend to the death your right to say it." These are not Voltaire's words, though the sentiment is Voltairean enough. Whether or not Voltaire ever said—or, more accurately, wrote—a similar sentence is a somewhat sticky question. When E. Beatrice Hall, writing under the name of S. G. Tallentyre, first put these words on paper, she did not claim they were Voltaire's; she offered them as a free paraphrase on a sentence from Voltaire's *Essay on Tolerance:* "Think for yourselves and let others enjoy the privilege to do so too."

The question is further complicated, however, by the fact that Norbert Guterman claims that Voltaire wrote in a letter to one M. le Riche ". . . I detest what you write, but I would give my life to make it possible for you to continue to write." The letter, says Guterman, was written February 6, 1770.

As things stand now, one can only say that as usually printed, the statement varies from Voltaire's written words while preserving, of course, their sense.

If she be not fair to me . . . . It is often quoted this way, but it is not the way George Wither put it in his "The Shepherd's Resolution." He wrote, instead: "If she be not so to me, / What care I how fair she be?"

If you use my name, I'll sue! There is no legal prohibition against the use of someone's name in connection with a newsworthy event in which he participated—with the exception, in many states, of juveniles and victims of sex crimes. But writers and publishers must be increasingly careful about the danger of invading a person's right of privacy. A public figure, especially one who seeks publicity, is deemed by the courts to have little right of privacy. But more and more the courts are recognizing the rights of privacy that belong to ordinary individuals. In fact, the whole issue represents the conflict between the right of the individual to protection and the right of the public to know.

Ignorance is bliss. This dictum is taken from Thomas Gray's "On a Distant Prospect of Eton College," though sometimes improperly attributed to either Oliver Goldsmith or Alexander Pope. Nor does Gray mean quite what these lines imply when taken out of context; he makes an important qualification: ". . . where [not "if"] ignorance is bliss, / 'Tis folly to be wise."

In other words, ignorance isn't *necessarily* bliss; where it is, then, true, " 'tis folly to be wise." Gray is by no means saying that it is always better to be ignorant than wise—though in popular usage that is what the phrase is often taken to mean.

IHS. These letters do not stand for "In this sign" (In hoc signo), nor "In this safety" (In hoc salus), nor "Jesus Saviour of Men" (Jesus Hominum Salvator), as is often thought. They are simply the common abbreviation, in Greek, for the name Jesus, and were used by the original transcriber of the New Testament into Greek.

This abbreviation comprises the first two letters and the last letter of the Greek word for Jesus, capitalized and Romanized.

Illinois west of the Mississippi. Yes, people can live in the state of Illinois and still be west of the main channel of the Mississippi River. Despite popular belief that Illinois lies east of the Father of Waters, Kaskaskia, Illinois, is indeed west of the Mississippi. It's the result of a nineteenth-century flood during which the river cut itself a new channel.

"I'll take you home again, Kathleen." This well-known song, which upon examination reveals no references to Ireland, is not an Irish ballad. It was not written by an Irishman, but by a Virginian named Thomas Paine Westendorf, living at the time in Indiana. Nor—as sometimes said—was Westendorf trying to cheer up his wife because she was ill and unhappy over the death of a son. As established by the researchers of Richard S. Hill of the Library of Congress, Westendorf was lonesome for his wife—they hadn't been married very long—who was visiting her home in Ogdensburg, New York, while Thomas was stuck in Plainfield, where he had a teaching job. Evidently he considered Kathleen a more romantic name than his wife's, which was Jennie.

According to the late Sigmund Spaeth, authority on popular music, Westendorf's direct inspiration was another song called "Barney, Take Me Home Again!" by Arthur W. French and George W. "Persley," whose real name was George W. Brown.

Immaculate Conception. Countless persons think that the immaculate conception refers to Christ's having been born of a virgin. It does not. The immaculate conception is the dogma that holds that Mary was free of original sin from the moment of her conception in the womb of her mother. This dogma did not become official until 1854 under Pope Pius IX, although it had been argued since the twelfth century.

impressionism. It is a widely held belief that the word *impressionism* was invented by a group of nineteenth-century French painters who wished to produce vague but pleasant glimpses of the world around them. Not true. They did not coin this word, and it is not properly descriptive of their work.

In April 1874, Claude Monet and other artists exhibited works of an experimental nature at the studio of the photographer Felix Tournachon, whose pseudonym was "Nadar." Among them was a painting by Monet entitled *Impression—Sunrise*. The critic Louis Leroy after seeing the exhibition wrote a review for *Le Charivari*, April 25, 1874, ridiculing what he had seen. He headed it *L'Exposition des Impressionistes,* a term meant to be both pejorative and sarcastic. Thus it was he, not the painters, who invented the term—a term not intended to be a serious description, but one of contempt. (He referred to Monet's brushwork on another canvas as "black tongue-lickings" which he could not identify.)

Furthermore, these painters did not have any theories of painting that bound them together. They were loosely associated, each going his own way. They were experimenting in a vigorous effort to get away from the sterility and insincerity of the French Academy. Far from trying to produce a merely pleasurable effect through indistinctness and vague impressions, they were searching for what they considered to be the real truth in painting through an entirely new understanding of light, color, and brushwork.

Later the impressionists did adopt the label for themselves, but in 1879 they abandoned it in favor of Group of Independent Artists, which we seldom hear. The word *impressionism* is firmly rooted in our vocabulary. With the triumph of their paintings the pejorative sense of the word has long since disappeared, but the idea that it basically means a vague impression of the world lingers on.

indentured servants. Often thought to be little more than slaves who performed the lowliest household tasks, indentured servants in colonial times were actually under contract, bound out to a limited term of service only, often to repay the cost of their passage to the New World. Many were artisans of considerable skill and experience, by no means "servants" as the term is commonly understood. They are specifically mentioned in Article 1, Section 3, of the Constitution as belonging with "the whole number of free persons" in "the several States."

An indenture was originally a special form of written contract, although the term is now commonly used for any deed or agreement. Originally, indentures were designed so that when torn into two parts, the torn edges were wavy, or indented; each party to the agreement kept one of the halves, which could be matched with the other if any questions of authenticity arose.

india ink. It's not from India; never was. It's from China, and really ought to be called China ink. As a matter of fact, that's what it *is* called—in France.

Indian fishing rights. Whenever a story appears in newspapers or on television implying that another Indian tribe has been deprived of its fishing rights in apparent violation of a treaty, many people conjure up the image of an aging chief peacefully setting out with his fishing pole to try his luck along some stretch of beautiful water immemorially "his," only to be arrested by a brutal and insensitive game warden.

But no game warden, or Fish and Game Commission, is likely to worry about such a case as this. The problem arises when Indians attempt to exercise their treaty rights by fishing *commercially*. And that is quite a different kettle of—well, of fish. There were no canneries in Alaska or along the Columbia River when most of the Indian treaties were negotiated; it never occurred to either Indian or white that in a few decades it would be possible for any group completely to wipe out a salmon run, for example, by employing the resources of twentieth-century technology. Nor was it imaginable that methods of preserving the salmon would become so efficient that wiping out a run would indeed be both possible and highly profitable.

Indians are not more greedy than anyone else, and most assuredly they have often been treated badly enough by whites. But any group of human beings is likely to have trouble, now and then, assessing the long-range effects of its actions. A tribe in need of money might well be tempted to overfish an area for profit, to the point where it would itself suffer in the future along with everybody else. It is for this reason that the United States Supreme Court has ruled that Indian fishing can be regulated as to manner, size of catch, etc., for the purposes of conservation.

The right of Indians to fish for their own consumption is not a problem. If Indians fished today for the same reasons (and with the same implements) as they did a hundred or so years ago, then there would be no "fish-ins," no protests, and no lawsuits.

Indian rope trick. This fable has existed in various versions for at least five hundred years. In one version the conjurer throws a rope straight up in the air, where it remains taut and firm. He then climbs up the rope hand over hand, pulls the rope up after him, and disappears. In another, simpler, version, the conjurer throws the rope up in the same fashion, climbs it, and slides down again, utters a few words, and the rope falls limp. Needless to say the whole thing is poppycock. The odd fact is that the legend persists, though no one has ever been able to see in India anything remotely resembling it that could possibly give rise to the report.

Indians as nomads. The fairly widespread belief that the Plains Indians of North America were always nomads is not true. Prior to the sixteenth century the Plains Indians could not venture long distances from the stream beds and water holes because they did not have means of transportation. When the Spanish brought horses to North America, all that changed. Then the Indians could travel extensively, and did. They could also pursue game, which previously they were obliged to stalk where the animals came to drink.

indulgence. To Roman Catholics, an "indulgence" is neither the forgiveness of sin nor payment therefor. It can only be granted after, not before, the sin has been forgiven; and it is remission in whole or in part of ecclesiastical penalties. The "sale of indulgences," which was indeed widespread during the Middle Ages, ought more properly to be called "sale of forgiveness."

inebriation myths. There are many myths about the kinds of intoxication that different kinds of alcoholic drinks will produce. "Champagne is more exhilarating, but produces a worse hangover." "Martinis make some people mean." "Beer on whiskey rather risky; whiskey on beer, never fear." "You can get away with more highballs than cocktails."

It is absolutely untrue that different drinks which contain identical amounts of absolute alcohol can have different intoxicating qualities. Thus a martini has no special qualities of inebriation that a whiskey sour of the same potency does not possess.

The degree of inebriation is the result of how much absolute alcohol is taken into the blood stream and how fast. Otherwise what the alcohol is mixed with has nothing whatever to do with the pharmacological effect.

There are many sociopsychological effects from drinking, and some people start to behave differently even before any alcohol has taken effect.

But when it comes to alcoholic intoxication, true intoxication in a chemical sense, there is only one thing that does it: absolute alcohol.

"Internationale." This revolutionary song does come from France —at least, it was first sung there—but it has nothing to do with the French Revolution. The "Internationale" goes back only to 1871.

"In the beginning was the word." This phrase is often misunderstood as implying God's authoritarian pronouncement. In the neo-Platonic sense, however, *word* (Greek *logos*) refers rather to communication *between* the divine world and the world around us. A better translation, perhaps, for modern eyes would be "In the beginning was the communication between the divine world and the world on earth."

"Invitation to the Dance." This is what Carl Maria von Weber called his romantically charming little piece of music, sometimes played as an encore by symphony orchestras and also popular in a piano arrangement—not "Invitation to the Waltz," as it is often referred to. The fact that the "dance" in the title happens to be a waltz is no doubt responsible for this common misconception.

"I only regret that I have but one life to lose for my country." See HALE, NATHAN—AND DYING WORDS.

Iran, name of. Those who think that Iran is a "new" name for Persia are quite mistaken. To the natives themselves, it has been known as Iran for centuries. "Persia" was simply what foreigners insisted on calling it, because that was what the Greeks called it when they first began trading with the "Persians" (from "Pars," the ancient name for one of Iran's provinces). The Iranians eventually tired of accepting somebody else's name for their own country, and in the mid-1930s announced that others would please now use the name they'd been using all along.

Irish elk. Fossil remains of the "Irish elk" from prehistoric times portray an animal six feet high with horns that sometimes measured eleven feet between the tips. The belief has persisted that this creature became extinct because its antlers were so cumbersome. This is not true. It died out because of the climate.

Furthermore the Irish elk was not an elk but a species of deer.

Finally, it was not exclusively Irish. It lived not only in Ireland, but in Great Britain, northern and central Europe, and western Asia.

iron curtain. Widely regarded as a phrase originated by Winston Churchill, it is anything but. There have been several instances of its earlier use, with substantially or exactly the same meaning, ranging from Queen Elizabeth of the Belgians in 1914 ("Between [Germany] and me there is now a bloody iron curtain which has descended forever!") to Josef Goebbels, who used the phrase "iron curtain" with reference to the USSR in February 1945. Churchill employed it in an address at Westminster College in Fulton, Missouri, on March 5, 1946, when he said, "From Stettin in the Baltic to Trieste in the Adriatic an iron curtain has descended across the Continent."

None of this necessarily means that Churchill deliberately "lifted" the phrase with the intention of passing it off as his own. It is quite common, especially on the part of those as widely read as Churchill, for a phrase to arise out of the unconscious mind without awareness of its origin; or it can be "original" with more than one.

Iron Mask, Man in the. Although he is better known as a fictional character, there really was such a person as the Man in the Iron Mask. He was a political prisoner of Louis XIV, but his true identity has never been determined. The mask he wore was not, however, of iron but rather of black velvet stiffened with whalebone and fastened behind the head with a padlock or by steel springs.

Istanbul. This word is not a "new" name for Constantinople, since the Turks themselves started calling the city Istanbul in 1453 and they've called it that ever since. Only foreigners used the name Constantinople. The original name Constantinople was given to Istanbul by the Romans; although they called it New Rome officially, it was popularly referred to as Constantinople after the emperor Constantine. The Turks finally got so annoyed at the stubborn insistence of everybody else to call the city by the wrong name that they simply returned all letters addressed to persons in "Constantinople."

"It is more blessed to give than to receive." In the words of Prof. David A. Jannsen of Portland State University, "We are oftentimes reminded that Jesus said it is more blessed to give than to receive. Doubtless He did in fact make such a statement, but one will look in vain for it in the four Gospels. It was probably a statement passed to Paul by those who had accompanied the Lord, since Paul is the one who gives us the expression . . . . The curious thing here is that most of us would immediately turn to the so-called Sermon on the Mount to locate these words. But though that may have been the occasion of their utterance, it is not so recorded."

Professor Jannsen also reminds us that the title "Sermon on the Mount" is one *we* have given it; it is never so identified in the Bible.

"Ivan Skavinski Skavar." Said to have been President Eisenhower's favorite song, "Ivan Skavinski Skavar" was not so called by its composer, who was not Frank Crumit, though some may recall his very popular recording back in the old 78-rpm days.

According to James N. Healy of Eire, author of a biography of the real composer, the song known as "Ivan Skavinski Skavar" was written by Percy French in 1877, when he was a student at Trinity College in Dublin. French called it "Abdulla Bulbul Ameer," who is another character in the narrative; sometimes the song goes by this title—often, however, incorrectly rendered as "Abdul Abulba Ameer" or "Abdul Abulbul Ameer."

"I would rather be living in Philadelphia." There are minor variations, but this phrase is popularly believed to be what W. C. Fields ordered placed upon his tombstone. But Fields's tombstone actually reads simply "W. C. Fields, 1880–1946." The "epitaph," funny as it may be—except, presumably, to Philadelphians—was one of a series of similar gags run by the old *Vanity Fair* magazine in the 1920s.

IWW. This abbreviation does not stand for International Workers of the World, in spite of the widespread belief to the contrary. IWW stands for *Industrial* Workers of the World.

J

Jackson Whites. The Jackson Whites, a mysterious group of hill people, have lived in the Ramapo Mountains of New York-New Jersey for several hundred years. They are not white, and no one knows where the name came from. Aloof and defensive, they have survived as a separate ethnic enclave in the pockets of the hills. They themselves do not know who they were or how they got there, to the perpetual fascination of writers and sociologists, who have delivered learned papers about them and written articles for the *New Yorker* and other magazines. There has been a general consensus that these people are a mélange of deserters from the American Revolution, Hessian soldiers, prostitutes imported for the British soldiers, Tuscarora Indians, and runaway slaves. In fact, it has been presumed that Jackson is a corruption of Hessian, or possibly the name of the entrepreneur who imported the prostitutes!

Now the researches of David Steven Cohen, sociologist at Rutgers, the State University, have proved without doubt that this theory of the racial potpourri has no basis in fact and that the Jackson Whites are among our earliest pioneers. Their forebears were black slaves originally owned by the Dutch and freed by them before the Revolution, more than two hundred years ago. They had Dutch names; they acquired land; they cleared farms.

Alas, in 1798 New Jersey passed a law which restricted the movements of blacks, and then, no doubt, they abandoned their lands and took to the hills—where they live today, 1500 strong.

Jaycee. This term does not stand for Junior Chamber [of Commerce], although many people think it does. For many years, true, Junior Chambers of Commerce were affiliated with "senior," or regular Chambers of Commerce. The informal word *Jaycee* was then an obvious acronym for Junior Chamber, or JC. But there is no longer any such legal affiliation on either a local or a national scale.

Now Jaycee does not "stand for" anything. It is no longer an acronym; it is a word. The official name now for what used to be the Junior Chamber of Commerce is Jaycees; a Jaycee is a member of the Jaycees. Neither is it in any sense slang, nor even "informal" usage.

Jerusalem artichoke. This plant has nothing whatever to do with Jerusalem, nor, as a matter of fact, with artichokes in spite of the implications of the name. The term is a corruption of the Italian *girasole articiocco,* or "Sunflower artichoke." The so-called Jerusalem artichoke does, in fact, belong to the sunflower family.

Joan of Arc. She was not French; her birthplace, Domrémy, was part of an independent duchy, that of Bar, which in turn was a part of Lorraine. And Lorraine did not itself join the soon-to-be-toppled Kingdom of France until 1776. Nor did Joan think of herself as French; as Sanche de Gramont puts it in *The French: Portrait of a People* (1969), "She said the archangel Michael told her: 'Go, go to France if you must.' " (Her father was so opposed that, according to the *Encyclopaedia Britannica,* he said he would drown her with his own hands if she went into France.)

Nor was she quite the poor peasant girl of legend. Her father, though of farming stock, was prosperous enough to be co-renter of a chateau, and was Domrémy's leading citizen. It was not until the nineteenth century that, with a large boost from Napoleon, the cult of Joan really emerged; and it was not until the twentieth that she was made a saint.

Johns Hopkins University. Those who know better than to refer to it as "John Hopkins University" often assume that it was named after two persons, a Johns and a Hopkins. This is not so. A Mr. Johns Hopkins (the spelling of the first name was a family tradition) left the money to found the university. Johns Hopkins Hospital, by the way, was founded by a separate Hopkins bequest and thus was not, in a sense, conceived of as part of the university but rather as a separate, though closely related, institution.

Johnson, Samuel, defines a fisherman as a fool. Dr. Johnson is credited with having defined the angler as a fool, but it is impossible to find this immortal statement in his own works, or in Boswell's biography.

William Hazlitt (1778–1830) in his *Essay on Egotism* attributes to Johnson, "A fishing rod is a stick with a hook at one end and a fool at the other." In 1859 an obscure writer named Hawker wrote in *Instructions to Young Sportsmen,* and attributed to Johnson, "Fly fishing may be a very pleasant amusement, but angling or float fishing I can only compare to a stick and a string, with a worm at one end and a fool at the other."

Devotees of the flyrod will be pleased to have this special consideration, even though dubious, from the eminent doctor.

Jones, Casey. Often regarded as a mythical folk hero, Casey Jones was actually an engineer, and from all accounts as brave as the song makes him out to be. His first name, however, does not derive from "K.C." for "Kansas City," as often said; he was born near Cayce, Kentucky, pronounced in two syllables, and from this fact came his nickname. (His real name was John Luther Jones.)

Nor was he a "rounder," in spite of the words of the ballad ("Casey Jones was the rounder's name"). A "rounder" in railroad parlance is a worker who moves from job to job; but Casey Jones stayed with his line, the Illinois Central, until his death.

The song most people know as "Casey Jones" is not a spontaneously generated folk ballad, although its origin may lie in an apparently original tune with words which (according to Casey's widow) his wiper,* Wallace Saunders, began singing a few days after the wreck. Overheard by an itinerant song writer, the tune was published with different words about 1902; in 1906 it was copyrighted by Shapiro and Bernstein of New York.

There is apparently no truth whatever in the lines sometimes

* Wipers—full title, "engine wipers"—kept things shipshape, so to speak.

added to the ballad ("Go to bed, children, and hush your cryin',/ 'Cause you got another papa on the Salt Lake Line"). Mrs. Jones, who outlived her famous husband by many years—she died in 1958 in Jackson, Tennessee, at ninety-two—spent much of her life protesting the implications of these apparently libelous words, and from all evidence she was quite correct in doing so. The fireman who saved himself at Jones' order by jumping also lived on for many years. His name was Simeon (Sim) Webb, and he died in Memphis, at eighty-three, in 1957.

Jordan almonds. Jordan almonds have nothing to do with either the river or the country called Jordan. They come from Spain; the name is a corruption of the Middle English *jardin almande,* the *jardin* in turn being simply the Middle French—and for that matter, also the modern French—word for "garden."

juggernaut. To most people a juggernaut is a moving force or thing which crushes everything in its path, especially people.

But Juggernaut, or Jagannath, is the name of a Hindu deity, not the cart in which his idol is carried. And the idea that vast numbers of persons were mercilessly crushed by this cart is erroneous.

Jagannath (Lord of the World) is one of the Krishna reincarnations of Vishnu. His temple is situated at Puri in Orissa, India. There his idol sits, made of wood with black face and red mouth, flanked by idols of his brother and sister. Once a year the three idols are placed in separate carts and with great effort dragged by numerous faithful worshipers to the country house of the god nearly a mile away. The cart, being forty-five feet high, must have seemed in the old days like a "juggernaut" indeed. Legend has it that many fanatical devotees threw themselves under the wheels to be voluntarily crushed, thinking they would be thus freed from the cycle of birth and rebirth. However, this was not part of the ritual and it is untrue. Accounts vary as to whether the occasional fatalities occurred because a member of the throng committed suicide through excess of zeal or was merely careless.

jury, unanimous verdict of, in capital cases. Nothing in the Bill of Rights or the United States Constitution requires a jury verdict to be unanimous in capital—or any other—cases. Nor does a jury have to be made up of twelve people, as is commonly believed.

Keats, John. That Keats was a pallid, withdrawn youth forced into the study of medicine against his will could scarcely be farther from the truth. As a boy in school, he was noted for his pugnacity; one contemporary account has him willing to "fight any one— morning, noon, and night." And while it is true enough that he was ultimately to abandon medicine for poetry, he worked hard at his medical education, ultimately qualifying for general practice.

Keats's decision to devote his life, or what was left of it, to poetry was apparently largely influenced by the praise given by Leigh Hunt and others to his famous sonnet, "On First Looking into Chapman's Homer" (see CORTES, BALBOA, AND THE PACIFIC OCEAN). Convinced, in his words, that he possessed "abilities greater than most men" as a poet—certainly true enough—he left medicine forever before taking his examination for Member of the Royal College of Surgeons. That his choice was not based on hatred of medicine but rather love for poetry seems obvious; all his adult life up to this point had been spent on his medical studies.

Unfortunately, he died of tuberculosis in his mid-twenties, only four years after this decision.

Kentucky rifle. The rifle, as distinguished from the smoothbore musket, first came into widespread use in America. Though it later came to be called the Kentucky rifle it was made in Pennsylvania, probably in Lancaster County, by Swiss colonists in the 1730s.

Klondike. Adventure tales notwithstanding, neither the general area known as the Klondike nor its best-known town, Dawson City, is in Alaska. Both are in Yukon Territory, which is in Canada. The Klondike, incidentally, is not a province. Nor is Dawson City the capital of the territory; Whitehorse is.

knots per hour. No sailor would think of using such a term, although many other people do. The knot is itself a measure of speed, and speed only—it means one nautical mile per hour. It is impossible for one place to be so many "knots" from another, any more than two locations on land can be so many "miles per hour" from each other.

As a matter of fact, there are three different versions of a nautical mile. Or even four, in a sense, because navigators treat a nautical mile as equivalent to the length of one minute of the meridian at the place where they are taking the reading. Otherwise, what a nautical mile is depends on whose standard you are sailing under. The British, or "Admiralty," nautical mile is 6,080 feet; the United States nautical mile is just a bit longer, at 6,080.20 feet. The international nautical mile is 1,852 meters, or 6,076.1033 feet.

Krakatoa as greatest volcanic eruption. Usually referred to as the greatest volcanic eruption in modern times, the explosion of Krakatoa in August 1883 is dwarfed by one that took place less than seventy years previously: the eruption of Tambora on Sumbawa Island, Indonesia, on April 5, 1815. Krakatoa is thought to have ejected some 50 million metric tons of ash into the atmosphere; Tambora is believed to have ejected about 220 million tons from 1811 to 1818, of which 150 million were in 1815 alone.

Another misconception involving Krakatoa is embodied in the title of the movie *Krakatoa, East of Java*. Krakatoa is east of Java only in the sense that a traveler would find San Francisco to be east of New York if he took the long way around the globe. Krakatoa is actually in the Sunda Strait, which is west of Java, not east.

Kremlin, the. Moscow has *a* Kremlin, but so do many other Russian cities; it's just that Moscow's is best known. In Russian the word signifies a citadel or fortress originally designed to protect the inner city from marauders. Moscow's Kremlin is not a specific building, as newscasters often seem to imply, but rather a complex within a large walled space.

Lady Godiva's ride. About the most one can say about Lady Godiva's bareback ride is that it cannot be proved that it didn't happen. There was such a person (she was baptized *Godgifu,* or "God's gift"), married to Leofric, the Earl of Leicester. The date of her death is uncertain, but it was either about the time of the Norman Conquest, 1066, or not long thereafter. Leofric does seem to have been a tough administrator; and contemporary accounts show Lady Godgifu, or Godiva, in a most favorable light: generous, philanthropical, religious.

No early chronicle as yet discovered, however, makes any reference to her famous ride. The earliest account known, by a Benedictine monk at St. Albans, appeared a century and a half after the occasion, if any. For an excellent account of the Godiva story in its ramifications, see Ashley Montagu and Edward Darling, *The Ignorance of Certainty* (1970).

Lancelot, Sir. The one knight of the Round Table everybody knows is not, as a matter of fact, a member of the original cast at all. There is no trace of Lancelot, or anyone like him, in the original British-Celtic legends of Arthur and his famous group. No one really knows how Lancelot made his way into the Arthurian cycle (and, of course, also into the *ménage à trois* which has become the dominant feature, to many readers, of the Camelot story). He shows up first in a twelfth-century French manuscript as the hero of a series of amorous adventures, none of them, however, involving anybody like Guinevere. As the Arthurian cycle grew in popularity during the Middle Ages, Lancelot appears simply to have moved in and taken over.

language. There are many misconceptions about language, a surprising number shared by otherwise well-educated people; indeed, there is probably no area, with the possible exception of so-called Freudian psychology, about which persons whom one would expect to know better are so grossly uninformed. Why this should be so is something of a puzzle; one possible reason is that our language, like our emotional drives, is so intimately a part of us that it is difficult to examine its phenomena objectively.

Still taken seriously by many are various "explanations" of the origin of language that, if not demonstrably untrue, still must remain, probably forever, in the realm of the unprovable. Among these are three that scholars like to call, with more than a trace of scorn, the bow-wow theory, the ding-dong theory, and the pooh-pooh theory.

The "bow-wow," or echoic, theory proposes that language arose onomatopoeically: that is, primitive languages were composed entirely of words that imitated sounds. It apparently derives by analogy with the presumed tendency of children to call dogs "bow-wows," ducks "quack-quacks," and so on. Certainly there are onomatopoeic words in English as in other languages: *buzz, snap, crackle,* and the *pow!* so common in comic strips are examples.

But echoisms cannot account for a language; they are simply imitations of sounds. They can become a part of a language only when they are involved in that great leap which distinguishes the mimicry of a parrot from the conversations of human beings. That is, they must evolve into abstractions; a dog is a bow-wow in terms of a language only if the mental picture—which is to say, the abstraction—of some kind of dog-in-general is evoked by the sound. In any case, children do not say "bow-wow" because that is what a dog sounds like when it barks; as a matter of fact, "bow-wow" is a fairly poor imitation of the sound of a dog's bark, as anyone who really listens can certify. A child calls a dog "bow-wow," for that's what the child's parents call it. It might further be pointed out that when a Frenchman describes in print the sound of a rooster crowing, he puts down "cocorico"; a German uses "kikeriki"; we write "cock-a-doodle-do." And let us not forget Orphan Annie's Sandy; *he's* evidently an "Arf!"

Primitive languages do not, as a matter of fact, contain more words of apparently onomatopoeic origin than do any others. There are certainly words which echo sounds, yes; but they form so small a part of any language, "primitive" or otherwise, that the bow-wow theory falls far short of accounting for the origin of language.

The ding-dong theory, in brief, assumes that humankind "naturally" responded to a natural stimulus and gave it a name; he saw a tree and said "tree"—or whatever ur-word it is assumed came to mind. This theory assumes a mystic relationship between things and words: when a human being perceived something, he responded as a bell responds when struck. It is obviously the least scientific of all conjectures about the origin of language.

"Pooh-pooh" got its name from the assumption that our earliest ancestors created a language out of their instinctive reactions against unpleasant experiences; they made a face accompanied by a sound, and finally the sound came to stand for whatever it was that caused the reaction.

And so on. As is fairly obvious, none of the theories is very satisfactory. And none really accounts for the beginnings of language. Unless some way is discovered to recapture, isolate, and analyze all the sounds ever uttered since the earth began—an impossibility which is itself a myth occasionally invoked by science-fiction writers—it will no doubt remain beyond reach to determine with any degree of scientific validity how our remotest ancestors first made the leap from random noise to language.

Frequently it is argued with some heat that animals have "languages" of their own. And now and then a human couple will "adopt" a baby chimpanzee in the hope that it can be taught its adoptive parents' language. No such attempt has succeeded. Certainly animals *communicate*—with each other and with human beings, as any pet owner can attest. But communication is not language. The essence of language is the creation and use of abstractions. A chimpanzee taught to make a noise like "banana" when he is hungry is simply illustrating a stimulus-and-response to which he has been conditioned. There is all the difference in the world between this and being able to discuss, let us say, whether bananas are fruits or vegetables. As Stuart Chase once remarked in another connection, when a dog buries a bone he is simply burying a bone; he is not concerned with the sacred principle of private bone ownership. One might go on to say that only if he could discuss with other dogs the danger that this principle may be subverted by Red Spaniels could he be said—for good or ill—to be using "language."

No doubt because we live in an age inundated by the printed word, it is often assumed that language is primarily what is written. It is not; language is speech. Writing is simply its capturing, in conventionally agreed-upon symbols, in more or less permanent form. Nor does "grammar," as so often assumed, form the foundation of language. Quite the contrary; grammar, or the study of the characteristics of language, must by its very nature be *ex post facto*. One cannot construct the grammar of a language that does not exist.

Springing from misapprehensions of what constitutes "grammar" is perhaps the most widespread misunderstanding of all: that grammar and usage are the same. They are not. The grammar of a language tells us little more of the way it is used by people who actually speak, write, and listen to it than the multiplication tables tell us about how people figure their income taxes. And just as a person trained in the use of transistorized computers might solve problems in arithmetic without any notion of what a multiplication table is, so might he speak and write to the entire satisfaction of the purist with no idea of the grammar of his native tongue.

It is not grammar that determines "correctness." It is, rather, that collection of linguistic conventions and prejudices lumped properly under the term "usage." A prime example is the word *ain't*. There is simply no rational or systematic—which is to say, "grammatical"—reason for the banning of *ain't* from educated speech and writing; indeed, as a contraction for "am not" it was considered quite proper not so long ago, and would today fill a most useful place in English as an alternative to the awkward "am I not?" or the unsatisfactory "aren't I?" which because of its subject-verb disagreement *is* actually "ungrammatical"—though a child who says "aren't I?" is certainly less likely to be reprimanded than the one who says "ain't I?"

None of this is to say that *ain't* is either correct or proper. The editors of *Webster's Third New International Dictionary,* though the attacks upon them for this reason were so grotesquely out of proportion as to raise wonder at such a case of overreaction, probably should not have implied that *ain't* is common in educated speech; at least, when not written or spoken playfully or ironically. For *ain't* is, quite simply, a shibboleth; educated people do not use it because educated people are not *supposed* to use it. There's no "grammar" involved.

Like as an adverbial connective ("Winston tastes good like a cigarette should") raises, if possible, even more fury among those who think of themselves as guardians of linguistic purity. There is no *rational* reason for the fury; adverbial connectives are nothing more than agreed-upon conventions. And linguistic conventions, like all others, change often enough without the heavens falling. But, like *ain't, like* used as above is forbidden by custom, not logic or "grammar."

Underpinning such linguistic prejudices as the *ain't-like* syndrome is the myth that lying behind all language is some mystic collection of principles with the force of authority—a kind of Mosaic law handed down from above, the violation of which is not merely a sin against "grammar" but also a moral dereliction. No reputable scholar believes such nonsense. Like humankind itself, language has evolved; it is what it is—more accurately, languages are what they are—because of a long chain of historical phenomena.

The invoking of this mystic authority most commonly takes the form of appealing to "the dictionary"—as if there were *a* dictionary, not any number of them. (See WEBSTER'S DICTIONARY.) If a word isn't "in the dictionary" then it "doesn't exist"—as if all dictionaries had to be unabridged. But dictionaries do not determine if a word exists; the existence of words, rather, determines the content of the dictionaries. Lexicographers are recorders and interpreters, not creators—as they are first to say, though sometimes it does seem that no one is listening.

Perhaps, as we struggle toward one of the oldest and also most difficult of injunctions—to know ourselves—we may ultimately come to know what our language means, and is. But until that day arrives, myth and misconception about language will continue to thrive.

largest United States city in area. No, it's not Los Angeles, as almost everyone would guess, but which doesn't even come close. As of 1972, Jacksonville, Florida, covered 827 square miles. Los Angeles comes straggling in with a piddling 458.2 square miles.

leap year. This event doesn't invariably occur every four years as is generally thought; rather, only when the year is exactly divisible by four—*except* centenary years not divisible by four hundred. There was no February 29, for example, in 1900, which was not a leap year. But the next centenary year, 2000, will have that extra day in it.

leathernecks. This term for members of the United States Marine Corps did not originate recently, nor does it have any reference either to the sunburn that might conceivably result from duty on the shores of Tripoli, or the kind of stiff military bearing often associated with the Marine Corps. It was, in fact, first applied to the light infantry, who were the elite of George Washington's army and wore dashing leather helmets with horsehair crests.

Leica as first 35-mm camera. The Leica was not the first camera to use 35 millimeter film for taking still pictures. It was, rather, the first *double-frame* "miniature" camera: that is, the first to combine two "frames" of 35 mm into one measuring 24 x 36 mm, to this day the standard size of a 35-mm negative.

Some of the pre-Leica miniature cameras were simply movie cameras modified so that they could take still pictures. But of course these pictures were the same size as a single motion-picture frame. Doubling the negative size lessened problems of grain and detail and also made for a camera easier to handle. The double-frame format of the first Leica was a sufficient innovation to insure that photographers would remember Oskar Barnack, the Leica's inventor. But inventor of the first camera to use 35-mm movie film for taking still pictures he was not.

Lenin's name. Lenin's first name was not Nikolai (or Nicolae or Nikolay), nor was his full name V. I. (for Vladimir Ilyich) Lenin, V. I. Ulyanov-Lenin, or any other variant, even though reference works sometimes so state. *Lenin* is itself a pseudonym; like many another Old Bolshevik, the man who was born Vladimir Ilyich

Ulyanov, son of a schoolmaster named Ilya Nikolaevich Ulyanov, early in his career used various pseudonyms, among them K. Tulin; Petrov; Frey; Karpov; Meyer; Starik; V. Ilyin; and Vladimir Ilyin. He finally settled on *Lenin,* sometimes signing it *N. Lenin.*

But the *N.* does not stand for "Nikolai," a legend perhaps spawned by knowledge of his father's middle name, Nikolaevich, or "son of Nikolai." In European and particularly in Russian writing, *N.* (possibly for *not* or in Russian *nyet*) is a conventional symbol for anonymity, thus a hint that *Lenin* is a pseudonym.

Unlike Stalin, who was born Joseph Dzhugashvili, Lenin did not, apparently, pick a pseudonym with any special meaning or derivation in Russian. (*Stalin* appears to be cognate with the Russian for "steel"; the name is sometimes translated as "man of steel," or some such.) One story, apparently originating with the writer Walter Duranty, is that Lenin adopted the name in honor of workers participating in a strike at the Lena gold fields. (Since this is often referred to as the "Lena Gold Strike," it is occasionally misunderstood as a "strike" in the common American miner's sense of "discovery." Named for the Lena, one of the great rivers of the world, the gold fields were originally the property of a private company, Lena Goldfields Limited. In an early instance of Communist-Capitalist economic negotiation, the Soviets acquired the company in 1934, after much haggling, for three million pounds.) But there can be no truth in this; *Lenin* was in use as a pseudonym long before the strike took place. It may be that *Lenin,* as sometimes speculated, is a kind of anagram or perhaps variant of *Ilyin,* from *Ilyich,* the middle name of the man who comes down in history as Lenin. In any case, the *N.* is not for "Nikolai" or any variation thereof.

leprosy. Counter to the impression so often given in Hollywood versions of biblical stories, lepers do not "rot away," nor do their fingers and toes fall off. Nor is it a highly contagious disease characterized by open running sores. And no one knows whether the leprosy mentioned in the Bible is the same disease as the one known today.

About a hundred years ago it was discovered that leprosy is caused by bacteria not unlike the type responsible for tuberculosis. Leprosy can take either of two forms: a relatively mild tuberculoid infection whose victims are invariably discharged from the hospital after a relatively short stay, and the lepromatous type which can persist for life. Much remains to be learned about leprosy, but one thing is certain: it is not, counter to almost universal belief, easily acquired by contact with sufferers. None of the nurses, nuns, or doctors at the United States Public Health Service Hospital for lepers at Carville, Louisiana, has ever contracted it; even where the disease is most prevalent, as in parts of India, only 5 percent of the population is affected. None of the many attempts by courageous doctors—or less courageous doctors who used volunteers—deliberately to infect themselves or others has succeeded.

Only one common belief about leprosy appears to have any basis in fact. It is true that one of the effects of the disease is to desensitize the skin. Thus when the camera moved in on the cigarette which, forgotten, was burning into the fingers holding it—an actual scene from a movie set in the tropics, years ago— this at least had some foundation, though it seems doubtful that the disease could have progressed so far as this without any previous indication.

"L'état c'est moi". ("The state, it is I"; or "I am the state"). Louis XIV is commonly believed to have said this, and it would have been a most suitable thing for him to say. But there is no documentary evidence that he ever did. Tradition has it that Voltaire *said* that Louis said it, but really made up the "quotation" himself.

Napoleon said the same thing while addressing the French Senate in 1814.

letters, literary rights in. Personal letters from famous people may be valuable as collectors' items, but the owners of the letters have no right to publish them. This is true even though the owner of the letter may also be the one to whom it was written. The author of a letter retains the same literary rights in it as if it were a short story, poem, or novel. Thus, to make public a letter from anyone, famous or not, is to violate his common-law right in a piece of literary property.

The law, thus, distinguishes between a letter as a material object, like a rare statue or a Ming vase, and as an original literary composition. As the former, a letter can be bought, sold, traded, given away, or willed to one's heirs. As the latter, it is subject to the same protection that applies to any unpublished manuscript: no one has the right to decide whether it should be published except the author himself.

"To publish" is not, incidentally, necessarily the same as "to print." Reading a letter aloud to a group, broadcasting it over the air, showing it on a television screen, or posting it in a public place so passersby could read it would constitute publication as the term applies in law.

"Let them eat cake." This remark, attributed to Marie Antoinette, and the only remark for which she is famous, could not have been original with her. In fact, she probably never said it at all; Alphonse Karr, writing in 1843, stated that a Duchess of Tuscany had said it in 1760 or before. Later, he said, it was circulated to discredit Marie Antoinette.

Certain it is that the remark occurs in the sixth book of Jean–Jacques Rousseau's *Confessions,* written in 1766. Rousseau was referring to an incident that had taken place in Grenoble about 1740, fifteen years before Marie Antoinette was born. "At length I recalled the thoughtless remark of a great princess, who, when she was told the peasants had no bread, replied, 'Let them eat cake.' "

libel, slander. Although often confused in popular usage, legally, libel is printed; slander spoken.

lie detector. The devices commonly called "lie detectors" do not, and cannot, actually identify lies. All they can do is to record certain physiological phenomena associated with lying—abnormal respiration, heartbeat, perspiration, for example. It is a crucial, not a frivolous, distinction to recognize that a lie detector's evidence, no matter how skilled the operator, is always inferential, never direct. That is why its findings are taken with a grain of salt by lawyers and judges.

And it can be fooled. Persons who are truly unaware that they are lying, when in fact they are, cannot be caught by such a device.

life preserver. What practically everybody calls a life preserver is, to the seafaring man, properly called a ring buoy. A life preserver, strictly speaking, is similar to what most people call a life jacket.

light bulb, inventor of. Many people think he was, but Thomas A. Edison simply improved upon a principle others had discovered and worked on for years. Electric lighting itself is much older than commonly supposed, although the earliest attempts involved arcs rather than filaments. As early as 1802 Sir Humphrey Davy produced an arc light, and in 1844, three years before Edison was born, Jean Foucault made an arc light strong enough to illuminate the Place de la Concorde in Paris.

An English physicist, Sir Joseph William Swan, made a crude light bulb as early as 1860. In 1878, he showed a successful carbon-filament lamp at Newcastle, some ten months before Edison managed to come up with his "original."

Lightning never strikes twice in the same place. This old saw is so often exposed as fallacious that probably not many educated people take much stock in it. But many are unaware that not only does lightning often strike twice in the same place; it is *more likely than not* to do so. Lightning, like all electric currents or discharges, follows the path of least resistance. Air is a very poor conductor. Thus, almost anything else helping to bridge the gap between ground and cloud—a high tree; or a building, especially one with a metal skeleton; an elevation in the landscape itself—will offer a more convenient path and thus "attract" the lightning.

To speak of a lightning "stroke" is not, incidentally, accurate. Lightning is really a succession of strokes, and often the most powerful move not from cloud to ground, but the other way: the so-called return stroke.

light-year. This is something of a misnomer, since the light-year is not a measurement of time, but of distance. In fact, it is the distance that a ray of light would travel in one year, or approximately 6,000,000,000,000 miles.

limericks. No, they are not named for the city in Ireland. Nor was the form invented by Edward Lear, though he certainly gave it a boost. (The characteristic Lear limerick, however, does not satisfy the contemporary connoisseur; Lear liked to repeat the last

word of the first line as the last word of the last line, now regarded
as old hat if not downright naïve.)

A fair amount of earnest scholarship has gone into the study
of the limerick. Langford Reed has suggested that eighteenth-
century Irish veterans returning from the Continent brought the
form back to their home base, which was Limerick. But his evidence is unimpressive. As a matter of fact Shakespeare may have
originated the form. In *Othello* (act 2, sc. 3, lines 71 ff.) , Iago
sings the following:

> And let me the canakin clink, clink;
> And let me the canakin clink:
> A soldier's a man;
> A life's but a span;
> Why, then, let a soldier drink.

Not perfect, true, by today's cultivated taste in limericks. But the
basic elements are all there; and who's to say that a tin-eared
Elizabethan printer (it did happen sometimes) is not responsible
for the faulty meter?

Lincoln, Abraham—and popularity as president. Sometimes a
myth will arise as the result of overly enthusiastic attempts at
debunking. One such is the statement sometimes made that Lincoln was not really a popular president. But in fact he was. Certainly he had enemies; a wartime president can scarcely hope to be
free from attacks arising out of the public frustrations and despair
which are a part of wartime. And the opposition press in Lincoln's
day, an era of journalistic vituperation scarcely equaled before or
since, was sometimes so extraordinarily vicious in its comments
that it is not always easy to remember they reflected only the
opinions of editors, not the public. It should also be remembered
that Horace Greeley, the most influential journalist in Lincoln's
time, was responsible for many of the attacks on Lincoln—possibly because Greeley had backed another candidate, Seward, for
the 1860 nomination, possibly because Greeley apparently had
the kind of temperament that seizes upon causes rather than issues.
(A blistering attack on Lincoln written by Greeley was scheduled
for appearance when the news of Lincoln's assassination reached
the New York *Tribune,* Greeley's paper. It was killed in Greeley's

absence by the managing editor, who explained to Greeley that the *Tribune* would have been wrecked by a mob if the editorial had been run—and that the *Tribune* would have deserved it.)

Lincoln was not, it is true, originally elected by a "majority"; his share of the popular vote was 39 percent. But he was running against not one, but three other candidates. And in fact, Lincoln's margin over Douglas, his leading opponent, was more than 500,000. When he was reelected in 1864, his lead over McClellan was about the same—some half a million. The population of those states which did not secede was about 22 million during Lincoln's tenure. Lincoln's popular majority in 1864, thus, represents a margin equivalent to about 4.5 million today. Whether or not the term "landslide," applied by some historians, is applicable, it is nonetheless true that Lincoln's victory over McClellan in 1864 was greater in equivalent terms than Franklin Delano Roosevelt's over Thomas E. Dewey in 1944. And this time Lincoln captured over 55 percent of the popular vote.

When Lincoln was assassinated, even those newspapers that had been most bitter in their comments while he lived poured forth a torrent of adulation. In the words of Robert S. Harper (*Lincoln and the Press,* 1951) , "It was no longer possible to determine the politics of a newspaper by what it said about Lincoln." Enemies Lincoln certainly had; no public figure can hope to escape them. But by the only standard that determines popularity on a statistical basis rather than a historian's opinion—the election returns—Lincoln was indeed a popular president.

links, golf. To the purist, only a golf course next to water is properly called a golf links. In the strictest possible sense, the course ought to be laid out amid sand hills next to a seashore, which is what *links* means to a Scotsman.

lion. Recent research has demolished a great many myths about the king of beasts, many of them given new life by *Born Free* and its pride of successors. After three years in Serengeti National Park, Tanzania, and almost three thousand hours of observation, Dr. George Schaller, an American biologist noted also for his studies of the mountain gorilla, has come to certain conclusions quite at variance with common belief.

Lions do not kill just to obtain food; sometimes they go on what amounts to a killing binge; and on occasion they will kill even when already gorged if the killing is easy. Nor is the kill quick and "merciful," accomplished by jumping onto the victim's back and breaking its neck with one mighty swipe of the paw; rather, the lion clamps its jaws on the prey's throat and strangles or suffocates it, a process that may take as long as ten minutes.

Surprisingly, it is the female which does most of the killing, while the male performs little more than 10 percent of the hunting; also, the lioness performs a dominant administrative role and provides much of the pride's leadership.

Most destructive of the noble image lions so often convey, however, is Schaller's discovery that lions are frequently scavengers, just like the much-maligned hyena; in parts of Africa they get more than half their food from carcasses killed by hyenas, wild dogs, or disease. Both males and females will sometimes eat their own cubs.

Lions are not, incidentally, an endangered species—as yet, anyway. They are still plentiful in Africa, and breed well in captivity.

liquids pumped upward into a tank. Those who have paid any attention to the refueling of jet aircraft often speculate on the extra power it must take to force the fuel upward into the tanks and wonder if it might not be faster and more economical to refuel from the top. As a matter of fact, it takes less energy to fill a tank with liquid by forcing it up through a hole in the bottom than it would take to fill it from the top. Any hydraulics engineer can explain why. The liquid entering the tank from the bottom does not lift the entire weight of whatever is above it in the tank, but only a column of the same diameter as the pipe and extending only as high as the surface. To fill an aircraft fuel tank from the top obviously requires the lifting of a column higher than the surface throughout the whole process.

Storage tanks on stilts, feeding the aircraft by gravity, would not, of course, make things any better: *they* would have to be filled before the aircraft could be fueled.

Little Bighorn, battle of. Sitting Bull did not participate in the battle of the Little Bighorn. He stayed in the hills, making medicine, while Crazy Horse took care of Custer. Further, the battle was not an Indian ambush, as many people think, but an attack by the soldiers on an Indian encampment. To Crazy Horse, by the way, the Little Bighorn was known as Greasy Grass River.

"Little Black Sambo." Though "Sambo," like "Rastus," has become identified with American racism, the Helen Bannerman story is set in India. For some reason, however, the characters have African-sounding names (Sambo's mother is called Black Mumbo; his father, Black Jumbo).

"Lizzie Borden took an ax / And gave her mother forty whacks; / When she saw what she had done / She gave her father forty-one." She did no such thing according to the jury that tried her. She was in fact acquitted, after only sixty-six minutes of deliberation.

That practically nobody seems aware that Lizzie was not found guilty probably can be blamed on Edmund Pearson, whose *Studies in Murder* (1924) suggested (Lizzie was still alive at that time) and whose *Trial of Lizzie Borden* (1937) said (Lizzie was dead now) that she did it. But a reporter and fact-crime writer, Edward D. Radin, in *Lizzie Borden: The Untold Story* (1961), maintains that Pearson ignored the evidence in Lizzie's favor, which Radin finds convincing. Radin thinks, in fact, that the guilty party was—who else?—the maid.

In any case, the fact remains that Lizzie was found innocent, not guilty; a matter of record.

Lloyd's of London. This famous institution is not an insurance company, as people often think, but rather an association of carefully selected underwriters who act as individuals. There is no such thing as a policy "issued by Lloyd's of London"; the association writes no policies itself, any more than the New York Stock Exchange sells stock as an organization.

log cabins and first American settlers. Firmly enshrined in American tradition is that the first colonists lived in log cabins or houses. They did not. John Smith, Governor Bradford, and the Founding Fathers never saw a log cabin, much less lived in one. As long ago as 1927, Henry C. Mercer and G. F. Dow, in separate studies, established that the log cabin was introduced to America not by the Puritans, the Pilgrims, or such Elizabethan adventurers as Captain Smith, but by Swedes who settled on the Delaware in 1638; and not until the eighteenth century did their innovation spread much beyond. (Later, German immigrants were to introduce the log cabin independently.)

The earliest English colonists, according to Harold C. Shurtleff in *The Log Cabin Myth* (1939), after first building such temporary shelters as "tents, Indian wigwams, and huts or cottages covered with bark, turf, or clay," then proceeded, as promptly as possible, to construct the kind of habitations to which they had been accustomed: framed houses. What Shurtleff calls "log-cabinitis" is the result of the nineteenth-century American tendency to romanticize—not without reason—early struggles against the wilderness. From log cabin to White House: the American dream. And it was exemplified, certainly, in Andrew Jackson and Abraham Lincoln, whose famous presidential campaigns did much to blur the difference between the earliest seaboard frontiers and the advancing western frontier of later years, where log cabins were indeed a common sight. But they were unknown to our founders; those depictions of Puritan forebears that show them, muskets on shoulders, returning to their log cabins after Thanksgiving dinner with the Indians have no basis in fact.

London Bridge. London Bridge is not the one most Americans think it is; it is usually confused with the Tower Bridge, which has tall, prominent towers that rise up above the Thames—and is not so called, incidentally, because of its towers, but because it is near the Tower of London, which in turn is not a tower, but a complex of buildings.

The Tower Bridge—the one often called London Bridge—is neither very old nor particularly historic. It was built in 1894.

The rather commonplace-looking bridge which was recently bought, brought over, and rebuilt at Lake Havasu, Arizona, though quite properly referred to as London Bridge, is not, of course, the London Bridge of verse and song. The famous London Bridge was built of stone in the twelfth century, to replace a wooden bridge of the tenth century. On it were houses, shops, and even a chapel. It was forever being damaged by fire, and what with its buildings constantly falling into disrepair, we have the nursery rhyme "London Bridge is falling down, falling down . . ." The buildings were removed from it in the mideighteenth century, and it was entirely removed in 1832 soon after the completion of the London Bridge that is presently in Arizona.

London police and guns. It is not true that the bobby is never armed. Not anymore, at least. About 5 percent of the London police force have qualified in the use of handguns; and eighty men, as rifle marksmen. Most London police stations have guns on hand just in case. Members of the Special Branch who protect important visitors carry guns as a matter of course, as do on occasion police constables guarding embassies.

lost art of hardening copper. It is sometimes said that certain ancient peoples knew how to harden or temper copper so as to make it usable for edged tools, etc. This is not so. Pure copper can be made harder by hammering or cold rolling, but it has to be alloyed with some other metal to achieve any great degree of toughness. Metallurgists could today produce copper tools as good as any found in Egypt or Peru, but there's no reason for it; steel is far superior.

"lost generation." Gertrude Stein is usually credited with the origin of this phrase, to describe the people who were in their twenties during the 1920s. Actually, Gertrude Stein records that she first heard it from Monsieur Pernollet, proprietor of the Hôtel Pernollet in Belley, where Gertrude Stein and Alice B. Toklas stayed in 1924. Something of a philosopher and a devotee of Lamartine, he employed the expression *une génération perdue* in seeking to describe the young men who had gone to war and had thus missed the all-important "civilizing process." He made the observation in reference to a young mechanic who was fixing Miss Stein's car.

Ernest Hemingway, spokesman of the "lost generation," credited her with the phrase's origin on the flyleaf of *The Sun Also Rises* (1926) and wrote his first version of its genesis in the unpublished preface (1925) to the book. His second, somewhat angry, version appears in *A Moveable Feast*. He mentions the mechanic, with whom Miss Stein was exasperated (but not M. Pernollet). Miss Stein, he says, applied the expression also to Hemingway in exasperation, saying that his was a generation that was drinking itself to death.

Loyalist side, Spanish Civil War. A surprising number of people assume that General Franco's was the established government of Spain when the civil war, which many believe presaged World War II, broke out there in July 1936. The exact opposite is the truth; Franco and his forces were the "revolutionaries"; it was they who rebelled. Perhaps the fact that the established church and the army, generally regarded as the forces of conservatism, were the rebels, while the Popular Front, or Loyalist government, composed of various liberal and radical elements, was in power has helped to foster the misconception.

Ltd. Sometimes adopted by American companies or mercantile establishments to add tone to the name, *Ltd.* or *Limited* has no such implication in England. Its significance is financial, not social. It means simply that the financial liability of each partner or stockholder is limited to the amount of his actual investment in the business.

Lucifer. This name for Satan has no biblical authority whatsoever, Protestant or Catholic, although the Bible is commonly given as its source. There is only one mention of a Lucifer in the King James (and also the Catholic) Bible—and it does not refer to Satan, but rather the king of Babylon. The biblical passage (Isa. 14:12) reads: "How art thou fallen from heaven, O Lucifer, son of the morning! how art thou cut down to the ground, which didst weaken the nations!"

Lusitania, **sinking of.** Misconceptions about the sinking of the *Lusitania* abound. The *Lusitania* was not an American ship. Its sinking did not "trigger" American entry into World War I; the sinking occurred on May 7, 1915, almost two years before the American declaration of war. It was not unarmed. It was carrying munitions, and among its passengers were Canadian troops. Nor was it sunk without warning; not only had the Germans declared the area where the *Lusitania* went down a war zone, but on the day of its sailing the German government printed in the New York press an official general warning with specific reference to the *Lusitania.* It would have been quite possible for every one of the 128 Americans lost, including Alfred Vanderbilt, to have transferred to a slower American ship that sailed two hours later than the *Lusitania* and arrived safely at Liverpool.

The *Lusitania,* a British Cunard liner, was armed with six-inch guns which, while obviously of little use against a warship, certainly could sink a submarine. Its own manifest listed more than 4,000 cases of small arms ammunition, plus 1,250 empty shrapnel cases and other contraband. Its captain, like all others in charge of British merchantmen at the time, had standing orders to ram any enemy submarine on sight. Whether or not it is actually true, as has been charged, that Winston Churchill, then first lord of the Admiralty, and others deliberately invited, in effect, the sinking of the *Lusitania* in order to inflame world and more particularly American opinion, the fact is that the Germans were quite correct in claiming that the *Lusitania* was far from being the unarmed passenger liner Allied propaganda made it out to be.

Another fact, of course, is that the sinking of the *Lusitania,* "justified" or not, was a very stupid act whose effect was to tip American opinion even more toward the Allied side. The German commander of the U-20 (who was not, contrary to legend, lying in wait; in fact, it was an unexpected change in her course that brought the *Lusitania* within range of one of his three remaining torpedoes) may have achieved a temporary victory. But the long-range effect of his action no doubt had more than a little to do with Germany's eventual defeat; for though, as said, America's entry into the war was not an immediate result of the sinking, the sinking nonetheless had enormous propaganda value for the Allies and played its part in motivating the ultimate entry of the United States into World War I.

M

macaroni. Americans mean by *macaroni* a type of pasta that is long and hollow and fairly thick, as distinguished from spaghetti, vermicelli, etc. However, in Italy *maccherone* (plural, *maccheroni*) is a generic term for at least eight kinds of pasta, including spaghetti, vermicelli, and half a dozen others.

Macaroon comes from the same source.

Magellan, Ferdinand—as the first to circumnavigate the earth in one voyage. Although many schoolboys will be surprised, it was not Magellan who performed this feat. Ferdinand Magellan sailed more than halfway around the earth, both east and west, in two separate voyages. (He was killed before finishing the second.) Sir Francis Drake was the first to make it in one trip.

male menopause. There is of course no such thing as "male menopause"—though it is commonly referred to. (Menopause is the cessation of menses.) The male climacteric, experienced by about 50 percent of the male population, involves physical manifestations, and very often emotional ones.

male sexual organs, size of as related to potency or virility. Despite popular belief, the size of male sexual organs has nothing to do with virility or potency. That this myth goes back at least as far as the days of the Roman Empire is illustrated in one of the "secret" paintings at Pompeii; behind a small door which, with a modicum of financial inducement, a tour guide will open is a rendition of a Pompeiian weighing his quite enormous penis on a scale; the Pompeiian wears also a smile of self-satisfaction.

But as Dr. David Reuben reminds us in his best seller, *Everything You Always Wanted to Know About Sex (But Were Afraid to Ask)* (1969), almost all orgiastic sensation in women is concentrated in the clitoris, labia, and related areas, within easy reach of practically any penis no matter its size. As Dr. Reuben goes on to say, in sexual intercourse it's quality rather than quantity that counts.

Malthus, Thomas. Those who invoke the name of Thomas Malthus (1766–1834) while advocating the various means of birth control that current technology has made available would certainly not have his blessing. Malthus—who was not, incidentally, either biologist or geneticist but rather historian and economist— advocated postponing the age of marriage and strict sexual continence as his remedies for the population explosion.

As a matter of fact, Malthus was quite wrong in one of his fundamental assumptions. What he took to be the cause of the great increase in British population during his time, a greater birth rate, turned out not to be the case at all. It was, rather, a fall in the *death* rate. Since the heart of Malthus's theories is his contention that population must increase at a geometric ratio while means of subsistence increase only arithmetically, this was a rather serious boner.

Not that Malthus found in his theory any particular cause for despair: to him, the constant struggle for life was not only God's will (Malthus had taken orders in the Anglican church and served for a time as a curate in Surrey); it was a means of insuring the triumph of good over evil. In *An Essay on the Principle of Population, etc.,* Malthus says, ". . . if those stimulants to exertion which arise from the wants of the body were removed from the mass of mankind, we have much more reason to think that they would be sunk to the level of brutes from a deficiency of excitements than that they would be raised to the level of philosophers by the possession of leisure . . . ."

man as a natural object. Only too frequently it is forgotten that to speak of the human race as if it were somehow an alien presence on this globe is utter nonsense. Mankind is as much a part of "nature" as are trees, glaciers, giant pandas, rocks, and rattlesnakes. As products of man's (perfectly natural) ingenuity, or whatever you wish to call it, skyscrapers and automobiles are every bit as "natural" as beaver dams. They may not, of course, be as attractive nor as nonpolluting as beaver dams. But there is no point in acting as if they were alien presences, for they are not. What mankind creates springs from mankind's nature.

mandarin. Whether used with reference to certain Chinese officials in an earlier time, to the language they spoke, or to the fruit called mandarin orange, the term *mandarin* is not Chinese nor does it spring from Chinese. It is, rather, derived ultimately from Sanskrit, one of a family of ancient languages not related to Chinese. The use of *mandarin* with regard to oranges of a certain kind may have come from an identification with the color of the robes Chinese mandarins wore. Or so, at least, the *Oxford English Dictionary* suggests.

man-eating plants. Everybody knows that there are some plants which attract and "devour" insects, but no plant or tree has ever been found that eats up men or large animals—despite scary stories to the contrary.

manor and landed estate. Although the term *manor* had long been used in England in a more general sense, in those American colonies during the seventeenth century where land grants were made, a distinction existed between a manor and a landed estate no matter how large. The lord of a manor had judicial powers; he could hold court, settle disputes between tenants and servants, and punish offenders.

Man Without a Country, The. *The Man Without a Country* is a story, once known to every schoolchild, about Lieutenant Philip Nolan, who "in a fit of frenzy," cries out, "Damn the United States! I wish I may never hear of the United States again!" Nolan is taken at his word, committed to the custody of the Navy, and sentenced to have his wish fulfilled. The author, Edward Everett

Hale, was so convincing in his detail that many readers then believed, and some even now believe, that the story of the man without a country is true, or based on truth.

It isn't; it's entirely fiction—except for the name of the protagonist, Philip Nolan, and a bit of the real Nolan's background. The real Philip Nolan appears to have been, if not something of a scoundrel, then certainly something of an adventurer and soldier of fortune. It is somewhat ironic, then, that Hale saw the real Nolan in an entirely favorable light.

Perhaps because he felt a bit of guilt at having used both his name and at least part of his early life in *The Man Without a Country,* Hale did actually write a book about the real person, *Philip Nolan's Friends,* published in 1876. "I have done my best," Hale said, "to repair my fault [against the real Nolan], and to recall to memory a brave man, by telling the story of his fate, in a book called 'Philip Nolan's Friends.' "

margarine and butter. Oleomargarine is not harder to digest than butter; the body digests and uses all food fats equally well. Nor would it do any good in terms of losing weight to substitute margarine; its caloric content is the same as butter's. Nor does margarine used continually have any effect on secondary sex characteristics as some believe; there is no evidence that it contains anything adversely affecting the building of hormones.

married priests (Catholic). It is quite possible for a Catholic priest to be married, even though a Catholic priest may not marry. Many Eastern Rite Catholic priests are, as a matter of fact, married, although their marriage must have taken place before ordination.

Under certain circumstances, however, even a Western Catholic priest may be married; as, for example, in the case of a married Anglican priest who is converted to Catholicism and becomes a Catholic priest.

Mars, canals of. It is sometimes said that the notion of "canals" on Mars derives from a mistranslation of the word used by G. V. Schiaparelli, the Italian astronomer whose years of birth and death exactly parallel Mark Twain's (1835–1910)—and who thus, incidentally, also came in with Halley's comet, and left with it.

Schiaparelli described the markings as *canali;* the debunkers point out that this means "channels," and, thus, the implication suggested by "canals," that they are the conscious contrivances of intelligent beings, has no foundation.

But the fact of the matter is that *canali* means *both* "channels" and "canals" in Italian. Further, Schiaparelli himself specifically refused to rule out the possibility that they might be the work of intelligent beings, though—like the good scientist he was—he qualified his statement by pointing out that there are plenty of straight lines and geometric shapes in nature. But there is no reason to assume that *canals* falsifies either Schiaparelli's meaning, or his intent.

"Marseillaise." The French national anthem was not, like "The Star-Spangled Banner," composed as a revolutionary song. The composer, Claude Joseph Rouget de Lisle, was a captain in the French garrison at Strasbourg, and a music amateur. The mayor of the city stated the need for a marching song, and de Lisle obliged, tossing it off, some say, in a fit of patriotic fervor after dinner one night. It was first entitled "War Song for the Rhine Army." However, it became known as the "Marseillaise" after soldiers from Marseilles sang it with great spirit as they marched on the Tuileries August 10, 1792. The irony is that Rouget de Lisle himself was a royalist and narrowly escaped the guillotine.

martial law. Although the term is used very loosely by some journalists, martial law is practically never invoked in cases of civil disturbance, and calling in the National Guard does not mean that martial law has been "declared." If a region is really under martial law, then all civil rights are suspended, and military courts are established in place of civil courts.

Marx, Harpo. There are doubtless still millions of viewers of Marx Brothers movies who are not aware that Harpo was just as capable of talking as the other brothers.

mathematicians and chess players. That mathematicians always make good chess players, or the converse—that good chess players are automatically good mathematicians—is an assumption without much apparent basis. Chess is a game of strategy and tactics, neither of which really plays much, if any, part in mathematics.

medal play (golf). No such thing, according to the rules of golf, which do not mention the term. The correct phrase is stroke play.

Mercedes-Benz. Nobody named Mercedes had anything to do with the production of the Mercedes-Benz. Instead, the name is that of the daughter of Emil Jellinek, an Austrian who habitually named his cars for her. (In 1900, three of his racing cars were called Mercedes.) Later, when he induced the Daimler automotive works to design a car for him, he again called it Mercedes. When the Daimler and Benz firms merged in 1926, they retained the name.

mess of pottage. This picturesque expression does not occur anywhere in the Bible. Nor does the Bible actually say that Esau sold his birthright to Jacob for pottage.

The incident occurs in Gen. 25:29–34. Esau came in from the field, said he felt faint, and asked Jacob to feed him some pottage. Jacob asked Esau to sell him his birthright. Esau replied that his birthright was of little use to himself as he would be dying soon. Thereupon Jacob required Esau to swear to him and Esau did sell his birthright to Jacob. At that point Jacob gave Esau bread and pottage of "lentiles." The implication is that a deal was made, but it is not precisely stated, and there is no mention whatsoever here of a "mess of pottage."

In Heb. 12:16 Paul, centuries later, referred to Esau, who "for one morsel of meat sold his birthright." *Meat* is here used in its now archaic sense, meaning simply "food."

metaphysics. An error of many centuries' standing has led to the common use of this term as meaning "supernatural," or "transcending"—that is, "beyond"—the physical world. It had no such meaning originally, nor does it yet in its original context: Aristotelian philosophy. Those works of Aristotle which in the common arrangement of his "books" followed the section called "Physics" were called "Metaphysics," or "that which comes after the Physics." The Greek *meta* does not mean "beyond" in any but the most literal sense: that is, "following" or "after."

Nor does Aristotle's "Metaphysics" deal with the supernatural.

Methinks the lady doth protest too much. Not only an inaccurate rendition of Gertrude's remark about the Player Queen in *Hamlet* (act 3, sc. 2, line 240), which in the Folios is rendered as "The lady protests too much, methinks" (in the Quartos it's "The lady doth protest too much, methinks"), but also usually misunderstood by those who do not know, or have forgotten, that "protest" here carries its older meaning of "proclaim." This meaning survives to some extent today in such expressions as "to protest one's innocence," where clearly the older meaning of "protest" is used.

milk. That milk is, as often said, nature's most nearly perfect food needs severe qualification. Many people do not possess the enzyme that makes the digestion of milk possible; the effect of milk on them is to induce diarrhea. Possibly as many as 75 percent of blacks in the United States are not able to digest the lactose in cow's milk. Any claim that milk is "good for everyone" is thus manifestly false.

milk in combination with other foods. Contrary to much folklore, milk and fish—or milk and anything else—are not poisonous or harmful when eaten in combination. If two foods can be eaten separately, they can be eaten together—at least in terms of safety. So if you happen to be fond of whipped cream on liver, feel free.

miniature (painting). A "miniature" is not so called because it is small, although of course it may be. The term has, in fact, nothing to do with size, but derives rather from the Latin *miniatus,* the past participle of *miniare,* which means to color with red lead. The Italian word *miniatura* originally had reference to the art of illuminating manuscripts, some of which were anything but "miniature" in the customary sense.

minutes of a meeting, etc. Despite what many think, this phrase is not related to the measurement of time. It stems, rather, from the Latin *minutus,* "small," since records of proceedings are—or were —generally taken down in miniature, to be transcribed into a fair hand later.

mirage. By many it is thought that a mirage is nothing but an illusion seen by a desert traveler delirious from thirst. This is not true. A mirage is an optical phenomenon which can be observed from the cool comfort of an air-conditioned car—and explained scientifically.

Also, it is thought that a mirage is completely illusory, that none of the elements are real and the entire picture can vanish from the scene. This, too, is incorrect. If there is a palm tree reflected in a pool of water, the reflection and the pool are illusory, but there has to be a palm tree there to begin with.

What happens is that a layer of very hot air forms over the sand, let us say, just as shimmering rays occur over a highway pavement. This layer of hot air can reflect the sky in such a way that it resembles a blue pool of water. It can also reflect nearby objects, like the palm tree. As the observer approaches and changes his angle of vision, the pool and the reflected tree disappear. The tree itself, of course, remains.

Not all mirages, however, are so simple as those described above. What is called the "Fata Morgana," occurring at the Strait of Messina, near the western coast of Japan, and sometimes over the Great Lakes in the United States, results when two different air density layers occur in rare proximity. It can transform an ordinary scene into a quite remarkable picture—from "simple cottage" to "wondrous castle," in the words of the *Britannica*.

missing link. The notion that there was a creature, yet undiscovered, who represents a "missing link" between man and ape is of course nonsensical on its face, as a moment's thought demonstrates. The evolution of man was an enormously long and complicated process in which, obviously, no one "link" could possibly vary so much from any other that it would stand out. Further, the notion of a "missing link" is based on a misconception of Darwinian theories of evolution. Darwin neither said nor implied that man is descended from the ape, as "missing link" implies; he merely postulated that man and ape evolved from a common ancestor. In his own words, "man is the co-descendant with other mammals of a common progenitor."

Note that Darwin does not limit to man and ape alone this "common progenitor"; his word is "mammals," and in fact, shortly before this remark from his *Descent of Man,* he calls attention to the "close resemblance" between the embryos of man and dog.

***Moby-Dick,* critical reactions to.** It is widely believed that Herman Melville's masterpiece either (a) fell with a dull thud upon an indifferent America or (b) inspired such an immediate storm of hostile criticism that Melville stopped writing and went into retirement. Neither belief is anywhere near the truth. *Moby-Dick* attracted wide attention when it was published, and the initial reactions were much more favorable than otherwise in the United States. In fact, the reviews were some three to one in favor, as Hugh W. Hetherington points out in *Melville's Reviewers* (1961), although "immediate reactions were so varied that it is possible, as has been done, to build up a case for an acceptance or for a rejection . . . ." Nor did Melville "retire" after *Moby-Dick;* he wrote and published several more volumes in the years immediately following its appearance.

It was the *delayed* reaction—that is, those criticisms of the book that appeared some months after what Hetherington calls "its peak of good fortune" in early December of 1851—that was primarily unfavorable. This, plus a disastrous fire at his publishers' in 1854 which destroyed several hundred copies of the book (though not, as often said, the plates from which it was printed), no doubt had some ultimate effect on Melville's "retirement" from the literary world.

Whether or not *Moby-Dick* should have received universal acclamation when it appeared is obviously a moot question today. But certainly it was neither ignored nor generally scorned.

moles in gardens. Since moles are entirely insectivorous, they pose no threat whatsoever to vegetation; they simply do not eat any type of vegetation. Unsightly as their tunnels may seem to be, they actually improve the soil by aerating it.

***Mona Lisa,* the.** The *Mona Lisa* (or La *Gioconda*) is certainly the most-talked-about work of art in the world. And with good reason: It is full of mystery and personality; it was Leonardo da Vinci's own favorite; it is a very great painting indeed. As if this were not enough, it has been weighed down with misinformation and spurious explanations of its greatness.

One story has it that the subject is the third wife of Francesco del Giocondo, that she was young and he was old. He was also harsh, and impotent. He pawned her jewels and made her wear mourning so that their absence would not be noticed. When Leonardo came along, he fell under her spell, for he was young, too. She became his mistress. Still she was sad, and in order to make her smile for her picture, he hired musicians and jesters. Then he painted her portrait, and in it he expressed through her sphinxlike expression the mystery and beauty of their romance.

Most, if not all, of this tale is nonsense. At that time Leonardo was not young; he was over fifty and looked about eighty. Furthermore, painters at this time did not paint portraits from live subjects. They made a sketch, or cartoon, from which they developed the painting in their shop. Leonardo probably made his master sketch in Florence about 1504, took it to Milan, transferred it to a panel and developed the painting (1506–1510), adding the costume, the veil, and the background landscape. The absurd story about hiring people to crack jokes while the lady was being painted from life seems to have been made up out of whole cloth by Giorgio Vasari, the famous art historian, who in 1550 produced this episode, along with numerous details about the hair, the flesh, the nostrils, etc., although Vasari had never even seen the picture himself. Finally, it is not at all certain that the Mona Lisa represents the third wife of Francesco del Giocondo. The reliable Cassiano dal Pozzo, writing over a hundred years after the painting was made, refers to "a life-size protrait, half length of a certain Giocondo," but we cannot be sure that this is really Francesco's third wife. The evidence is scanty.

Of course the lady's expression comes in for perennial comment. Tourist guides like to say that if you stare at her long enough, she will smile back at you, and that it requires great genius to paint this kind of a furtive smile. Leonardo had achieved this ability; therefore it is a great painting. Again, this is nonsense. This kind of ghostly smile was not at all uncommon among painters in that period: Andrea del Verocchio for instance. The painting is one of genius, but that is not where the genius lies.

Tourist guides also like to say that the eyes will follow you around the room, as if this too were an accomplishment reserved only for the greatest painters. The eyes-that-follow-you trick is a simple one, used by innumerable artists in everything from posters to billboards.

If La *Gioconda* could hear what people say about her she would doubtless not smile; she would laugh out loud.

Money is the root of all evil. In fact, it should read, "For *the love of money* is the root of all evil." That's what Paul wrote to Timothy in 1 Tim. 6:10. There is a difference.

Monitor **and** *Merrimac.* Every schoolchild knows of the first battle between ironclad naval ships, the *Monitor* and the *Merrimac* (sometimes spelled *Merrimack*), which took place March 9, 1862, at Hampton Roads, Virginia. In fact, this most famous naval engagement of the United States Civil War did not involve two ships named *Monitor* (North) and *Merrimac* (South). It took place between the *Monitor* and the *Virginia.*

The ship popularly called the *Merrimac* had indeed borne this name originally—as a Northern ship, a wooden frigate set afire and abandoned in 1861, then raised by the South and rebuilt as an ironclad. But she was at once renamed the *Virginia,* and it was as the *Virginia* that she fought. The popular term for the battle represents a triumph of alliteration over history.

Morris, William, and his morris chair. William Morris is well remembered for his revival of medieval crafts and concepts. Also, he is credited with having been a very practical man, for didn't he invent the morris chair, which has survived to this day?

No he did not, as a matter of fact. The morris chair was designed by Morris's colleague, Philip Webb, and was made by Morris and Company, the firm that Morris and his friends had established. It was then copied by Americans such as Gustav Stickley, prominent in the crafts movement of that time. Finally the morris chair that we know emerged from mass-produced, commercial furniture that imitated the Stickley product.

Morris, who insisted on hand craftsmanship, would not be pleased to find his name attached to the factory-made contraption that used to grace every American den.

In the Victoria and Albert Museum (London) there is a morris chair that bears no resemblance whatsoever to the American version. Its back and arms are of rather slender wooden elements painted black; the seat is of rush. This light chair was produced after a traditional design found in Sussex by Warington Taylor.

moss growing on north side of trees. The old belief that, if lost, one can at least establish compass directions by noting where moss grows on trees and taking this for north is false and, in a quite literal sense, misleading. Ironically, it is true that on level land in a dry area a tree growing by itself may have moss on just the north side. In dense forest or on lowlands, however, moss tends to grow on all sides of the tree. The moral seems obvious enough: if one is to get lost, he should arrange to do so in open, dry country.

moth-eaten. Moths, contrary to the popular notion, do not eat clothes. Some, as a matter of fact, don't eat anything at all during their adult lives, which are (not surprisingly) brief. It's the larvae that do the damage; by the time moths are flying out of the closet, it's too late.

Mont Blanc, location of. It's not in Switzerland, as many think. It's in France.

Mount Ararat. Noah's ark did not come to rest on Mount Ararat. It came to rest on the *mountains of* Ararat. There is no reference to a single mountain called Ararat in the Bible. See Gen. 8:4.

Mozart's funeral, weather conditions at time of. The romantic notion that Mozart was buried in a raging Viennese blizzard was demolished in 1960 by Nicolas Slonimsky in the January *Musical Quarterly* (vol. 46, no. 1, pp. 12 ff.) . Mr. Slonimsky, the distinguished musical historian, demolished it by the simple but ingenious expedient of writing to the Vienna Weather Observatory, whose records go back to the eighteenth century. Mozart was buried on December 6, 1791. Not only does the record show that there was little wind and the temperature on this day did not fall below 37.9 degrees; in the course of his research Mr. Slonimsky also uncovered an entry in the diary of one Count Karl Zinzendorf, kept in the Austrian State Archives, which describes the weather on the day of Mozart's funeral as mild, with frequent drizzle or mist.

It is not impossible, of course, for snow to fall at temperatures above freezing; and one can imagine that a few wet flakes conceivably might have been mixed in with the count's "drizzle." But under no conceivable circumstances could a blizzard have occurred when Mozart was laid to rest.

An interesting sidelight mentioned in Mr. Slonimsky's account involves the often-told story connected with the burial of that other great Viennese composer, Beethoven. It turns out to be quite true. Entirely in the romantic tradition, there really was a violent thunderstorm the day *he* was buried.

Mrs. This title is not really an abbreviation at all, though it is widely regarded as such by almost everybody, including dictionary-makers. Once, true, it stood for "mistress." But "mistress" and "wife" certainly do not mean the same thing now, nor have they for many years. *Mrs.* simply cannot be spelled out in standard usage; unlike an abbreviation, there is no "full" form for *Mrs.* (*Missus,* or some such, is merely a nonstandard effort at a phonetic rendition.)

Mr., on the other hand, is a true abbreviation, standing for "Mister."

Mrs. O'Leary's cow. Mrs. O'Leary's famous cow could scarcely have kicked over the lantern while being milked; Mrs. O'Leary was in bed at the time the Chicago fire broke out, having milked the cow some time earlier. As a matter of fact, a reporter named Michael Ahern admitted that he made up the whole story to add color to his account of the fire.

Murphy bed. The Murphy bed is made, it is true, by a company called the Murphy Door Bed Company. But counter to almost universal usage, its proper name is In-a-Door. At least that's what the Murphys call it.

mushroom cloud. Although this term has become synonymous with the atom bomb and its various appalling relatives, it does not define a unique characteristic of nuclear explosions. Any very large blast above ground and in calm air, even if caused by conventional materials like TNT, will be followed by a mushroom-shaped cloud as air displaced by the explosion rushes back in, collides with itself, rises to form the "stem" of the mushroom and then billows out above as its force becomes dissipated.

Music has charms to soothe a savage beast. Not the way William Congreve (1670–1729)—no, it isn't from Shakespeare—put it.

He said "breast." It's from his play *The Mourning Bride,* also notable for "heaven has no rage like love to hatred turned, / Nor hell a fury like a woman scorned," customarily if somewhat inaccurately rendered as "Hell hath no fury like a woman scorned."

mustard gas. This most wretched of World War I weapons is not a gas but rather an atomized liquid. And it has nothing to do with mustard; its color and smell gave it its name.

my cup runneth over. Hundreds of sermons have been preached on Ps. 23:5, ". . . my cup runneth over." Much is made of the fact that this verse portrays the cup that is not only full but overflows. However, that is not what the original Hebrew says. Literally translated it says, "my cup [is] full." The meaning of "something extra"—the whole point of so many sermons—is not there at all.

"my wife having left my bed and board, I will not be responsible for any debts contracted by her." Since husbands are not generally responsible for their wives' debts nor wives for their husbands' in any case, this or a similar notice is usually quite irrelevant, although it is often seen. In case of a separation, either party may be held responsible for the maintenance, support, and education of any children of the pair; but such a notice would not relieve a spouse of this responsibility.

Obviously, it takes a lawyer to determine the specific circumstances and obligations in a specific state. Merely inserting such a notice in the newspaper as many do, without benefit of counsel, may well be a waste of time and money.

Napoleon brandy. See BRANDY.

natural oils as unsaturated fats. Advertising slogans notwithstanding, not all vegetable oils, nor those derived from plants
rather than animals, are of the kind which minimize cholesterol
buildup. Coconut oil, for example, is very highly saturated; one
would certainly do himself little good by changing from lard or
butter to a coconut-oil product.

negatives (photographic), right to reproduce prints from. Ownership or possession of a photographic negative does not automatically bestow the right to reproduce it, although some people think
it does. For example, a commercial photographer hired by a
patron to take a picture may keep the negative in his files, but
he has no right to reproduce it. It's the patron who has this right,
barring, of course, some special arrangement to the contrary.

New Deal. Many believe that this expression—so much a part of
the FDR vocabulary—was invented by Franklin D. Roosevelt.
Others think that it is a hybrid formed from Teddy Roosevelt's
Square Deal and Woodrow Wilson's New Freedom. Still others
attribute its coinage to Raymond Moley, a leader of the original

"brain trust." All are wrong. The term originated with Stuart Chase, whose book *New Deal* was published in 1932.

news. Reporters like to believe that the word is an acronym for north, east, west, south—the four points of the compass from which all news comes. It isn't, of course. Its derivation is easy to trace: the Old English word was *nīwes,* from *nīew,* meaning "new." The spelling looks strange, but the pronunciation was almost the same as that of *news* today.

nice. "Nice" has had an interesting history. Deriving from the Latin *nescius,* "ignorant" (from *nescire,* "not to know"), its meaning in the fourteenth and fifteenth centuries commonly was "foolish" or "wanton." To refer to someone as a "nice person" was no compliment in Chaucer's day. Through a process linguists sometimes call elevation, the word has gradually, over the centuries, achieved its present largely favorable connotations.

However, something of the old meaning is still preserved in the expression "a nice distinction," which does not really signify a valid distinction, but rather a somewhat nit-picking, or foolish, one. ("Well, now, *that's* a nice distinction, I must say.")

nightmare. Has nothing to do with horses. The "mare" derives from Old English *mara,* or a specter which, it was said, perched itself on the breast of a sleeper and deprived him of motion and speech.

ninety-five theses of Martin Luther. Martin Luther's famous ninety-five theses were the opening gun of the Reformation, and it is recorded that he wrote them out and nailed them to the door of castle church, Wittenberg, on October 31, 1517. This dramatic aspect of the story is slightly erroneous, for Martin Luther, according to scholar Erwin Iserloh, did not nail them to the church door; he sent copies to a few selected friends. It is thought that the church-door story was created by Melanchthon.

noble savage, origin of concept. Almost always attributed to Jean-Jacques Rousseau, both the expression and the concept of the noble savage long antedate his birth. Tacitus's *Germania* (A.D. 98) expresses the notion; and twelve years before Rousseau was born, John Dryden wrote, "When wild in woods the noble savage ran."

No love lost between them. This phrase is taken today in a sense exactly opposite to its original meaning, illustrated in the old ballad, "The Babes in the Wood":

> No love between this two was lost
>   Each was to other kind:
> In love they lived, in love they died,
>   And left two babes behind.

Northern Ireland. This region really ought to be called "Northeastern Ireland." Surprisingly few, except for the Irish and the British, seem to realize that Donegal, to the north and west of Northern Ireland, is a part of Eire. There are spots on the Donegal-Northern Irish border where one would need to travel due south, even southwest in places, to cross into Northern Ireland. Parts of Donegal are considerably north of Northern Ireland.

O

oarsmen and longevity. The belief that crew racing is a dangerous sport because it leads to "athlete's heart" and an early death has no foundation in fact. Quite the contrary: far from dying young, oarsmen outlive their classmates some six years, according to a study by Dr. Curtis Prout of the Harvard University Health Services reported in *Time* magazine, July 31, 1972.

According to *Time,* the belief that oarsmen die young was challenged as long ago as 1873 in a study of almost 300 British rowers. But the myth persisted. Dr. Prout's study is based on a comparison between 172 graduates of Harvard and Yale who had competed at least once in the four-mile varsity race between 1882 and 1902, and an equal number of their classmates picked at random. The 90 Harvard crewmen lived to an average age of 67.79 years, and the 82 Yale men to 67.91. The control groups averaged 61.54 and 61.56 years respectively, and only half as many rowers as nonrowers died before 60.

octane rating, gasoline. Advertising claims have confused many, but in fact gasoline octane rating has nothing to do, at least directly, with the amount of power a given gasoline can produce. A high-octane rating is simply an indication that the gasoline will have less tendency to preignite, especially in a high-compression engine. (Preignition means that as a result of the heat created in the cylinder by compression, the fuel-air mixture will tend to burn "spontaneously," before the spark plug has fired.) Preignition has the effect of throwing the engine out of time; the mixture, or some of it, will burn at other than the optimum point at which the most thrust is created on the piston. Preignition, under extreme conditions, can actually damage an engine. It is evidenced as the familiar knock, or ping, all drivers have at one time or another encountered. The best gasoline for a given engine is the one which just barely prevents preignition, or knocking. It is a waste of money to go any higher in the octane scale.

The addition of tetraethyl lead to gasoline has been the universal means of increasing octane ratings—though it is not the only possible means. Because lead in gasoline is a major source of pollution, however, and because high compression engines require a higher octane, lead-rich gas, compression ratios in United States automobile engines (and engines of cars imported into the United States) have been recently lowered. Neither engineers nor manufacturers have liked this very much because high-compression engines are more efficient than low-compression ones. It was done as an antipollution measure, so that less lead would need to be added to gasoline, and gasoline with a lower octane rating would become satisfactory for today's cars.

O.K., origin of. Those who do not believe that the origin of *O.K.* is shrouded in mystery are likely to think that it derives from a misspelling of "all correct" ("oll kurrect") attributed to Andrew Jackson, admittedly not the most literate of our presidents.

As a matter of fact, the origin of *O.K.,* has been known since 1941, and is accepted without question by almost all authorities. According to Allen Walker Read, writing in *Saturday Review of Literature* for July 19, 1941, *O.K.* first made its appearance in the New York *New Era,* March 23, 1840, as part of a name: The Democratic O.K. Club. The club, composed of supporters of Martin Van Buren, used *O.K.* as an abbreviation for Old Kinderhook, New York, Martin Van Buren's birthplace. (Van Buren had previously been associated publicly with Old Kinderhook, having been known, for example, as the Kinderhook Fox.) In *The American Language: Supplement I,* H. L. Mencken indicates that later in 1840, the *New Era* "stated categorically" that *O.K.* stood for "Old Kinderhook."

Partly because *O.K.!* became a sort of rallying cry for Van Buren supporters, the term caught on at once. The various false explanations of its origin seem to have sprung from attempts at derisive belittlement of the Van Buren cause. The attribution of "oll kurrect" to Andrew Jackson appeared in a newspaper opposed to Van Buren, who was a devoted follower of Jackson. Mencken mentions also a Tennessee tradition that when Jackson was serving as a court clerk, he marked "O.K." on legal papers approved by the judges. There are two things wrong with this explanation. First, Jackson was never a clerk of the Tennessee court. Second, it was not O.K. that appeared on the papers, but O.R., or "Order Recorded." But then, of such stuff is folk etymology made.

It should be added that at least one standard dictionary—the Popular Library edition of *Webster's New World Dictionary*—accepts the "oll kurrect" explanation, though without attributing it to Jackson. Of various other explanations, or perhaps more accurately speculations, the only one that seems possible is the suggestion that O.K. may have roots in certain Black English forms (ultimately African) : Jamaican *oh ki*, c. 1818; and a Surinam expression *okee*, though the latter was first recorded in the early 1880s. In any event, it can be said with assurance that "oll kurrect" is most certainly oll inkurrect as explanation.

Old English. Geoffrey Chaucer (1340–1400) did not write in Old English. Nor did Sir Thomas Malory, the fifteenth-century compiler of the stories of King Arthur and his Round Table in *Le Morte d'Arthur,* write Old English. Certainly William Shakespeare did not write in Old English; both he *and* Malory, in fact, wrote in Modern English. Nor are the various illustrated (or "illuminated") manuscript pages or imitations thereof often sold in gift shops Old English.

Old English is, in fact, a language completely different from Chaucer's, or that of anyone else mentioned in the preceding paragraph. It's a foreign language in spite of its name; Chaucer himself probably could not read it, though Chaucer was a proficient enough linguist to write in French and to translate from Latin and Italian. A student setting out to learn Old English today would expect to spend at least as much time mastering it as if he were to train himself to read German or Russian.

Scholars divide the history of the English language into three broad periods: Old English (A.D. 450–1100) ; Middle English, the language of Chaucer (1100–1500) ; and Modern English (1500 to the present). The language of Malory is often called Early Modern English, sometimes abbreviated eMnE. The dates are approximate; the historical factors which determine them are the invasion of England by the Angles, Saxons, and Jutes, who brought their Germanic tongue with them, usually dated A.D. 449; the Norman Conquest, which occurred in 1066; and the introduction of printing to England by William Caxton in 1476.

The only manuscript of any length that survives from the real Old English period is that of *Beowulf*—and it is sheer luck that it does survive, since it was very nearly destroyed by a fire in the library of Sir Robert Bruce Cotton, a well-to-do antiquarian and collector of Shakespeare's time. One can still see the charred edges of the manuscript today.

Following is a reproduction of one of the pages of this literally priceless manuscript, which illustrates what Old English actually looks like.

That Old English bears little resemblance to the popular conception is amply demonstrated by the reproduction above of part of one of the manuscript pages of *Beowulf*. A literal translation of a highly inflected (or, as linguists say, "synthetic") language like Old English into an "analytic," or noninflected language like modern English is almost impossible. But at least it will show how very different Old English is from the "Ye Olde Gifte Shoppe" variety so often miscalled Old English.

Transliterated into ordinary modern type without utilizing any special characters, following are all but the last few words of the first four lines of the manuscript excerpt above, with translation.

Beowulf mathelode bearn ecgtheowes
[Beowulf spoke, son (of) Ecgtheow:]
hwaet we the thas saelac sunu healfdenes
[Lo, we (to) you this sea-booty, son (of) Healfdene,]
leod scyldinga lustrum brohton tires
[Lord (of the) Scyldings (with) joy (have) brought; glories*]
to tacne the thu her to locast . . .
[As token which you here at-look (i.e., look at) . . .]

Put very briefly, the reason Old English is so unlike today's—or, for that matter, Chaucer's, Malory's, or Shakespeare's—language is that following the Norman Conquest, England officially became a French-speaking nation—and remained so for several centuries. The profound influence of Norman French, the language of William the Conqueror, upon the "native" Old English brought by the Germanic Anglo-Saxons when they themselves invaded Britain about A.D. 450, is responsible for the radical alterations which took place in English between *Beowulf* and *The Canterbury Tales*.

In any event, what practically everyone calls Old English today is really Middle English or even Early Modern English.

oldest city. Most people, if asked what the world's oldest city is, would probably answer "Rome." Rome, the Eternal City, was traditionally founded in 753 B.C., making it more than 2,700 years

---

* Strictly, "*of* glories."

old. Damascus, Syria, on the other hand, was in existence before the time of Abraham (Gen. 14:15, 15:2). It is undoubtedly the oldest continuously inhabited city in existence and probably was flourishing a couple of thousand years before Rome was founded.

oldest living thing. Hundreds of thousands of visitors have flocked to Sequoia National Park in California to contemplate "the oldest living thing"—the giant redwood named the General Sherman. It is three thousand years old, and has been considered for generations to be the largest—and oldest—living thing on the face of the earth.

But the General Sherman has yielded first place in longevity to a much older and much smaller tree in the White Mountains of California. It is the bristlecone pine. Here there are dozens of trees aged 2,000 to 3,000 years; nine trees more than 4,000 years old; and one tree aged 4,600 years.

The ages of trees can be accurately ascertained, without doing any harm, by use of the Swedish increment borer. This removes a thin cylinder of wood from the trunk, whose rings can be carefully counted.

old school ties. Eton, Harrow, and similar posh "public" schools in England do not have their own ties; such ties are, rather, characteristic of associations or clubs connected with the schools. The old school tie of Harrow is actually the tie of the Harrow Association, to which not all Old Harrovians belong. It is even possible to belong to the association, and thus wear its tie, without being an Old Harrovian.

onanism. This term is commonly used as if it meant "masturbation." But there seems little question that the word, which derives from the name of the biblical character Onan, actually means *coitus interruptus,* or withdrawal on the part of the male before ejaculation. Here is the biblical account of Onan's "sin," from Gen. 38:8–9 (King James translation):

> And Judah said unto Onan, Go in unto thy brother's wife and marry her, and raise up seed to thy brother.
> And Onan knew that the seed should not be his; and it came to pass, when he went in unto his brother's wife, that he spilled it on the ground, lest that he should give seed to his brother.

Dictionaries list *coitus interruptus* as one meaning for onanism, while conceding that "masturbation" is what it is commonly taken to signify. Roman Catholic interpretations of the Bible agree that onanism is not the same as masturbation.

"One touch of nature makes the whole world kin." Like many other Shakespeare lines, especially when taken out of context, this one is completely misunderstood by practically everybody. This is what Ulysses, in Shakespeare's play *Troilus and Cressida,* is actually saying to Achilles (act 3, sc. 3, lines 175–184):

> One touch of nature makes the whole world kin,
> That all with one consent praise new-born gawds [trifles] . . .
> Then marvel not, thou great and complete man,
> That all the Greeks begin to worship Ajax;
> Since things in motion sooner catch the eye
> Than what not stirs. . . .

Or, to put it another way: There's *one* natural trait we all share: we praise the superficial, the novel, whatever will "catch the eye." It's a rather cynical remark, really. The customary interpretation is about as far from Shakespeare's intent as it is possible to get.

opossums. A good deal of nonsense about opossums is firmly believed, often enough, ironically, in areas where opossums are most abundant. Baby opossums do not hook their tails around the mother's tail curled up over her back, though drawings sometimes show this as the means by which the babies are carried. The baby opossum actually rides on its mother's back by clinging to her long hair with its claws; the mother, like all opossums, walks with her tail pointing backward for balance.

Nor do opossums hang by their tails from branches or sleep in this posture. It is true that the opossum is the only North American mammal with a prehensile tail: that is, one that can be used for grasping; and it may indeed wrap its tail around a branch for balance and support. But it cannot support its weight in this fashion and could never sleep this way.

Among the most fascinating, if outlandish, folk myths about opossums is that both impregnation and birth take place by way of the female's nose. The male, so the myth goes, achieves sexual union by placing his penis in the female's nose; at birth, the female "sneezes" her young into her pouch. It may be that this myth arose because the sexual organs of opossums are, in truth, rather interestingly constructed; the male has a double-headed penis and the female a forked vagina and two uteri. Whether or not this natural back-up system accounts for the proliferation of opossums wherever they are introduced, the fact is that the penis is designed, obviously, to fit the double vagina, not the nostrils.

Opossums breed in the normal mammalian fashion. The sneeze theory of opossum parturition probably also results from faulty conclusions based on mistaken observation. The female opossum, before giving birth, inserts her nose and mouth into the pouch—opossums, like kangaroos, are marsupials—and licks it clean. She also licks her vulva as the young are born and cleans each baby as it emerges. But the baby opossums climb into the mother's pouch by themselves.

The most persistent and widespread belief concerning opossums is, of course, that they invariably "play possum," that is, act as if dead, if chased. Anyone who has cornered an opossum inadvertently or otherwise knows that this is by no means so; a common response is to hiss and snap. If handled, it may try to bite. Occasionally, an opossum may, it is true, collapse in a kind of catatonic state of immobility. But most scientists believe this is not something an opossum does deliberately; it is, rather, a response rather like the shock a human accident victim often suffers. In an opossum, this state of shock may have some survival value, but often enough it simply condemns it to death by a predator. In any case, most opossums will try either to escape or to defend themselves when in danger.

organic fertilizers. Regardless of the mystique surrounding "organically grown" food, there actually is no such thing as an organic fertilizer in terms of what the plant absorbs by means of its roots. No matter what it is, from manure to the latest synthesized product of the laboratory, any fertilizer is reduced to an inorganic form before it is taken up by the plant. Barring some form of radio isotope "tagging," there is absolutely no way to tell, after the fertilizer has done its work, whether it was originally organic or "chemical."

No scientific evidence exists that so-called organically grown foods are "safer," more nutritional, or of higher quality than plants grown by other means. Pesticides, of course, are another matter; their presence in or on a plant can be determined and many of them are certainly not well suited to human or animal consumption. But apart from this, though organic gardening may be an interesting hobby it has no bearing on safety or health.

Many "unnatural" fertilizers or soil conditioners are, in fact, merely duplicates of what can be found in nature. Manufactured urea is the same as the kind found in nature, for example; and when the superphosphate which is made by composting rock phosphate with elemental sulfur and soil—a process acceptable to the organic gardener—is used in gardening, bacteria convert the sulfur into sulfuric acid which then reacts with the rock phosphate. Which is exactly what takes place in the fertilizer factory.

"O Romeo, Romeo! Wherefore art thou Romeo?" One of the most perdurable and exasperating misconceptions extant, at least to those who know Shakespeare, is illustrated in a scene often repeated. It is, let us say, the annual amateur hour. Out onto the stage pops a character wearing a rag-mop wig and holding aloft a lantern while he peers elaborately about and cries, "Romeo, Romeo, wherefore art thou, Romeo?"

Wherefore did not mean "where" in Shakespeare's day and does not mean "where" now. It means "why." Nor do the lines from *Romeo and Juliet* make any sense if it is taken to mean "where." Here are the lines in question—among the most famous in the play (act 2, sc. 2, lines 33–36) :

> O Romeo, Romeo! Wherefore art thou Romeo?
> Deny thy father, and refuse thy name;
> Or, if thou wilt not, be but sworn my love,
> And I'll no longer be a Capulet.

Since it has already been amply established in the play that the lovers' problem is that Romeo is a Montague, that Juliet is a Capulet and that the two families are engaged in a bitter feud, obviously Juliet is asking why it must be that Romeo has to be Romeo. As the lines make clear, she is suggesting that either he "refuse thy name," or, if he won't, then *she* will "no longer be a Capulet." That she could scarcely be looking for him is further emphasized by the fact that at this point (it is the famous "balcony scene") , she has no idea that Romeo is in the neighborhood. He's still hiding in the shrubbery of the "orchard," or garden. Finally, note that as Shakespeare wrote the lines, no comma follows the word "thou."

It does seem regrettably true, however, that the annual hijinks will very likely continue to feature that rag-mop wig, that exaggerated search, that lantern. As Shakespeare's friend and contemporary Ben Jonson said (*Every Man Out of His Humour*, act 1, sc. 1) , "Art hath an enemy called Ignorance."

ostriches and their diet. Popular belief to the contrary, ostriches cannot eat just anything and survive, as many a zoo keeper will testify. They do need grit for the gizzard, just like chickens, and since ostriches are large, they need lots of grit. It is for this reason that they do look for gravel and such-like. Moreover, they may swallow, to their misfortune, trinkets fed to them by children of any age. But they do not ordinarily choose tin cans and coronets, neither of which they would be able to digest.

ostriches burying their heads in the sand to "hide." They don't. The persistence of error is well illustrated in this myth, which goes back a couple of thousand years or so. No matter how many biologists and zoologists continue to deny the truth of this belief, it's still with us. Ah, well, it creates a useful metaphor, and as Vilhjalmur Stefansson reminds us, in *Adventures in Error* (1936) , "Consider . . . what trouble we should get into if we did not have the literary ostrich and wanted to convey picturesquely the idea of that sort of wilful blindness from which we ourselves never suffer but which curiously afflicts our opponents. In pursuit of suitable analogy we might vainly canvass the whole animal kingdom. The ostrich-by-definition is, therefore, not only less trouble to deal with than a real bird; he is actually more useful and instructive than any real bird or beast. When we consider how often he has been used in sermon and precept we must admit that this model creature has contributed substantially not only to the entertainment and instruction of nations but also to the morality and general goodness of the world."

Owens, Jesse—vs. the horse. Jesse Owens, the great black runner who made proud the hearts of his countrymen and annoyed the

"Nordic"-loving Hitler by winning four gold medals in the 1936 Olympics, could outrun a racehorse. Or at least so popular belief has it. Nor is the belief entirely without foundation; Owens did beat racehorses in the 100-yard sprint.

But it does turn out that there was a trick to it—by Owens's own admission. As the great Jesse explained it, he and the promoters of the exhibition always made sure they got a properly high-spirited thoroughbred; no plug horses. Owens and the horse would line up together—with the starter and his gun next to the horse. When the gun went off, the horse would naturally rear and, in Owens's words, "I would be off with a tremendous break and by the time he came down I was 50 yards down the track, and at that point even though he would be covering 21 feet for every 7 I covered, it was too late; I would win."

owls. Owls have been given some quite inappropriate names.

In the first place, there is no variety that goes by the name of hoot owl. The barred owl's call is a hooting one, as it says—omitting the consonants—"Who cooks for you?" (It is sometimes confused with the great horned owl.)

The one that is really maligned, however, is the screech owl. The screech owl does not screech; it utters a soft wail.

owls, daytime vision of. Contrary to popular belief, owls can see in the daytime; some, in fact, do their hunting primarily during the day. Most of them do hunt at night, but the reason is that they depend upon stealth instead of speed; also, their main prey, mice and rats, are more active at night.

oxygen. Oxygen is not, contrary to popular opinion, inflammable. It is essential to combustion, true. But it does not, of itself, burn. And though it is, of course, necessary to life on earth as it presently exists, it is essentially a poison gas to which human beings and other organisms have adapted, but which would actually *prevent* the origin of life on earth under today's conditions.

oysters and the "r" months. The old belief that oysters are safe to eat only during the months that incorporate the letter *r* in their names is pure fiction. True, oysters tend to be watery during the summer, but that poses no danger to health.

In spite of folklore to the contrary, by the way, oysters are no special help to virility or potency. They are a pretty poor source of energy in any sense; a half-dozen raw ones of the kind commonly grown along the Atlantic coast add up to only some sixty calories.

P

Pago Pago. People who have not traveled among the Pacific Islands are apt to pronounce this American Samoan name the way it is spelled: Pāgo Pāgo, or at best, Pägo Pägo. The correct pronunciation is actually Pängo Pängo, and that is the way it is pronounced there.

In the islands they tell a rather interesting story which explains this peculiarity. It seems that when the missionaries came out to this part of the Pacific, they dutifully provided printed materials in the native language, transliterating the local speech into the Latin alphabet. However, there were so many sounds that needed to be represented by *n* in combination with a following consonant, that to set them all in type would have used up the whole supply of *n*'s, and more. (Every type font has so many *a*'s, so many *b*'s, and so many *n*'s, etc.) To solve the problem the missionary typesetters left out the *n* that occurred in combination with a consonant.

So to this day Pango Pango is Pago Pago, and Nandi is Nadi, and so on.

Paige typesetter. In spite of popular opinion, the marvelously complicated machine into whose development Mark Twain poured so much money was not the principal cause of his bankruptcy. It was the failure of his publishing company that drove Mark Twain to the wall—and, incidentally, revealed the stuff of which his character was made. He determined to pay off his creditors a hundred percent and did, by returning to what he had come to hate: the lecture platform.

Nor was the Paige typesetter quite the mechanical absurdity it has been made out to be. True, it was very complicated; but so is the Linotype. By 1890, the Paige typesetter had been developed to the point where Twain said of it, in a letter, "I guess we've got a perfect machine at last. We never break a type, and the new device for enabling the operator to touch the last letters and justify [that is, even up the right-hand margin of] the line simultaneously works to a charm."

Only in retrospect does Twain's investment in time and money seem foolish. It was apparent, by the closing years of the nineteenth century, that a mechanical typesetter was on the way; and the race had actually narrowed down to the Paige machine and the Mergenthaler Linotype. The Linotype won out largely because Twain permitted the eccentric genius James W. Paige to continue in a crazy search for absolute mechanical perfection, twice modifying or tearing down his machine when it was already performing satisfactorily enough—and doing so, in each instance, just when large investors were particularly interested. It has even been argued that Paige and Twain did not really want their typesetter to be marketed; Paige for obvious reasons (he'd be out of a job), Twain because the search for mechanical perfection had come to mean more to him than the presumed financial goal at its end.

In any case, the Mergenthaler people took the Paige machine very seriously indeed. At one point, they offered to trade stock-for-stock with Twain and Paige, so that no matter which machine won, both parties would profit. Twain, typically, refused; it was to be all or nothing for him. It turned out nothing. But it is hardly likely that the Linotype forces would have made such an offer had they not believed the Paige typesetter to be a formidable competitor.

Panama Canal, direction of. The Panama Canal, quite contrary to popular belief, does not cross the Isthmus from east to west (or, if you prefer, from west to east). It doesn't even come close to doing so; from Limón Bay to Gatun Lake it runs due south, then takes a turn eastward. Its "western" or Pacific terminus is actually more than twenty miles *east* of its Atlantic beginnings. A ship traversing the canal, thus, actually doubles back on its course, losing some twenty miles of headway.

Panama hats. They are not from Panama as the name implies but from Ecuador, originally. (Panama was a distribution center for the hats.) Nor are they woven under water, though during the weaving both fibers and fingers are kept moist.

Panay. On December 12, 1937, the United States gunboat *Panay* was sunk by Japanese aircraft while lying at anchor in the Yangtze.

The Japanese government claimed that it was a mistake, and their apology was accepted. However, it has been well demonstrated that this attack was not an error. The *Panay*'s position had been carefully announced by its commander.

Many people in the United States claimed that it was convoying three Standard Oil tankers. This, also, is not true. The Yangtze was an international waterway by treaty, and the *Panay* was not on convoy at all.

Parnell, Charles Stewart. Charles Stewart Parnell, "uncrowned king of Ireland," the great nineteenth-century leader of the Irish nationalist movement, was as close as Roman Catholic Ireland had come to a national hero under whom all could unite in their struggles against the British. But he was neither Catholic nor Irish as most Irish men and women of the time would have defined the term. His mother, in fact, was American, the daughter of Commodore Charles Stewart of the United States Navy, and his family had its roots in England. Further, as one of the landowner class, Parnell would have seemed to stand for all that the nineteenth-century Irish hated and despised, particularly in view of the fact that Parnell himself was educated at English private schools and at Cambridge.

It was apparently from his American mother that Parnell acquired that hatred of the English which, combined with his own fierce sense of Irish nationalism, were to spur his rise to an eminence from which, however, he was tumbled following the O'Shea affair. (Parnell married the wife of a Captain O'Shea, once his friend and agent, following her uncontested divorce.) It was not, however, the O'Shea divorce *per se* that caused Parnell's downfall, although it certainly was enough to alienate many if not most of the Irish clergy; the English shrewdly used the divorce against him, exploiting the reservations Irish church-men had always felt about a Protestant leader.

parsimony, principle of (logic). Sometimes called "Occam's Razor," after William of Occam, a fourteenth-century philosopher, this principle does not mean that the simplest explanation is always the best. It means, popular opinion notwithstanding, that the simplest explanation *which covers all the circumstances* is the best. Complicated circumstances may call for a complicated explanation, but if it is the only one that deals, or attempts to deal, with all the known facts, then it still may be consistent with the principle of parsimony.

Parsons table. Although it looks like the kind of table a backwoods parson might have: simple, easy to knock together, and rugged, a Parsons table has nothing to do with men of the cloth.

A Parsons table comes out of the backwoods of Manhattan, circa the early 1930s, and was developed by the Parsons School of Design.

"Pat-a-cake, pat-a-cake, baker's man!"

> Pat-a-cake, pat-a-cake, baker's man!
> So I will, master, as fast as I can:
> Pat it, and prick it, and mark it with T,
> Put it in the oven for Tommy and me.

This nursery rhyme has appeared in various forms for the last three hundred and fifty years or more.

Most people take it for granted—naturally enough—that the *T* stands for Tommy. However, the name Tommy does not occur in all versions, and it is much more likely that the T was intended to be the sign of the cross rather than the initial of a little boy's name. As early as the Middle Ages it was the custom to mark various baked goods with the sign of the cross, a pleasant reminder of which is hot cross buns.

patented articles made for one's own use. It is just as much an infringement to make for one's own personal use an article which has been patented as it would be to manufacture and sell it. In fact, it is an infringement even to make it, whether or not it is sold or even used. A patent grants the patentee the exclusive right to make, use, *or* sell the patented device.

patent medicines. Few proprietary medicines, especially during their heyday in the latter half of the nineteenth century, were actually patented. The reason is simple enough: in order to obtain a patent, the "inventor" would be required to list the ingredients of his "medicine," and few if any of the nostrums sold then would survive such a revelation. The term is really a misnomer.

Paul Revere's Ride(s). Longfellow's poem "Paul Revere's Ride" ("Listen, my children and you shall hear . . ." [The Landlord's Tale, from *Tales of a Wayside Inn*]) has made Paul Revere better known for his midnight ride than anything else. (Besides his large role in the American Revolution he was perhaps America's greatest silversmith, an engraver, political cartoonist, iron founder, and inventor. Also, he did a bit of dentistry.)

Longfellow succeeded in writing the most popular poem in American historical literature. To do this he felt the need to compress and change the facts, and it is interesting to sort them out.

Paul Revere was intensely interested in the revolutionary movement, and he did a great deal of horseback riding in this connection. Having taken part in the Boston Tea Party, he made a long horseback journey in 1773 to report it to the Sons of Liberty in New York. For Boston's Committee of Safety he made trips to New York and Philadelphia. He became the official courier of the Massachusetts Provincial Assembly and was a familiar figure on the landscape, so familiar to the British that his name appeared in London newspapers.

Paul Revere made at least three important rides with respect to military action. He rode to Durham and Portsmouth, New Hampshire, to warn the New Hampshire citizenry that General Gage planned to carry away the munitions from Fort William and Mary to protect them. The colonists raided the fort. This was their first act of aggression.

He made two rides—not one—in April 1775. The first was on April 16 to Concord to warn the patriots to move the munitions from there to a safer place. It was on this occasion (not April 18–19, as Longfellow says) that he arranged for lanterns to be hung in the steeple of the North Church ("One, if by land, and two, if by sea").

However, according to Revere's own account the signals in the church tower were not for *him* when he reached the opposite shore of the Charles River (as Longfellow has it) but to send the message to others in case Revere could not make it across the river or over Boston Neck. They were apprehensive about a messenger being able to get across. Furthermore, as the British came both by land and by sea, one can't help wondering just how the lanterns were set up. It is the second ride of April 18–19 that Longfellow describes, telling us how Revere mounted his "steed" on the opposite shore, spread the alarm through every Middlesex village and farm, and eventually "came to the bridge in Concord town." But Revere this time never made it to Concord at all.

What really happened was that Revere did go in a boat "with muffled oar" to the Charlestown bank. (The oars were muffled with a woman's petticoat, but Longfellow does not mention that.) Although he did rouse the countryside en route, his main purpose was to tip off John Hancock and Samuel Adams and carry the alarm to Concord. He got to Lexington by midnight, went to the house of the Rev. Jonas Clarke, and warned Hancock and Adams, who departed forthwith. He then made for Concord in company with William Dawes and Samuel Prescott. The three were spotted by British scouts. Prescott jumped over a fence, and managed to bring the alarm to Lincoln and Concord. Dawes headed back to Lexington. The troops kept Revere, but he sufficiently impressed them by saying the countryside was aroused against them that they let him go—but without his "steed." He got back to Lexington and devoted himself to rescuing a trunk full of documents that Hancock had left behind. Thus he missed the battle of Lexington. It is also recorded that Revere was paid five shillings by the colonists for his night's work.

Pearl Harbor and the sitting-duck theory. Firmly fixed in the popular consciousness is a belief that had the Japanese not caught the Americans flat-footed at Pearl Harbor on December 7, 1941, the loss of ships and men would have been much less. But as Leo Rosten said in *World* magazine (Aug. 1, 1972), after Fleet Admiral Chester Nimitz, the exact reverse is the case. Bad as Pearl Harbor was, had the Pacific Fleet been at sea it would have faced a Japanese Carrier Task Force the speed of whose ships was at least two knots greater than that of the American ships; the Americans would have had very little if any air cover (one carrier, which could scarcely have arrived in time, against six Japanese carriers) ; and instead of being lost in shallow water from which ships could be—and were—raised and repaired, all losses would have been irrevocable. Further, and most important, far fewer men were lost precisely because, in Rosten's words, "they *were* in the harbor."

pearls in oysters. Don't count on paying for your meal at an expensive New York or San Francisco restaurant by finding a pearl in an oyster. At least, not unless the oysters came from tropical waters. No pearls of value are ever found in North American edible oysters.

Peking Man, the. Usually believed to represent a single humanoid creature, the 400,000-year-old remains found near Peking in the 1920s actually represented bits and pieces of some forty people. Regarded as one of the great anthropological-archaeological finds of modern times, the fossils disappeared, incidentally, shortly after the attack on Pearl Harbor when a group of American marines, preparing to take the remains from Peking to Tientsin for safekeeping, was captured by the Japanese. The remains are still missing.

Pennsylvania Dutch. The so-called Pennsylvania Dutch do not have their roots in the Netherlands, but rather in Germany, from which their forebears emigrated. The confusion arose, as it also has in other contexts, because the German word for "German" is *Deutsch*. In German, Germany is *Deutschland*. The misapprehension is an old one; as long ago as the sixteenth century Englishmen commonly referred to the Germans as "Dutch."

The Pennsylvania "Dutch," then, are German in origin and tradition—though they have heard the term applied to them for so long that they have perforce resigned themselves to it. Dutch men and women themselves prefer "Hollander" or "Netherlander." Recalling what happened to the Netherlands at the hands of the *Deutsch* during both World War I and World War II, it is not surprising that "Dutchmen" are not particularly fond of the word.

penny. Officially, there is no such coin; to the United States government and its mints, it's legally a "cent."

perfect bridge hand, the. Long as the odds are of being dealt all the cards in a given suit in bridge—or, for that matter, being dealt a full house or a royal flush in poker—they are exactly the same as the odds against getting any *other* hand in any card game, as a moment's thought will demonstrate.

permission to publish anything. Many people appear to believe that there is, or ought to be somehow, a prior restriction possible on what can be published, though this would fly straight in the face of the First Amendment to the Constitution. "I don't see why they permitted them to print such garbage," or some similar statement, reveals an ignorance of our first constitutional principle: no agency has the power to restrict the freedom of the press.

Of course, writers and publishers can be, and are, held responsible for what appears *after* it has been published; they may be hauled into court if they commit libel, for example. But nobody—from the president on down—has the constitutional right to forbid the publication of anything.

Pershing, Black Jack. Though General Pershing apparently was not notable for either sweetness or lightness, his nickname did not reflect any aspect of his character or his complexion. It derived, rather, from his several years of service with what was then called a colored regiment, the Tenth United States Cavalry. He was first known, in fact, as Nigger Jack. That this repulsive sobriquet quietly faded away is a tribute to the sensitivities of our forebears.

perspective as a function of focal length. It is widely believed that wide-angle lenses distort and foreshorten perspective whereas telephoto or long-focal-length lenses flatten it. This is not true. Perspective is not determined by the focal length of a lens, but rather by where the photographer stands with respect to his subject. At close range, "exaggerated" or "distorted" perspective results—with any lens. (Actually, the human eye will also "distort" perspective when it is close to its "subject"; it's just that we don't notice it unless we make a conscious effort.) If the photographer shoots far-off objects, then he or she will get "flattened" perspective. But it's because of the distance, not the lens. Perspective, in other words, is not a function of focal length. It's the position of the lens with respect to its subject that determines perspective.

petar(d), to be hoisted by or on one's own. A petar, or petard as it is also spelled, is not some kind of derrick, as one might think, nor does Hamlet actually speak of being "hoisted by" or "hoisted on" one. His reference is not to King Claudius, by the way, but to his boyhood pals Rosencrantz and Guildenstern, who intend, as Hamlet now suspects with every reason, to betray him. Here are his exact words (act 3, sc. 4, lines 205–209) :

> [Rosencrantz and Guildenstern will] marshal me to
>   knavery; let it work;
> For 'tis the sport to have the engine[e]r
> Hoist with his own petar; and 't [it] shall go hard
> But I will delve [dig] one yard below their mines
> And blow them at the moon.

Perhaps Hamlet's use of *with* where today we would, in fact, commonly say *by* has contributed to the misunderstanding of *petar*, which was actually a kind of bomb, or "mine," commonly used to blast open gates of buildings under siege. In other words, Hamlet metaphorically proposes to plant his own bomb beneath theirs and thus "blow them at the moon." And he does, at least metaphorically; when it turns out that Rosencrantz and Guildenstern are carrying sealed letters from King Claudius ordering Hamlet's death, Hamlet opens the letters and simply substitutes their names for his own.

Peter Rabbit. Many readers, brought up on the animal stories of Thornton W. Burgess, credit that author with the creation of the immortal Peter Rabbit. Actually, the original Peter Rabbit was created by author-illustrator Beatrix Potter, whose *The Tale of*

Peter Rabbit appeared in England in 1902. The name of the Thornton W. Burgess rabbit was Peter Cottontail, although Burgess did refer to him as Peter Rabbit, too.

petrified wood. The wood itself does not turn into stone, though that is what many believe. Rather, the minerals in water which infiltrate wood, under certain conditions and over a long period of time, *replace* the wood cells, which act, thus, as a sort of mold. But no organic material "turns to stone," in spite of what the Greeks said Medusa could do.

Philomel(a). A misconception that runs throughout the whole of English poetry is reflected in the universal poetic use of Philomel or Philomela as a name for the nightingale. Even T. S. Eliot, surely the most scholarly of poets with the possible exception of John Milton, refers to the transformation of Philomel into a nightingale in his most famous poem, "The Waste Land."

The Greek myth which tells the story of Philomela does not, however, deal with the transformation of Philomela into a nightingale; it is her sister, Procne, who is so transformed. Briefly, the story involves the gruesome revenge of Procne, sister of Philomela, upon Tereus, husband of Procne. Tereus had cut out Philomela's tongue and left her to languish in a dungeon for years. When Procne discovered this, she killed her young son, Itys, and served him to his father, Tereus, for dinner, surely the most repellent instance of cutting off one's nose to spite one's face in literary history. When she told Tereus what he had eaten, he was immobilized enough in horror to enable the two sisters to make their getaway.

But Tereus recovered his mobility, pursued and caught up with them. However, as he was about to wreak his own revenge with a sword, the gods intervened and turned Procne into a nightingale and Philomela into a swallow. As Edith Hamilton, the mythologist, points out, the swallow, because Philomela's tongue was cut out, can only twitter, never sing; whereas the nightingale has the sweetest and saddest song of all birds because she can never forget the son she transformed into a ragout.

It is true that Roman writers, notably Ovid, made the mistake of confusing the two sisters and identifying the tongueless Philomela as the nightingale, clearly an impossibility. Their error has simply been repeated over the centuries.

physicians treating members of their own family. There is no legal or ethical consideration whatever that forbids a doctor from treating his or her spouse, children, or any other relatives, although this is a widespread belief. Doctors sometimes hesitate to do so, particularly in cases of serious illness or injury, because they are only too aware of the human tendency to lose one's objectivity where there is emotional involvement. But they will not be hauled into court or hailed before a professional conduct commission if they prescribe for their wives or husbands.

pigs as "dirty" animals. The pig's reputation for being dirty is ill-deserved. Even in fairly close confinement a pig will select a place in which to defecate and repeatedly use that spot and that spot only. Most domestic animals are indiscriminate in this respect.

In America the pig early received the reputation of "liking" filth, because in New England it was usually kept in the worst place on the farm—in a dark sty under the barn. In their natural state, pigs are forest-roaming creatures.

When the day is hot, pigs will wallow in the mud—but not because they like dirt. The reason is that pigs have no perspiration apparatus, and this is their way of lowering the temperature of the skin.

Pigs are sometimes maligned for eating garbage. In captivity, of course, they eat what they are fed. It is well to recall that of all domestic animals their preferred diet is closest to that of human beings.

Finally, it is often said that pigs cannot swim, because if they try they will cut their own throats with their forehooves. This, also, is nonsense. They can swim perfectly well.

Ping-Pong. This is by no means the same as table tennis, at least in terms of its use as a descriptive phrase. *Ping-Pong* is a registered trademark. It is not the generic name of the game everybody knows, and this accounts for the almost universal use of *table tennis* instead of you-know-what in publications. *Kodak, Coca-Cola* (and also *Coke,* which the Coca-Cola people were clever enough to register as a trademark before it became a common noun) , *Frigidaire, Kleenex,* and so on all fall under the same general rule: if you use it, capitalize it (and, to be entirely legal, indicate that it is a registered trademark) . Referring to a "coke" in a story or article which appears in a national magazine is likely to result in a polite letter from a company lawyer suggesting that, in future, the word at least be spelled with a capital letter. The reason for this apparent fussiness is that names, titles, phrases, etc., are not—and cannot be—copyrighted. But that's a good thing, from a corporate point of view, for they *can* be registered as trademarks. And trademarks go on forever, unlike copyrights, which expire in twenty-eight years and can be renewed only once. A trademark which passes into the language as a common noun, however, loses its proprietary standing.

Trademarks do sometimes pass into the common language, sometimes as the result of a court decision (see CELLOPHANE) , sometimes because company lawyers are not vigilant enough. Few are aware that the word linoleum was coined to describe a substance patented in England in 1863 by Frederick Walton; it is now a common noun. Somewhat ironically, the more successful a coinage turns out to be, the greater the danger that it will be lost as a proprietary term; Xerox is a good example. Because it fills such a useful place in today's language (photocopy seems a clumsy synonym) , its proprietors must be constantly on guard lest it lose its identification with the Xerox Corporation.

A great deal of time and money are spent by corporations precisely because they have been so successful in turning the name of a product into a "household word." ("If it isn't an Eastman, it isn't a Kodak," or "Frigidaire—made only by General Motors.")

Pittsburgh vs. Pittsburg. There is no such place as Pittsburg, Pennsylvania. There are Pittsburgs in California, in Kansas, in Kentucky, in New Hampshire, in Oklahoma, in Texas. But in Pennsylvania it is Pittsburgh, and that is the only Pittsburgh in the country.

pizza. There are those people who say that our pizza did not come from Italy and those who say that pizza here is the same as it is in Italy. Both are wrong.

In Italy pizza is a thin bread, flavored with oil and salt. In

Naples this was spread in the middle with tomatoes, anchovies, etc.—a regional dish, often served as an appetizer, and called *pizza alla napoletana*. In this country the Neapolitan pizza has become larger, more elaborate—and ubiquitous.

pledge of allegiance to the flag. So firmly fixed in the public consciousness is this ritual statement that few realize it did not exist until 1892, and that it was first published in substantially its present form in a magazine for boys, the *Youth's Companion*. Written by Francis Bellamy, one of the staff members of the *Youth's Companion*, it was part of a promotion celebrating, somewhat oddly, Columbus Day.

plurals of proper names. A look at any middle-class suburb reveals an astonishing variety of misinformation regarding what happens to be one of the simplest and least open to exception rules of usage, the formation of plurals of proper names. Embellishing many a mailbox, or suspended proudly beneath in wrought iron, are such identifying signs as The Robinson's, or The Smith's or even The Jone's.

Yet few grammatical processes in English are easier than the pluralizing of proper nouns. All one need do is add the letter *s*, or *es* if the name already ends in *s* or in *x*. Thus, properly, The Robinsons; The Smiths; The Joneses; The Marxes.

Pocahontas. Pocahontas was by no means a mythical creature, though many seem to think she was. She became, in fact, a considerable celebrity in England, to which she traveled in 1616, the year of William Shakespeare's death, after marrying John Rolfe, an Englishman. She died in England only a year later; her son, Thomas Rolfe, returned to Virginia and founded a line which was to include the second Mrs. Woodrow Wilson.

However, the story of her "rescue" of Captain John Smith when she was a child of eleven (not, as often assumed, a young adult) has often been regarded with considerable skepticism, partly because of Smith's reputation as an embellisher of tales, if not on occasion an outright braggart, and partly because Smith did not mention the episode in *A True Relation of Such Occurrences and Accidents of Note as Hath Happened in Virginia,* the first book written in America to be published in England. It appeared in

1608, shortly after the episode happened—if it did. Not until 1624, in *The General History of Virginia,* did Smith tell the story of his "rescue." A further reason for skepticism is that Smith's 1608 account presents Powhatan, Pocahontas's father, as uniformly friendly; not until the 1624 *History* does he portray Powhatan as a potentially dangerous savage.

At least one scholar is inclined to think that if the episode happened, it was not at all what it appeared to be. Says Philip L. Barbour in *Pocahontas and Her World* (1970):

> The ceremony of which Smith had been the object was almost certainly a combination of mock execution and salvation, in token of adoption into Powhatan's tribe. Indian boys in their early adolescence were subjected to far more fearful rites when they entered into manhood. They had young braves to "protect" them. In Smith's case, Powhatan himself was possibly his foster-father, but Pocahontas had been chosen to act in his stead . . .
>
> Smith could not understand, much less know, this. He simply regarded Pocahontas as his savior.

Mr. Barbour's case does seem fairly strong, particularly in view of the ritualistic nature of the episode: the two large stones placed in position, the "executioners" at the ready with their clubs, and especially the pause which must obviously have been so timed that Pocahontas, Smith's "protector," could place herself in position to "spare" him. Lending further credence is the unlikely possibility that, if Smith's execution were really intended, even (perhaps "especially") the daughter of the chief would scarcely have dared interfere. But she would be playing an entirely appropriate role if Barbour's thesis is correct.

It might be added that although Barbour does not mention the possibility, it is consistent with John Smith's tendency toward romanticizing his adventures to suppose that even if he did know the whole thing was merely a tribal ritual, it made a far better story if told straight.

poison ivy, poison oak, poison sumac. Sensitivity to these common plants is acquired, not innate; it is not present at birth. Nor are all persons sensitive to them; only about half of the adult population becomes sensitive to poison ivy and its cousins in areas where these plants grow. This may, perhaps, account for a highly dangerous myth involving what is often said to be an "old Indian remedy": that one can achieve immunity or cure by eating the leaves of the offending plant. Nothing could be farther from the truth, of course; anyone who is sensitive and attempts this "remedy" will likely end up in a hospital.

Products which are claimed to provide immunity are of doubtful, if any, worth. Their value probably lies in their inducing greater awareness, and thus caution, among those who take them. The oils of the plants cause the irritation; the smoke from burning poison ivy carries this oil and can easily cause the same symptoms as direct contact.

Neither the blister nor the rash is contagious or infectious. Nor does scrubbing with soap and water help unless it is done within a few hours of exposure; after the rash appears it will only make matters worse.

Pompeii, destruction of. The common notion that Pompeii and its neighboring cities Herculaneum and Stabiae were destroyed by molten lava is quite erroneous. Had this been the case, excavation would not only be virtually impossible, but little could be discovered as a result of it.

Actually, there were two disasters involved in the fate of Pompeii. In A.D. 63, a great earthquake very nearly destroyed the city. Its occupants were still engaged in rebuilding when, in 79, sixteen years later, the eruption of Vesuvius occurred. (Notable as it was, this was by no means the worst Vesuvius could do. In 1631, some 18,000 are believed to have died as a result of a truly cataclysmic eruption. Estimates of those who died at Pompeii generally center around the figure 2,000.) However, it was not lava, but rather noxious fumes and ashes, that covered the city and its inhabitants. Those killed by the fumes, often very quickly, were covered by the ash and other small volcanic particles which then hardened, as the result of water from above, to a substance not unlike plaster of Paris. This is how the moulds of corpses and other items, of such fascination to the tourist, were created.

"Pop Goes the Weasel." In spite of its association with barn dances, backwoods fiddlers contests, and American square dancing, "Pop Goes the Weasel" was originally a London music-hall ballad.

Nor is it particularly old as ballads go; it was composed in the 1850s, probably by a W. R. Mandale.

Those thousands who have heard it played and sung while wondering how or why a weasel goes "pop" should know that the "weasel" in the tune was a hatter's tool; "pop" was London slang for "pawn." When one realizes that the Eagle was a music hall on City Road, then the quatrain which follows makes entire sense.

> Up and down the City Road,
> In and out the Eagle,
> That's the way the money goes—
> Pop goes the weasel!

porcupines shooting their quills. Porcupines cannot shoot their quills. They may slap at a tormentor with their tails, dislodging some quills. But they have no means of propelling them through the air.

pores of the skin breathing. Despite pseudo-scientific advertisements for various cosmetics and soaps, the pores do not "breathe," nor is there any need to go to special efforts, under ordinary circumstances, to "keep the pores open." Among related fallacies is that painting or gilding the whole body closes up the pores and thus causes a quick death by suffocation. No truth in it. Keeping one's body gilded for any length of time would not, obviously, be desirable. But any ill effects would certainly not show themselves at once—assuming, that is, the absence of a toxic substance in the gilt.

portland cement. This material has nothing to do with either the Maine or the Oregon city, although the name has often led people astray. As a matter of fact, it does not have any direct connection with the Isle of Portland in England, from which the term *portland cement* does, however, derive. The material was so named merely because it happens to resemble in color a building stone which *is* found on the Isle of Portland.

posh. Widely believed is the story that *posh* is an acronym for "Port Outward–Starboard Homeward." According to this explanation, when upper-echelon British civil servants or administrators were sent to India on the famous P & O line (Peninsular and Oriental Steam Navigation Company) in the days when the sun never set upon the empire, they would specify that their staterooms should be on the port, or left, side of the ship on the voyage out, on the starboard side on the way home after their tours of duty: these being, respectively, the shady sides of the ship.

Unfortunately, this explanation is almost certainly what linguists call folk-etymology; that is, contriving an explanation not because it is demonstrably true, but because it sounds as if it ought to be. The P & O line cannot produce evidence that the expression was ever used by any of its officials, although its records go back to 1849.

As defined in an 1897 slang dictionary mentioned by the *Oxford English Dictionary*, *posh* had no sea-faring implications, meaning rather merely "a dandy." The first quotation cited by the OED goes back only to 1918, and there, again, it appears not to have any reference to the sea. Nor does the most prestigious of American dictionaries, the Merriam-Webster, accept the "Port Outward–Starboard Homeward" etymology.

Brewer's Dictionary of Phrase and Fable, published by Cassell and Co., Ltd., of London, does accept unquestioningly "Port Outward–Starboard Homeward" as explaining *posh*. Its entry, however, is not documented nor does it include any citations.

postal cards and postcards. These items are not the same, at least not to the men who run the United States postal service. A postal card is one that has the stamp printed on it; a postcard is what the tourist buys at a newsstand and must stamp for himself.

potato. The "Irish" potato did not originate in Ireland, as some people suppose, nor was it introduced into the British Isles by Sir Walter Raleigh. The word *Irish* was attached to the white potato to distinguish it from the so-called sweet potato. Indeed the origins of both kinds of potato are somewhat confused by the failure of old accounts to differentiate between the two.

It is now pretty well agreed that first cultivation of the white potato took place among the Incas on the upland slopes of the Peruvian Andes, that it was brought to Europe by the Spanish explorers, and was carried to America by the colonists.

At one time it was maintained that the true potato somehow

got from South America to Virginia and was taken from there to Europe by Sir Walter Raleigh. However, it actually did not reach Virginia until a century after Raleigh. Also, Sir John Hawkins was supposed to have brought the potato to Europe in 1565, but that turns out to be the sweet potato.

The Germans in Offenbach were so grateful to Sir Francis Drake for bringing back the potato from his round-the-world voyage that they erected a statue to him as the "Introducer of the Potato into Europe." However, there is not the slightest evidence that potatoes were aboard his vessel, the *Pelican*.

pouring oil on troubled waters. No phrase like this occurs in the Bible. Both Pliny the Elder (A.D. 23–79) and Plutarch (A.D. 46?–120), however, refer to oil as having a soothing effect on rough water. And Bede, often called "the Venerable Bede" (A.D. 673–735) tells of one Bishop Adain who, in the seventh century, gave to some travelers oil for casting into the sea in case of rough weather. The bishop's oil, however, was not designed to smooth troubled waters; it was holy oil, with the miraculous ability to make the wind stop blowing.

predestination. Commonly a club with which to belabor Calvinists, predestination is by no means an exclusively Calvinist doctrine. It is every bit as Augustinian as it is Calvinist; and indeed, predestination *must* be a part of any theology, Christian or otherwise, which assumes an omnipotent and omniscient—that is, all-powerful and all-knowing—God.

Without attempting to resolve disputes which go back even before Christianity—the Greeks argued about it too—it can be said, broadly, that *predestination* as usually defined implies that some will be saved (the "elect" in Calvinist terms) and some will not; that God knows which are which; and that nothing an individual can do will guarantee his "election."

To which, at many a sophomore bull session, the scornful reply is: What's the point, then, in living a "good life"? Some will be saved, some won't; God knows who—and only God; and since it's already been decided, one might as well live it up; what's the difference? The theologian answers: Ah, but you confuse God's knowledge with God's will. God *must* know, if He is assumed to be omniscient, who is to be saved. But He does not will an individual's salvation or damnation; these result from the individual's free moral choice. (It is a heresy in both Catholic and Anglican terms to believe that God *predetermines* one's salvation. This amounts to a belief in fatalism, a pagan doctrine.)

To put it another way, a God who is all-powerful cannot, by definition, be held to a bargain. One cannot "earn" salvation by good works; for this proposes, in effect, a denial of God's absolute power. No one is privileged to say to St. Peter "You must let me in, for I have lived a good life." It has to be entirely up to God—unless, again, one commits the heresy of denying God's omnipotence.

It is easy to see why practically everybody at one time or another has argued the paradoxes implied in predestination. But it might be added that, in a sense, a belief in predestination is among the noblest of doctrines. For it places the emphasis not on goodness as a lever to insure some future paradise, but as valuable for its own sake. To live the good life without regard to what's in it for you comes close to the ultimate in altruism.

pregnancy, myths about. It would be a never-ending if not hopeless task to try to assemble into anything less than several volumes all the misinformation regarding pregnancy. But certainly some of the most common myths can be exploded. Old wives' tales abound, of course: that eating ice cream will cause the baby to "catch cold" or to get cold; that the baby may be "marked" if the mother is frightened; that getting the feet wet will flood the baby with "water"; that reaching for something on a top shelf will wrap the umbilical cord around the baby's neck, and so on and so on.

None of the above is true. Nor is it so that broad-hipped women necessarily have easier births than the narrow-hipped—it's internal, not external, measurements that count. Nor will wearing high heels cause cross-eyed children, though some actually believe this.

Certainly not all beliefs about pregnancy are untrue; as the thalidomide tragedy revealed, what the mother ingests may have drastic consequences. Most of the folklore of pregnancy, like superstition in general, results from coincidence; if, only once in several generations, a "marked" or malformed child is born following a frightening experience on the part of the mother, then it is likely to be remembered and passed on from generation to generation, with the "exceptions" unrecorded and unremembered.

prepositions, ending sentences with. When told that one must not end a sentence with a preposition, Winston Churchill is said to have remarked, "This is something up with which I will not put." In fact, there is no such "rule."

pretzels, origin of. Both the Granny Goose Pretzel Company ("The only pretzels made to music") and Martin Abramson, a free-lance writer, are responsible, no doubt among others, for the quite charming—and entirely false—story of how the pretzel originated. Granny Goose's explanation is printed on the back of the bag. Abramson's account in *Best Western Way* (Spring 1972; *Best Western Way* is the house organ of Best Western Motels) is basically the same, though somewhat embellished.

Some time near the beginning of the seventh century, so the story goes, a monk, either by accident (Abramson) or design (Granny Goose) formed some strips of dough, a spin-off from his bread-baking duty, into a looped twist. (Granny Goose, though not Abramson, says that the design was meant to represent the folded arms of children at prayer. But even by a considerable stretch of imagination it is hard to equate a pretzel's shape with the usual position of the arms at prayer. It's easier, perhaps, if one imagines the arms folded across the chest. But that's the conventional coffin arrangement, which raises hob, of course, with the whole tone of the story.)

Given to children who were faithful in their religious observances, the bits of twisted, baked dough came to be called *pretiola,* the Latin for "little reward." From *pretiola* to *pretzel* is only a small step, especially for those who have had no training in linguistics. Ergo, the pretzel.

It does seem rather a shame so heartwarming a tale should fall so far short of the truth. But it does. Merely a quick trip to the dictionary reveals that *pretzel* derives, prosaically enough, from the German word for "branch" (ultimately derived from Latin, but not the Latin for "little reward"). This is no doubt because a pretzel looks a little like a tree's intertwined branches.

prices ever rising. It is usually taken for granted that prices of everything were always lower in the old days. Indeed, Andrew

Jackson is credited with having forecast the country's ruin with bacon up to four cents a pound! It is interesting to observe, however, that in 1933 the per-bushel prices of wheat and corn in America were lower than they had been three hundred years before.

Pride goeth before a fall. Perhaps it does, but that isn't quite the way the Bible puts it. According to Prov. 16:18, "Pride goeth before destruction, and an haughty spirit before a fall."

professor, as title. Not everyone who teaches in a college or university is a professor, and the common use of the title indiscriminately reveals either insecurity or ignorance. Academic titles are, in fact, as rigid in their significances as are military ranks, though with one difference: anyone who holds the rank of assistant professor or higher can properly be addressed, in speech or writing, as "Professor."

In terms both of pay and prestige, the order on American campuses is as follows, from highest to lowest:

> Professor (sometimes called Full Professor)
> Associate Professor
> Assistant Professor
> Instructor
> Fellow
> Assistant (rarely, Associate), Teaching Assistant, Graduate Assistant, or something similar.

Lecturer is sometimes used as an academic title, but varies in its significance. In the above list, it would hover somewhere around Instructor, in terms of rank.

In England very few of those teaching even in universities may properly be called professors, as the term is reserved for the highest echelon.

pronunciation, correct. Many millions of people believe that there is actually (or should be) a difference in sound between such pairs of words as *miner-minor, alter-altar,* and *council-counsel;* that indeed there is, or should be, a difference in sound between *all* unstressed (or, as often said, "unaccented") vowels in such words as *history* and *geography.*

The fact, confirmed by a vast body of research, is that in normal, connected discourse (that is, conversation or speech-making as it takes place under customary informal circumstances) there is absolutely no distinction made in American English between the sounds of any of the unstressed vowels. *All* unstressed vowels in American English, in other words, sound the same: a sort of indeterminate short grunt, or "uh," often represented in dictionaries by the symbol [ə] or "schwa." Thus the sound of the unstressed syllables in the following words is the same: *alone, sofa, system, easily, gallop, circus, banana, collect, abut,* etc. To teach a child that the vowel sound of the second syllable of *system* should somehow be different from the vowel sound of the second syllable of *easily* or *gallop* is, quite simply, nonsense.

In situations other than normal discourse—sermons or Bible readings of the formal variety, for example, or in singing—it is true that unstressed syllables are sometimes given values which would be false in conversation. This occurs particularly in terms of endings like *-est, -em, -en. Purest* and *purist* are identical in sound—in normal conversation. But a singer may be taught *pure-est* and *pure-ist,* and to sound the word *heaven* not as it is said in conversation ("heavn"), but rather as if it were "hevvenn."

psychiatrist, psychoanalyst. These terms are often confused in popular usage, and indeed sometimes in not-so-popular usage. Psychiatrists, always holders of the M.D. degree, do not use the couch as an invariable accessory in treatment, usually preferring to see their patients face-to-face across a desk. Psychoanalysts, on the other hand, who may or may not be holders of the M.D., do use the couch if they practice the "classic" psychoanalysis associated with Freudian principles. A psychoanalyst is someone who has himself undergone psychoanalysis and studied its principles. There are, today, various "psychoanalytic" methods of treatment which do not, however, necessarily derive from strictly Freudian principles and may not involve the intensive probing of the past which is a part of historical Freudian psychoanalysis.

A psychiatrist may also be a psychoanalyst, if he has himself undergone psychoanalysis. But psychiatrists, whether analysts or not, use many varying techniques: medication, behavior modification, supportive therapy, electric shock either as treatment or as means of enabling them to "reach" a patient, and so forth. Though Freud himself was a physician, he trained nonmedical persons as analysts and even postulated that a medical background might actually hinder doing psychoanalysis.

Trained social workers (that is, those who hold the M.S.W. degree) and psychologists often use the techniques of psychiatry and/or psychoanalysis.

Perhaps the most prevalent misconception is that psychiatry and psychoanalysis deal with intellectual problems; indeed, intellectuals themselves tend to believe this—unless, that is, they are themselves under treatment, at which point they soon enough learn that psychotherapy deals not with the "mind," but with the emotions. Indeed, if the intellect could solve our problems, surely they would long since have vanished. As far back as one can go in history, logical arguments against war are common; it simply has no intellectual defense. So why do we still have wars?

"Psychologist" is a more inclusive term than either "psychiatrist" or "psychoanalyst." Psychologists engage in a variety of activities: marriage counseling, testing, dealing with emotional problems, research, consultation, teaching. Like "social worker," the term "psychologist" is sometimes used by lay persons with less precision than professionals employ. Clinical psychologists are customarily holders of the Ph.D. and are more likely to engage in psychotherapy than are psychologists who hold the Ed.D., or Doctor of Education. Unlike psychiatrists and most psychoanalysts, psychologists are not doctors of medicine.

Puritans. *Puritan* has come to have such pejorative connotations that it is difficult to realize how many false conceptions contribute to its use as a generic term for antiscientific, reactionary, teetotaling moralists as deficient in education as in sophistication. Derived to a considerable degree from two sources, Nathaniel Hawthorne and H. L. Mencken, who coined the phrase "Bible Belt" and whose 1917 essay "Puritanism as a Literary Force" made him the high priest of the Puritan haters, many myths surrounding the Puritans and Puritanism have fixed themselves firmly in the contemporary American consciousness.

It should first be said that *Puritan* is not subject to exact definition; Puritans came in many shades of belief and did not represent a party or creed in the strictest sense. Arising out of a desire to "purify" the Church of England of its "papist" or "Romish" practices, the movement attracted adherents as different from each other as John Milton and Michael Wigglesworth, the author of a collection of abominable doggerel enormously popular in seventeenth-century America, called *The Day of Doom, or a Description of the Great and Last Judgment, with a Short Discourse about Eternity.*

Puritans in colonial America never constituted anything more than a small minority, although admittedly the Puritan influence was considerable in terms of early American literary (but *not* political) tradition. It is, however, often forgotten that the work from which so many derive their notions of Puritanism, *The Scarlet Letter,* was written in the middle of the nineteenth century, two hundred years after the events Hawthorne purports to describe, by a man so haunted by guilt at the part one of his ancestors had played during the Salem witch trials that it does not seem excessive to refer to it as neurotic. (And, as a matter of fact, the part this remote ancestor played was not even a particularly important one; see HA[W]THORNE, "JUDGE" AT SALEM WITCH TRIALS.)

Likely also to be overlooked is that the Puritan movement, which originated in England, was not a minor rebellion on purely theological grounds. It involved political considerations of such major import that the very institution of the monarchy itself was toppled: something that had never before happened in English history and has not happened since. In present-day terms, the Puritans were politically the liberals, not the conservatives; what they fought was a repressive Establishment (and it was repressive enough), both religious and secular—or, perhaps more accurately, the religious-secular Establishment.

Much has been made of Puritan objections to the theater. And it is true enough that if the Puritans had come to power in England only a few decades earlier, William Shakespeare certainly would not be remembered as a playwright, for he would have had no theater to write for. But this is not to say that English Puritans objected to the theater solely because of its "immorality"—though in truth theater people in Shakespeare's day were not always of the sort sometimes described as "desirable."

For the great age of the English theater was, paradoxically—or ironically—also a time when the theater was closely watched and controlled by the Royalist–Established Church power structure to which the Puritans were so adamantly opposed. No play could be produced without the approval of the Master of the Revels, accountable to the reigning monarch, who very much acted the political censor. Shakespeare, Christopher Marlowe, Ben Jonson, and the lesser greats of Elizabethan times understood this, and perforce accepted it; they had no choice. In a real sense, thus, the theater, if not quite an arm of the monarchy, was certainly enjoined by the authority of the Master of the Revels, whose approval was essential, from speaking out against it.

It would inevitably seem to opponents of the Establishment that an institution forbidden to attack it must therefore, to one degree or another, be its friend, even its partisan. And it is true enough that many a passage in Shakespeare's plays, as in those of other playwrights of his day, must have enraged the Puritans not because of its bawdry, but because of its pro-Establishment bias. One need not elicit the dozens of relevant citations to conclude that Shakespeare was certainly sympathetic to both the fact and the concept of monarchy as well as the "divine right" of kings, that bitterest pill of all to swallow for those who believed that it ought to be possible to speak against injustice without also speaking against God.

And even though it is true that Puritan objections to the theater made much of bawdry, objections based on political grounds have often enough—either for expediency or to attract a wide base of support or both—disguised themselves, at least in part, as objections to "immorality"; attacks upon political leftists or radicals today are often accompanied by attacks upon their presumed sexual license, use of drugs, and so on.

That the Puritans certainly did not hate literature is evidenced, clearly enough, by John Milton, the greatest Puritan writer of them all—and one to whom we often turn for his vigorous defense not only of a free press and free speech (in his *Areopagitica*) but of civil liberty—a phrase used by Milton himself—in general. Sixty-three years before Jean–Jacques Rousseau was born, Milton wrote, in his revolutionary defense of the right of the people to depose, even to execute, tyrants ("The Tenure of Kings and Magistrates"), "No man, who knows aught, can be so stupid to deny, that all men naturally were born free. . . ." This is scarcely the kind of sentiment associated, in the popular mind, with Puritanism.

Of course, Milton was a genius, thus impossible to force into a narrow category; and his Puritanism would no doubt have been suspect to a Wigglesworth, for Milton had reservations with regard to the theological strictures of the philosophical father of Puritanism, John Calvin. Even in America, however—and it should be remembered that those who ended up in Massachusetts Bay represented an extreme segment, the *Separatist* Puritans— Puritans were by no means the somber killjoys so many think they were.

At the very site of the house where the darkest chapter in colonial Puritanism opened, the home of the Reverend Samuel Parris, in Salem, recent excavations have revealed hundreds of broken wine bottle fragments, one with Parris's initials on the seal; many beef and pork bones; and many clay pipe bowls and stems. The early American Puritans drank—in fact, drank a good deal, from contemporary accounts; they ate well when they could; and certainly they had no objection to smoking.

That Puritans in the colonies dressed always in black is another myth. They liked bright colors. Even Hawthorne makes much, in *The Scarlet Letter,* of the rich dress favored, on occasion, by many of his characters. Hester Prynne, it will be remembered, made her living by her skill at elaborate needlework. Nor were the Puritans either antilearning or antiscientific, at least as science was understood then. It was, after all, the Bay Colony that founded Harvard, whose charter specified its objective as the advancement of good literature, arts, and sciences.

A point often overlooked, especially by those under the Mencken influence, is that American Puritanism was not a peculiarly vicious and repressive offspring of the English-European variety. As Rod Horton and Herbert Edwards remark in *Backgrounds of American Literary Thought* (1967), nothing could be more inaccurate than to assume that immediately after the Reformation the rest of Europe leaped at once from the sixteenth century into the twentieth, leaving Puritans far behind in superstitious ignorance and die-hard conservatism. If anything, American Puritans were less in such intellectual bondage than their English counterparts. Twenty persons were hanged as witches in Salem in 1692; but in England alone one witch-finder was responsible for three hundred hangings in just two years (1645–47). Four Quakers were hanged in Boston; but under Elizabeth I three thousand dissidents died in prison. Roger Williams was banished; but as Horton and Edwards remind us, he could have been summarily beheaded in England for saying less.

It should be recalled also that Jonathan Edwards's famous sermon, "Sinners in the Hands of an Angry God," was not delivered to colonial Puritans, though the impression persists that it was. Often taken, though inaccurately, as a symbol of seventeenth-century American Puritanism, it was actually spoken in 1741, more than a hundred and twenty years after the landing of the *Mayflower* (only some forty of whose hundred passengers, by the way, signed the famous compact). It was a revivalist sermon. And, along with other similar sermons, it probably cost Edwards his job at the Northampton Church, as a matter of fact; he was dismissed in 1750 because of the severity of his doctrines.

A final myth arises from ignorance of colonial Puritan belief. Neither the Separatists who arrived on the *Mayflower* in 1620 (the Pilgrims) nor the much larger group of Massachusetts Bay colonists who arrived ten years later (the Puritans—though both groups were essentially Puritan in belief) had any notion of instituting the kind of political system established after the American Revolution. The Pilgrims and the Puritans were not interested in a republican form of government, and certainly not in separation of church and state; they simply wanted to be left alone to establish their own form of authoritarian theocracy. They were not much easier on Dissenters than had been the hated English Royalists.

Purple Heart. Often believed to be a World War II creation, the Purple Heart medal was actually originated by George Washington in 1782. It was then intended to honor distinguished military service; only three or four were awarded during the American Revolution. Now, of course, it is commonly granted to servicemen who have been wounded in line of duty.

pyramids. Many believe that the dimensions, position, measurements, and so forth, of the pyramids of Egypt contain or reveal mysterious formulae that are the keys to hidden knowledge. Similar beliefs are often expressed concerning STONEHENGE, Mayan and Inca structures, the stones at Carnac, and so on. Almost any structure with pretensions to antiquity has been, at one time or another, exhaustively analyzed by scientists, pseudo-scientists, science-fiction writers, mystics, or journalists in an attempt to prove a pet theory.

What is often forgotten is that, as Winifred Needler remarks in a *Popular Archaeology* review (October 1972) of Peter Tompkins's *Secrets of the Great Pyramid* (1971), "a formula constructed with sufficent complexity may fit a given phenomenon and yet prove nothing." The *ex post facto* fallacy is well known to logicians: that is, the assumption that because *B* follows *A*, it must therefore have some causal connection with *A*. As an old proverb has it, if a cat has kittens in the oven, that doesn't make them biscuits. If, let us say, an ancient tomb turns out to consist of 365 stones atop which is a smaller structure containing 28 stones, this cannot be taken to "prove" that the builders of the structure were aware of the length of the year and the period of the moon's revolution around the earth. They may simply have run out of rocks.

There are two further dangers in such inferential reasoning: the difficulty of fitting in observations that do not confirm the theory, which often leads to suppressing or ignoring data not in conformity with it; and the overlooking of an elementary principle of logic usually referred to as the principle of PARSIMONY, or Occam's Razor. This principle holds that of all possible explanations, the simplest (*not* the most complicated) is most likely to be true—always assuming it covers all the facts. And though logic and "common sense" are often enough at war with one another, in this instance common sense is thoroughly on the side of the bishop of Occam. If one's automobile stops without warning, the wise driver checks his gasoline gauge before taking the carburetor apart or disassembling the distributor.

A further illustration, admittedly contrived, may show how easy it can be to err when examining phenomena with a view to proving a point—and how persuasive "evidence" can seem to be even when quite false. If, at some remote time in the future, linguists were to attempt to establish the etymology of *TV*, it would be only too easy to show that the *T* stands for the conventional shape of the television antenna, and the *V* is simply an adaptation of the electronic engineers' symbol for the kinescope, or television picture-tube: V or <. Thus an expression which we know to be phonetic-acronymic could be ingeniously "proved" to be a form of picture-writing, on which basis who knows what further theories might be built?

The SHAKESPEARE-BACON "CONTROVERSY" is a prime illustration both of Needler's remark, quoted above, and of assumption based on "selective" data. It all depends on what one is looking for, which only too often determines what one will find. When it was fashionable to seek some kind of divine formula or rationale for the Great Pyramid, such rationale was discovered easily enough. Then followed the usual counterreaction: the debunking of any such notion as "divine inspiration" for the Pyramid. Since 1971, however, when Peter Tompkins published *Secrets of the Great Pyramid,* the "secrets" argument has taken the form of a presumably scientific (and elaborate) rationale for the Great Pyramid: that it was built as a kind of laboratory/observatory.

The reexamination of old data by trained researchers can obviously be of value. But one should remember that trained researchers prefer to base their conclusions not on ground already plowed, but upon the fresh fields of newly discovered data. It may be that somewhere as yet unknown (like the Dead Sea Scrolls before they were discovered) lies an explanation for the "secret" of the Pyramid. And it may be that there is no particular secret after all.

We know, today, that the famous Watts Towers of Los Angeles were simply the expression of one man's rather eccentric, and certainly eclectic, philosophy. If, at some remote time in the future, this fact is forgotten, then it will be easy enough to elaborate upon a vast construct which "proves" that the Watts Towers were —well, were almost anything, including an observatory.

Quakers. Quakers don't mind being called Quakers, at least not any more. But it is not the name of their faith; Quakers belong to the Religious Society of Friends.

Nor is it true that the term *Quaker* was first applied to the Society of Friends, founded by George Fox in the middle of the seventeenth century. Although George Fox himself thought that the term was given to him and his followers in 1650 by a Justice Bennet "Because I bid them, Tremble at the Word of the Lord," there is extant a letter written in 1647 which applies the word *Quaker* to an obviously foreign group bearing no relation to the Society of Friends: ". . . a Sect of Woemen (they are at South-werke) come from beyond the sea, called Quakers, and these swell, shiver, and shake, and when they come to themselves (for in all this fitt Mahomett's holy-ghost hath been conversing with them) they begin to preache what hath been delivered to them by the Spiritt."

quarter horse. Not so named because of its lineage, but because of its speed in running the quarter-mile.

Queen Anne style. Queen Anne had nothing to do with the Queen Anne style except to lend it her name. Much of the decorative style of the period was influenced by Sarah Jennings, first Duchess of Marlborough and a forebear of Winston Churchill, who had a large role in the queen's private as well as public life.

It also designates—unsuitably—a style that Richard Norman Shaw contrived in the mid-1870s. He needed a corny style for English country houses and produced a potpourri of elements from Elizabethan cottages, romanesque and Flemish renaissance. It was unveiled at the British Pavilion of the 1876 Philadelphia Centennial Exposition, and may be seen in the row houses of New York City dating from the 1880s and 1890s.

quicklime and corpses. No matter the number of crime stories, whether fiction or purported fact, that involve the destruction of corpses by burial in quicklime, the fact is that quicklime simply does not "eat" human or animal bodies. As a matter of fact, it is more likely than not to act as a preservative. It seems more than likely that there have been murderers convicted *because* of quicklime rather than in spite of it.

quicksand. Quicksand does not suck you under or pull you down, popular belief notwithstanding. Since its density is greater than that of water, quicksand, as a matter of fact, is *more* buoyant than water, not less. In other words, a man's body will not sink so far into quicksand as it would into water.

But—and it is a large "but" indeed—quicksand is nevertheless highly dangerous stuff. In spite of the periodic debunkings that appear in popular magazines, its reputation as a killer is well deserved.

Quicksand is sometimes said to be differentiated from the sand found at seashores and in golf-course bunkers by the shape of its granules: instead of being rough and irregular like those of ordinary sand, they are round, like ball bearings; thus its peculiarly seductive behavior. But this is not the case. Any kind of sand becomes "quick" under a certain somewhat unusual but by no means uncommon circumstance: water under rather weak pressure from underneath. As described in an excellent account by Gerald H. Matthes, in *Scientific American* for June 1953 (pages 97 ff.), quicksand is nearly always limited to a relatively small area where an underlying spring maintains pressure. It may sometimes be found *under* water where, for instance, a spring below the stream bed exerts an upward pressure.

The effect of the upward water pressure is to create a super-saturated condition in which the sand, round-granuled or not, becomes suspended and frictionless and will not support weight. There is no way to identify quicksand by eye; it may be crusted on top and look perfectly firm but collapse under a person's—or animal's—weight.

The belief that quicksand exerts a positive pulling action derives from the fact that any attempt to struggle out of it only makes matters worse. As Mr. Matthes says in a later issue of *Scientific American* (October 1953, p. 4), ". . . any effort that is made to pull one foot up and out only serves to sink the other foot deeper. Since quicksand contains no air—all spaces between sand grains being filled with water—the pulling up of a foot creates a strong suction for lack of air to take its place." It is this suction created by the victim himself, not the sand, that is responsible for the common misapprehension.

In any event, the victim will not go completely under. He may, however, end up with only his head showing; and if (in the classic melodramatic tradition) he waves his arms wildly, then it may happen that instead of his head being above the sand, only his arms will be. In either case, the prospect is not appealing.

A wagon or an automobile may, it is true, completely disappear, because wagons and automobiles weigh more than human or animal bodies. A man wearing a heavy pack may also, of course, sink to the bottom if he does not (or cannot) shed it quickly enough. The advice Mr. Matthes and other experts have for those unfortunate enough to encounter quicksand is simple enough: lie flat on your back. (If you wait until the quicksand is above your knees, it's obviously too late.) Then either roll or "crawl" your way ashore. But it's exhausting business, as Mr. Matthes points out.

Quicksand is not a myth. Ironically, however, for all its perils it is not nearly so deadly a hazard as what Mr. Matthes calls its "dangerous relative," the alkali bog. An alkali bog is formed by spring-water seeps that contain alkaline salts leached from a soil rich in them. In Mr. Matthes's words:

> Such bogs are far more treacherous than quicksand because they are apt to occur in unexpected places—on a hillside as well as in or near a river—and because they contain clay or colloidal matter which gives them the consistency of soft soap.

Most alkali bogs can be recognized by the white efflorescence of salts along their edges or over their surface. A man or animal mired in an alkali bog sinks more rapidly than in quicksand, and quick work is required to get out of one. There are bogs in the West which are littered with the bones of animals that did not move promptly enough.

R

raccoons washing their food. The belief that raccoons wash their food in water because they have no salivary glands is untrue. Raccoons do have salivary glands.

rainfall and air pollution. The prevalent notion that "a good rain will clear the air" has very little truth in it. Rain has only a very slight effect on air pollution, and certainly will not "purify" the atmosphere.

rape, ease of. The widespread and cynical belief that most cases of rape either are invited by the victim or are reported as such out of motives of revenge is often accompanied by the belief that rape is very nearly impossible unless the woman "cooperates."

What is forgotten is that rape is not merely forcible entry, which a struggling woman beneath a lone attacker might well make difficult, if not impossible. Rape involves not just the use of, but the *threat* of violence, even death. A woman who allows her attacker to achieve sexual union because the attacker may otherwise kill or injure her is no more "cooperating" than is the victim of a hold-up man who hands over his wallet rather than risk being shot.

rattlesnakes, age of; warning of. This cannot be determined by number of rattles, in spite of the common belief that each rattle represents a year. True, the rattles result from the sloughing off of skin. But rattlesnakes shed their skins at varying intervals; usually they slough off the old skin three or four times a year.

There is a common belief that rattlesnakes always warn the victim by rattling before striking. In fact, William Bartram (1739–1823), a botanist and ornithologist, called the diamondback "the magnanimous rattle-snake." Recent, more thorough studies have demonstrated that this is not true: the diamondback is quite capable of striking without warning.

Perhaps the diamondback can be excused for this, for he is totally deaf, and does not know whether he is rattling or not.

re. This is not, as often thought, an abbreviation for "regard" or "reference" when used in a business letter. It's the ablative of the Latin *res,* meaning "thing" or "matter."

***Reader's Digest* as a reprint magazine.** That *Reader's Digest* depends almost entirely on outside sources for its material has not been true for many years. Indeed, the first of the Digest "originals," or pieces written directly for the magazine, appeared in the 1930s. Today, most of its articles are written either by its own editors or by established writers who have been directly commissioned.

Digest editors do keep a watch out for suitable material that can be condensed and reprinted, for which they pay good rates—in addition, of course, to whatever the author got from the magazine or newspaper in which his work first appeared. However, most of its editorial content (barring, of course, special departments specifically aimed at reader contributions, like "Life in These United States") is from its own editors; established writers whose contributions are frequently solicited; and—in an arrangement apparently pioneered by the *Digest*—from magazines or newspapers with which the *Digest* has a working agreement. In this latter case, a writer will be commissioned to do a piece which the *Digest* will offer to the cooperating publication; after its first appearance there the *Digest* will then reprint it.

Red Square (Moscow). Red Square was not so named by the Communists, although many people think it was. In fact, it had been known as such long before the revolution that toppled the Romanovs and ultimately resulted in the establishment of the Soviet government.

reindeer. They do look like deer, and because of their name, many think they belong to the deer species. But they don't. Reindeer belong to the caribou family.

rent for trenches and cemeteries. There may still be a few old-timers around who believe that the United States paid the French government rent for the use of battle trenches in World War I, and both British and French governments a rental fee for land used as cemeteries for fallen soldiers. There's no truth in either story.

restrictive ("pointing-out") and nonrestrictive phrases and clauses. Teachers of English often explain, with an air of sweet reasonableness, that one of the "logical" distinctions in our language is that between the punctuation of restrictive and nonrestrictive modifiers. The former, sometimes called a "pointing-out" modifier, is illustrated in the old proverb "A bird in the hand is worth two in the bush," in which "in the hand" and "in the bush" do point out the specific kind of bird in question: that is, they are restrictive modifiers. Thus, they are not set off by commas.

Similarly, a restrictive *clause* (distinguished from a phrase because it has a subject and predicate) is not set off by commas: "The lady who just went out has come back." In this instance, "who just went out" identifies the particular lady in question and is thus "restrictive." If we already know who the lady is, or if there is only one lady in the vicinity, then we should write "The lady, who just went out, has come back." All very reasonable; we tend to speak the first version without pauses, the second with; and commas commonly indicate pauses in speech.

The only trouble is that German, which Germans regard as a much more logical language than English, makes no such distinction. In German, no matter whether we know the lady or not, the sentence is invariably punctuated by commas: "Die Dame, die gerade ausging, ist zurück gekommen." To put it another way, logic and sweet reasonableness have naught to do with the punctuation of restrictive modifiers in English; it's just a matter of usage, or custom.

Revelations. Actually, there's no such book in the Bible. The one that is there is called Revelation.

Revere, Paul. See PAUL REVERE'S RIDE (S) .

reversing wheels to stop a locomotive. Though not so commonly seen since the advent of the Diesel engine, occasionally a news item will refer to an engineer's "reversing the wheels" in order to stop a train in an emergency. Actually, maximum braking is assured, as in automobiles, just at the point before the wheels lock. Spinning or sliding wheels, regardless of the direction of rotation, are less effective, not more so. Certain devices on some automobiles, in fact, are designed to insure against wheel lock-up; and skilled drivers have long known that pumping the brakes will stop the car quicker than locking the wheels. Putting an automobile into reverse on an icy road or lake would insure against any adhesion whatsoever between tire and ice.

It may be that the common practice on ships or boats of reversing engines in a panic stop, or in airplanes of reversing pitch of propellers or jet-thrust, which does make sense, is responsible for the "reverse wheels" misapprehension.

Rhine, J. B. The famous experimenter in ESP, or extrasensory perception, Dr. Joseph Banks Rhine, was not trained as a psychologist, although almost everyone assumes this to be the case. His Ph.D. is, in fact, in botany; for a time, Dr. Rhine taught botany at West Virginia University.

rice paper. This material is not made from rice, as its name would seem to indicate, but from the pith of a tree called the rice-paper tree, a small Asiatic tree of the ginseng family.

Richard I. Richard the Lion-Hearted had good press agents in the troubadours, who touted him as a great hero, so that he became a famous figure of chivalry. His reputation was further enhanced in Sir Walter Scott's *Ivanhoe* and *The Talisman.* As these two books were required reading in school, he became the idol of a generation or two of children.

Actually, however, he was about the worst king that England ever had. He certainly did not fulfill the ideals of chivalry. He was excessively cruel. He bled England to pay for his wars, and he did not sponsor a single measure of benefit to his country. As a warrior he was superb, and he wrote tolerable lyrics.

Richard III, as hunchback. There has been much argument as to whether Richard III resembled in any important particular the deformed and malignant villain of Shakespeare's famous play; indeed, the Richard III Society, founded in England in 1924 under the name Fellowship of the White Boar (the white boar was Richard's emblem) devotes most of its considerable energies to correcting what it regards as the injustices done Richard by Tudor propaganda. (An American branch of the British organization, the Richard III Society, Inc., was founded in 1969 with similar objectives.)

Exactly what kind of person Richard III really was may never, of course, be entirely established. But one misapprehension can surely be laid to rest: he was not a hunchback, no matter how Shakespeare describes him or actors portray him. None of the contemporary portraits of Richard III, and they are several, shows any sign of "deformity."

richest street in the world. What is the "hottest" shopping street in the world? Where is real estate the most costly? Fifth Avenue? Bond Street? Rue de la Paix? No. It is a street in Zurich only half a mile long that used to be a frogs' ditch. It goes by the rather ordinary name of Railroad Station Street (Bahnhofstrasse). Here are clustered some of the famous Swiss banks, watch companies, jewelers, and hotels. So intense is the competition for space here that land sells for upwards of $1,000 per square foot.

right of the first night. The *jus primae noctis* (Latin: "law of the first night") or *droit du seigneur* (French: "the lord's right") is widely believed to have been a custom that existed in medieval Europe whereby a potentate (and the word is used advisedly) had the right to sleep with all new brides of his vassals on their wedding nights. However, there is no sound evidence whatsoever that such a law was ever enforced, or, indeed, was ever prevalent in Europe. A decree of the Seneschal of Guyenne, 1302, is the only document which represents it to have been in effect, but that decree is itself suspect. Certainly this was never a part of the life-style of the Middle Ages in Europe, yet as a belief it has been popular for centuries.

Such practices have occurred in some primitive societies in South and Central America and Africa.

right to keep and bear arms, the. The second article of the Bill of Rights of the United States Constitution reads—in whole, not in part, italics furnished—*"A well-regulated militia, being necessary to the security of a free State,* the right of the people to keep and bear arms, shall not be infringed." Nothing in the Constitution, thus, forbids the right of federal or state governments to make any gun-control laws they wish in terms of an individual who is not a member of a "well-regulated militia."

ripe and green olives, calories of. Don't count on saving much in the way of calories if you reach for the green ones instead of the ripe ones, as many dieters will tell you to do. Two giant green olives contain fifteen calories, two giant ripe ones sixteen. The ripe ones do have more carbohydrate content, however.

rivers flowing north. It is often said that the St. Johns River, in Florida, is the only major river in the United States to flow north. This is manifestly untrue; the Willamette in Oregon, which is major enough for ocean-going vessels, flows north for almost all its length, taking a northwesterly turn only when it reaches the town of Rainier, some fifty miles from its mouth.

robin. The American robin is actually a thrush; *robin* derives from *robin redbreast,* the common British term for a bird of another species. The scientific name for the bird Americans call the robin is *turdus migratorius,* which may account for the American preference for "robin."

"Rose is a rose is a rose is a rose." That's what Gertrude Stein actually wrote—not *"A* rose," etc., as many think. And she said it three times, not twice. It's from her poem entitled "Sacred Emily."

Ross, Betsy—and "Old Glory." Betsy Ross was indeed born in Philadelphia in 1752 and died in Philadelphia in 1836. Her husband's uncle, General George Ross, was one of the signers of the Declaration of Independence. But whether she actually made the first flag falls in that category scholars must label "not proved." Historians are suspicious of the story every schoolchild knows: the visit from George Washington, Robert Morris, and General Ross with the request that she try her hand at making a flag, the rough diagram of which they had with them; her demonstration that a five-pointed star could be made with a single clip of the scissors though her illustrious visitors had thought a six-pointed star would be easier; then, later, the final design and her commission.

The story is suspect for two reasons. First, it was not told until 1870, when Betsy Ross's grandson presented it in a paper before the Historical Society of Pennsylvania. And second, no one has ever found any contemporary documentary evidence to back it up. Still, no one has produced a more convincing claim.

In any case, Betsy Ross was almost certainly not the first to call the flag "Old Glory," though this is also a somewhat murky area. According to the daughter of one William Driver, a sea captain from Salem, Driver invented the phrase.

Rough Riders. Rough Riders is the popular name for the First Regiment of U.S. Cavalry Volunteers in the Spanish-American War, and it is popularly supposed that Teddy Roosevelt was their commander and led this band of adventurers uphill and down dale in death-defying cavalry charges.

Theodore Roosevelt did organize the group, but its command went to Leonard Wood, who had military experience. The horses had to be left in Florida and the "Rough Riders" fought mainly on foot!

royal purple. Purple to most of us connotes a dark blue with some red in it. Royal purple, about which we read so much in ancient history, was really a crimson. The best royal purple came from Phoenicia, especially Tyre. It was made from a tiny Mediterranean shellfish, the *murex*. The color could be altered by mixing it with urine and other ingredients.

rub out. As a synonym for killing, this saying surprisingly goes much further back than gangster cant of the recent past. According to Samuel Eliot Morison's *The Oxford History of the American People,* the phrase was first used by white trappers of the early nineteenth century in exactly its present meaning.

run away, handling the child who wants to. Firmly enshrined in popular mythology is the belief that if a child is determined to run away from home, then the proper course for the parents to take is to put no obstacles in the way: fix a lunch, help to pack a bag, say a polite "good-bye" and "write us if you have time."

Few folk-beliefs bring such helpless tears of rage to the trained social worker as this one. For of all possible ways of treating the potential runaway, this is the worst. A child runs away, or tries to, because he or she feels unwanted. To embark on a course of action which can only encourage this belief is to court real psychological damage.

running the gauntlet. It is naturally assumed by most people that "running the gauntlet" in some way originated from a meaning of gauntlet, or glove, akin to "throwing down the gauntlet." This is not the case. The "gauntlet" which is a glove comes from a medieval English word taken from medieval French: *gantelet,* "glove."

The "gauntlet" one runs, as when schoolboys form a lane between two rows and force their victim to run between them while enduring the blows of his tormentors, owes its origins to a case of mistaken identity. An earlier form of the word gauntlet, meaning glove, is gantelope, sometimes spelled gantlope. Because of its resemblance to a Swedish word, *gatlopp,* which means "lane run" and does indeed describe running the gauntlet, "gantelope," or in its later spelling "gauntlet," came to be applied to the "lane run." Thus there are really two words, spelled the same, derived from the same source—one of which, however, came by way of the kind of error scholars call folk etymology to be mistakenly identified with the Swedish *gatlopp.*

running water purifies itself. In these ecology-conscious days, probably not very many believe this old chestnut. To some degree it is, of course, true enough; given a choice between swimming at a raw sewage outfall and a point ten miles downstream, few would choose the former. If, however, it were really so, then a great many municipalities have wasted untold millions of dollars on riverside treatment plants.

Ruth, Babe—and the dead ball/larger ballparks theory. The notion that Babe Ruth's record as the Home Run King would "really" stand forever because he played when baseballs were "deader" and ballparks larger has no foundation in fact. According to Joe Reichler, baseball historian and member of the commissioner's staff, the ball was actually livelier in Ruth's day than it is now; indeed, the Ruth years are often referred to as the "live-ball" era. Further, baseball parks today are larger, not smaller, than they were in Ruth's time. Ruth played nearly half his games at Yankee Stadium, where the distance down the right-field line was only 296 feet.

It might be added that another popular misconception involving Ruth is that the still-popular candy bar was named for him. But the bar is called Baby Ruth, of course. This is sometimes incorrectly accounted for as the result of legal complications making it impossible to call the candy by Ruth's exact name. It was actually named after a child whose first name was Ruth.

S

sailing at the speed of the wind. Although it seems impossible, not only can certain kinds of sailing craft travel at the speed of the wind; they may actually exceed the wind's velocity by a very considerable margin. An iceboat with its minimal friction can even travel four times as fast as the wind.

St. Andrews (golf). American visitors to the holiest shrine in golfdom, The Royal and Ancient Golf Club of St. Andrews in Scotland, are always pleasantly surprised to learn that it is a public course, municipally owned, with exceedingly low greens fees even by American public-golf course standards. There are even clubs available for rental, again at very reasonable cost.

No American golf course, obviously, equals St. Andrews in prestige. Those that may be considered at least approximately analogous, in American terms, are invariably private, restricting play to members, guests, or visitors who are themselves members of other private clubs, and charging greens fees ranging upward from ten dollars.

salmon, death after spawning. Of the ten or so species of salmon, only the United States Pacific Coast variety invariably all die—males and females alike—after spawning. Perhaps because this one species does, many think that every species dies after spawning.

saltpeter as anaphrodisiac. Surely there can be few who have ever lived in a college dormitory, fraternity or sorority house, military barracks, or for that matter lumberjack camp, who have not at some time encountered the firm conviction that the coffee has been doctored with saltpeter. Why? Because it inhibits sexual feelings or performance.

Of course there isn't a smidgen of truth in the belief. It's a bland substance, known to chemists as potassium nitrate, or KNO_3. Pharmacologically, it is considered a diuretic, which somehow must account for its undeserved reputation.

Samson and Delilah. Most people may not believe it but Delilah did not cut Samson's hair—nor is this statement based on the technicality that Samson's head was shaved rather than clipped. She was simply not the one who removed his locks, by whatever means. According to Judg. 16:19 Delilah made Samson "sleep upon her knees; and she called for a man, and she caused him to shave off the seven locks of his head. . . ." It might also be added that Samson succumbed to Delilah's pleadings not because he loved her, but because she nagged him until "his soul was vexed unto death."

San Francisco Earthquake of 1906. Many nonwesterners call it that, but native San Franciscans don't; they call it the San Francisco Fire of 1906. And it is true that most of the casualties, and as much as twenty times the damage, were caused by the fire which followed the quake whose shock, incidentally, extended all the way from Los Angeles to Coos Bay, Oregon, and as far east as Winnemucca, Nevada, some three hundred miles.

sap rising in spring. Sap neither rises in the spring nor falls in the fall, common terminology notwithstanding. It moves in and out, from center to surface and back; not up and down.

sardine. As applied to a specific living fish, there really is no such thing. A sardine is anything you get out of a sardine can, since the term applies to any of several small fish which are suitable for preserving, commonly young herring or pilchard.

sauterne. O.K. in English; the French spelling, however, if you want to be fancy, is always *sauternes,* after the French region,

Sauternes, near Bordeaux. In French, *sauterne* is no more the singular of *sauternes* than *sou* is the singular of *sous* or Pari the singular of Paris.

scapegoat. This term is commonly used to refer to the one in a group who gets caught although his own offense is no greater than, or perhaps not so great as, that of the others. William Calley, for example, was often referred to as a "scapegoat" following his conviction in connection with the My Lai massacre during the Vietnam war. But a scapegoat is actually himself innocent; he is sent out into the wilderness with the sins of *others* upon his head, not his own. Actually, two goats are involved in the Mosaic ritual. One is symbolically laden with the sins of the people and set free: the (e)scapegoat. The other is sacrificed.

scarlet fever and scarlatina. The notion that scarlatina is a different disease from scarlet fever is quite false—even perhaps dangerous if it leads to the further assumption that scarlatina is not contagious or infectious. Scarlatina is a mild case of scarlet fever.

scorpions stinging themselves to death. An old belief has it that a scorpion surrounded by a ring of fire will commit suicide. This is not so. Some scorpions possess immunity to their own venom; others can be killed only by massive doses.

Scotch, Scots. Although the adjective is often used in the United States, those who have visited Scotland, or number Scotsmen or women among their friends, are well aware that only in conjunction with Scotch whiskey is the adjective *Scotch* acceptable to natives of Scotland. Why this should be so is not easy to determine. But it probably reflects the historical fact that *Scottish,* later commonly changed (or abbreviated) to *Scotch,* was the original *English* appellation.

Actually, both Robert Burns and Sir Walter Scott used the term *Scotch* (even when it did not refer to the whiskey) regularly. But during the latter half of the nineteenth century, for whatever reason—perhaps the growing power of Victorian England and its concomitant tendency to overshadow the Scots and the Welsh —the term *Scotch* fell more and more out of favor. See also BRITAIN AND ENGLAND.

Scotch whiskey "blends." The words *blend* or *blended* when applied to Scotch whiskey should by no means be confused with American usage. Almost all good Scotch is a blend of various kinds of Scotch whiskeys. In America, a blended whiskey is one in which straight whiskey has been combined with grain neutral spirits in order to reduce costs. The term *blend* thus means quite a different thing when applied to Scotch, and it is in no sense an implication of economy or shortcuts in manufacture; quite the contrary.

Scotland Yard. At one time there were two Scotland Yards. Neither had anything to do with the London police force. A tenth-century king of Scotland was given a plot of land in London for a castle, though not without conditions (the Scottish king was required to visit the castle once a year as a form of homage to England). By the seventeenth century, when England and Scotland at last shared the same king, James I, the original site was divided into two areas, Great Scotland Yard and Middle Scotland Yard. But it was not until 1829 that the Metropolitan Police Force (of London), which is the official term for the organization now loosely called "Scotland Yard," was formed.

And then it was not located in what had come to be called simply Scotland Yard, but in a nearby location the official address of which was simply No. 4, Whitehall Place, not "Scotland Yard." New Scotland Yard, and New Scotland Yard South, were names applied toward the end of the nineteenth century to the *buildings* which then housed the headquarters staff. Thus, "Scotland Yard" as an address is meaningless, particularly now when various metropolitan police stations are scattered all over London.

Many people have the notion that to "call in Scotland Yard" is to invoke a mysterious crew of specialists who exist in a rarefied atmosphere quite apart from that of the regular London police. This is not true. Though *Scotland Yard* is, narrowly, the term used for the headquarters of the London police, it also is collectively applied by natives to the London force in general. The lowliest police constable is as much a part of Scotland Yard as the commissioner himself.

Nor is Scotland Yard in any sense a national police, like the FBI; it's strictly a London outfit. True, there is the rather grimly named Murder Squad, described by Peter Laurie in *Scotland*

Yard: A Personal Inquiry as "a team of experienced detectives who are available to provincial or colonial forces, for dealing with difficult crimes." But Scotland Yard has no more authority over the rest of Britain than the Washington, D.C., police force has over the rest of the United States.

Seeing Eye. In spite of its wide usage, this is not a generic term for dogs especially trained to lead the blind. The Seeing Eye, in Morristown, New Jersey, is only one of several organizations devoted to training such dogs; its dogs may, of course, be referred to as Seeing Eye dogs. But there are also Guide Dogs, which come from a group in California, and Leader dogs, out of the Midwest. Perhaps the fact that there is no common term for a dog trained to lead the blind has encouraged the use of *Seeing Eye*. Still, it's worth knowing that more than one organization devotes itself to training the remarkable animals that, for some blind at least, help make life easier to manage.

Seine River, pronunciation of. Almost universally pronounced "sane" by everybody except the French. *They* pronounce it "senn."

self-determination. Although it is commonly supposed that this great concept of Woodrow Wilson is one of his Fourteen Points, it is not among them. The Fourteen Points began with (1) "Open covenants openly arrived at," and ended with (14) "A League of Nations." Self-determination as a principle was not mentioned.

sex the year round. There is an old saying that what makes man different from the animals is that he drinks when he is not thirsty and has sex all year round. Actually not all animals confine themselves to one mating season. In warm climates, for instance, mares come into heat in most of the months of the year.

"Shake and shake / The catsup bottle. / None will come, / And then a lot'll." This was not written by the late Ogden Nash, though such notables as Edwin Newman, Hugh Downs, and Ann Landers have publicly attributed this amusing quatrain to him. It was written by Richard Armour and is included in the collec-

tion *Light Armour* (1954). The definitive text above was supplied by Mr. Armour, also the author of the foreword to this
volume.

Shakespeare-Bacon "controversy." There isn't any such thing. Not
among Shakespeare scholars, anyway, no single one of whom has
ever seriously proposed that anybody but William Shakespeare
wrote the plays attributed to him. It is not putting things too
strongly to say that a belief in Bacon's—or anyone else's—authorship of Shakespeare's plays is akin to a belief that the world is flat
or the moon made of green cheese.

In essence, the argument that Shakespeare could not have written his plays boils down to a misunderstanding of the creative
process flavored with more than a little intellectual, or pseudo-
intellectual, snobbery. (It is ironic that Mark Twain, who was
born in a tiny frontier village and left school at the age of eleven,
argues that Shakespeare couldn't possibly have written the plays
because he was a country bumpkin lacking in education.)

But literary genius—as Mark Twain so clearly demonstrated in
terms of his own career—has little to do with formal education,
nor even "experience" as usually defined. In any case, the notion
that Shakespeare was extraordinarily knowledgeable about practically everything—the law, sailing, soldiering, history, etc.—does
not hold much water. There are no legal terms in Shakespeare's
plays that a layman, especially one who had been involved as we
know Shakespeare was in litigation, would not know or could
not easily pick up. And a well-placed "Yare!" or two, a "Heave-
ho!" now and then, are about all we get of seamanship in his
dramas. His military tactics, like his history, he could easily have
got out of any number of books widely available in Elizabethan
England.

As for the best subjective argument against the Bacon theory,
surely no one who has slogged his way through Bacon's essays
could possibly believe that the same person was capable of writing
Hamlet or *King Lear*. Sir Francis Bacon was, without question, a
great man. But his cast of mind was scientific, logical, philosophical. And, withal, also political. He was neither poet nor playwright.

In any case, the assumption that Bacon—or anyone else—
somehow wrote Shakespeare's plays assumes also a conspiracy so

vast as to stagger the imagination: a conspiracy involving just about every segment of English society in the late sixteenth and early seventeenth centuries, from the rector of the Stratford church where records of Shakespeare's birth and marriage, the baptism of his children, and his death were kept (anyone who wishes may go take a look at them) to the courts of Queen Elizabeth and King James themselves, before whom we know, again from written records, that plays of Shakespeare were presented.

And we must assume also the connivance not only of Ben Jonson, the most famous Elizabethan writer next to Shakespeare himself, but also of the two dozen or so members of the acting company with which Shakespeare had long been associated. For, seven years after Shakespeare's death in 1616, these people, among a good many others, collected his plays into an elaborate volume, the famous First Folio, and published it at a price clearly indicating the prestige associated with the Shakespeare name. Ben Jonson wrote an introductory tribute (incidentally, one of the finest such ever composed by a literary genius in honor of one of his fellows) ; the volume was dedicated to two well-known titled Englishmen of the day; and is prefaced by the names of twenty-six members of the acting troupe, then known as the King's Men, that Shakespeare had both written for, and probably on occasion acted with. Shakespeare's own name heads the list of twenty-six.

The outlandish assumptions pile up *ad infinitum.* What, for example, of the fact that Shakespeare was buried not in the churchyard, but actually inside the church? An exceedingly rare privilege today, it was equally so in Shakespeare's time. A dilemma poses itself. If the "Shakespeare" buried inside the Stratford parish church was really an imposter, then the name under which he was buried would have had to be prominent enough to enable the conspirators to get away with interring him in so prestigious a location. Are we to assume that somebody else named William Shakespeare was so famous that he would be entitled to burial within the church? If so, who? And, most important, why?

It is, of course, foolish to state flatly that such-and-such cannot possibly be so under any circumstances. It is conceivable, if one tries very hard, to imagine that the astronauts have engaged in a conspiracy to conceal the fact that the moon is, after all, made of green cheese: sneaking those rocks (perhaps created in a secret laboratory) aboard before blast-off, faking the television transmissions, somehow preloading the still cameras with convincing negatives and slides. After all, everything they have shown us corresponds pretty much to what we thought the moon was like all along.

And so one must admit that, yes, to a person prepared to entertain this possibility, it may be possible to believe that Bacon, or somebody else, wrote the plays attributed to Shakespeare. But it does seem, to put it most mildly, unlikely in the extreme.

shall and will, use of. Old-fashioned grammarians, or those committed passionately to what they regard as "proper usage," like to point out that in first-person sentences *shall* is used to express "simple futurity"; *will* to express determination. *I shall be with you shortly* and *I will never give in!* illustrate this "rule."

But the fact is that both American and British usage has for many years been exactly the reverse. When General MacArthur left Corregidor, he said, "I *shall* return." And surely determination, not "simple futurity," was implicit in Winston Churchill's famous and ringing remarks: "We shall not flag or fail . . . . we shall fight on the beaches, we shall fight on the landing grounds, we shall fight in the fields and on the streets, we shall fight in the hills; we shall never surrender." The popular marching song goes not "We will overcome," but "We *shall* overcome."

sheet (or heat) lighting. Although it looks different, in fact sheet lighting is the same as any other kind; it's just so far away that you see only the diffused reflection. Obviously, the word *heat* has no significance as a descriptive term.

Sherlock Holmes. At no point in any of the fifty-six short stories and four novels that Arthur Conan Doyle wrote about his famous detective does Holmes say either "Elementary, my dear Watson," or "Quick, Watson, the needle!"

shingles encircling the body. It is popularly believed that if the eruption called shingles, or herpes, makes its way completely around the body, the patient invariably dies. There is no truth in the belief. Not often is the body completely encircled; but if it should happen, death is not the inevitable result.

ship auger. The long augers which antique dealers call ship augers have nothing to do with ships at all. They were used in the construction of *log* "ships"; that is, log rafts that floated timber to the mills.

ships suspended halfway between surface and floor of ocean. An old belief has it that a ship will sink only so far in deep water: until it reaches the point where the increasing density of the water is balanced by the density of the ship. But water is virtually incompressible; its density is only slightly more at great depths than at the surface. Thus, a ship that sinks at all will go all the way.

ship's tonnage. When the average landlubber reads the tonnage of a ship, he quite naturally assumes that the figure represents the number of tons the ship itself would weigh if it could be placed on a pair of scales. But this is quite wrong: the whole subject of rating ships can be very confusing to the layman, as there are at least six different methods. These three are the most common:

1. Gross tonnage, used for passenger ships: a measure of the enclosed capacity of the vessel. The enclosed space is figured in cubic feet, divided by 100 (a hundred such cubic feet being considered one ton). The result is the gross tonnage. Thus the old *Queen Elizabeth* did not weigh 83,673 tons; it had 8,367,300 cubic feet of capacity.

2. Deadweight tonnage, used for freighters and tankers. This has nothing to do with the weight of the vessel because that is excluded. Deadweight tonnage is the total weight in tons avoirdupois of everything the ship *can carry* when she is fully loaded. Thus if you loaded your car (fully) with junk to sell, drove onto the scales, unloaded and recorded the weight again, the difference between the two figures would be your car's "deadweight tonnage."

3. Displacement tonnage, used for warships. In this case the figure represents total tons avoirdupois of the ship *and* its full load. It is computed by taking the number of cubic feet of sea water displaced by the ship when she is loaded down to the loadline and dividing by 35 (a ton of sea water occupies 35 cubic feet) .

Not one of these ship's measures represents the weight of the vessel itself.

Confusion in tonnage ratings has been going on for about three hundred years. In seventeenth-century France one ton avoirdupois was considered to be equivalent to the capacity of four wine tuns (or 42 cubic feet on the average) . The word "ton" itself has been a constant source of confusion, sometimes relating to the wine tun, and sometimes to the avoirdupois ton.

shooting stars. In spite of their name, these phenomena are not stars, of course, but meteorites, or small masses heated to incandescence as they pass through the earth's atmosphere.

Siamese twins. This is not to say that there are no such things. The name, however, is something of a misnomer, since it was first applied to Chang and Eng who, though born in Siam in 1811, were actually three fourths Chinese, the father being Chinese, the mother one half Chinese. Their story is indeed a fascinating one. They ended up as American citizens, taking the name Bunker, and before the Civil War were slaveholders in North Carolina.

Many who know Mark Twain's account of a "Siamese" pair, *Those Extraordinary Twins,* assume that he made up out of whole cloth the tale of Luigi and Angelo, particularly the typically Twainian touch of seeing to it that one (Luigi) was a heavy drinker while the other (Angelo) was a teetotaler. But the fact is that the real Chang was actually a heavy drinker—and the real Eng was a teetotaler. And, apparently, it did cause problems.

One would assume, incidentally, that there must be alive today descendants of Chang and Eng: Chang had seven daughters and three sons; Eng, seven sons and five daughters. Speculations as to methodology are left to the reader.

sideburns. Many people think that the term was coined to describe the location, but originally the word was *burnsides,* after the Civil War general who liked them, Ambrose E. Burnside. No doubt because the *side* in his name can indeed so easily be taken for the location of sideburns, the two elements got turned around.

side-slip. The maneuver by which aircraft, particularly the small single-engined variety, kill some of their altitude and airspeed when approaching for a landing is not so called by pilots. It's called a forward slip. And for good reason; an airplane that truly slipped sidewise would be in a very bad situation indeed. Airplane wings are not designed to provide lift when presented endwise to the atmosphere.

signing of the Magna Carta. The event which so many hail as the first step to English democracy did not take place. The Magna Carta was not signed; it is even a matter of considerable doubt whether King John could write. It was, however, "sealed."

Sign of the Four, The. Not the title of the second of the Sherlock Holmes novels. In *The Complete Sherlock Holmes,* described in a note to the reader as "the only complete, definitive edition of these famous stories," and published by Doubleday under arrangement with A. Conan Doyle's estate, the title is given as *The Sign of Four*—no second *the.*

silver fox. In spite of its name, which implies something else, the silver fox is not a separate species; it belongs to the red fox family.

sin, original. Has nothing whatever to do with sex. "This First Book proposes, first in brief, the whole subject,—Man's disobedience, and the loss thereupon of Paradise, wherein he was placed . . ." So says John Milton, in the "Argument," or preliminary synopsis, for Book I of *Paradise Lost.* He puts it much more grandly, of course, in those wonderful, soaring words with which Book I actually opens:

> Of Man's first disobedience, and the fruit
> Of that forbidden tree, whose mortal taste
> Brought death into the world, and all our woe,
> With loss of Eden, till one greater Man
> Restore us, and regain the blissful seat,
> Sing, heavenly Muse . . .

So it's obvious what the original sin was: disobedience. Indeed, if one stops to think about it, the only "sin" possible in Eden *was* disobedience; one can scarcely commit a "conventional"

sin when living in ignorance of good and evil. Or, to put it another way, how could either Adam or Eve have done wrong when
they didn't know what *wrong* meant? Of course, it can be argued
that even disobedience was scarcely a sin under these conditions;
but that's a problem Milton himself, along with just about every
other theologian, wrestles with, and it is not proposed to solve it
here.

sirloin, **origin of.** The origin of the term *sirloin* for steak—expensive steak, that is—has given rise to a widely accepted myth.
As the tale goes, some medieval or renaissance prince or lord is
served an unusually good piece of meat. Hauling out his sword,
which presumably he wears at dinner, he touches the steak and
proclaims, "I dub thee Sir Loin!"

The whole tale is nonsense, although it does provide a classic
example of folk-etymology, or the contriving of an explanation
for the origin of a word not because it is correct, but because it
sounds as if it is.

Sirloin derives in perfectly plain fashion from two French words
which mean "above the loin," because that's where sirloin comes
from. The original spelling, which was *surloin,* makes it more
obvious; it was a variant of *sur* ("above") and *loigne,* or *loine*
("loin").

six-guns and the fast draw. Western movies are more sophisticated than those of a generation or two ago; concomitantly has
emerged a debunking of many Old West myths. But there still
persists the notion that gunfighters shot from the hip. They did
not. Neither, of course, did they take the careful two-handed aim
modern marksmen employ in today's peaceful target shooting
contests.

According to Wyatt Earp himself, as quoted in Stuart N. Lake's
Wyatt Earp: Frontier Marshal (1931), the successful gun handler
was the one who took the time to aim (time measured, however,
in split seconds), not the one who was the first to get his gun out
of its holster. And the gun was fired at about the level of the waist,
arm extended with elbow half bent. Earp maintained that shooting from the hip, and likewise "fanning" the gun as sometimes
shown in the movies, were certain paths to death or defeat.

Nor did gunfighters ever shoot two guns at once, from the hip or anywhere else. They often *carried* two: one in reserve. And sometimes the "border shift" might be employed, which meant transferring the loaded gun to the hand which held the emptied one, though Earp says it was rare.

The tendency to debunk has certainly reminded us that men who kill other men either for sport or money are not likely to be admirable figures, during any era. However, some of the debunking itself needs to be taken with a grain or two of salt. The famous fight at the O.K. Corral is a case in point. It certainly did take place; it was certainly not an ambush; and although there were two opposed factions in Tombstone, Arizona, where the fight took place in 1881, one of which included the sheriff (apparently in cahoots with rustlers) and was bitterly anti-Earp, the fact remains that the three Earp brothers and Doc Holliday were legally cleared following attempts to "get" them on a murder charge. Virgil Earp, Morgan Earp, and Holliday were all wounded, the latter only superficially, at the O.K. Corral, which makes the "ambush" theory unlikely, to say the least.

Another myth about the Old West is that it was common practice to carve a notch on a gun butt for each victim. Only "outlaws who killed for the sake of brag," said Earp, ever did this. The myth may have gained much of its currency through Bat Masterson who, like Earp himself, was finally to leave the West for "civilization," Masterson to New York, Wyatt Earp to Los Angeles where he died at eighty, peaceful and prosperous, in 1929.

Apparently a New York collector had pestered Masterson for one of his frontier six-guns. Masterson finally obliged him by buying an old Colt at a pawnshop and then, as a joke, carving twenty-two notches on the butt.

Finally, those who amuse themselves while watching a movie or TV special by counting the number of shots from a "six–gun" before reloading is necessary should be aware that most gunfighters in the Old West could actually shoot only five times before reloading. Especially since actions were often modified for hair-trigger sensitivity, it was common to leave the hammer resting on an empty chamber to avoid the embarrassment of accidentally shooting one's self in the foot or thigh.

skunks spraying scent. Anyone who believes the old myth that a skunk cannot spray its scent if held off the ground by its tail could be due for an unpleasant surprise. The muscles by means of which skunks spray their scent can constrict whether or not the skunk has its feet on the ground.

skyscraper, first appearance of. New York was not the location of the first skyscraper, as is commonly supposed. The first building to be called a skyscraper and built on an all-steel skeleton was the Auditorium building of Chicago, designed by L. H. Sullivan and completed in 1889. It boasted ten stories. However, the next year, 1890, the World Building was finished in New York. It had twenty-six stories and was 375 feet high.

skyscrapers swaying in the wind. It is widely believed that tall buildings may sway as much as eight feet or more in a strong wind. It has been said in Chicago that tenants of the John Hancock Center, some 1,000 feet high, get seasick in a high wind; one tenant was reported by *Time* (January 4, 1971), to have said that during one storm there were whitecaps in his toilet. When the Woolworth Building in New York City was built, it was said that on a breezy day it might sway as much as eighteen inches; and some New Yorkers believe that the Empire State Building can sway eight feet.

The fact is that no high-rise buildings sway more than a matter of a few inches. In fact, they probably do not "sway" at all in the usual sense of the word (that is, a regular movement back and forth, like an inverted pendulum). They may, it is true, deflect from the vertical. In 1934, Alfred Bossom described in *Building to the Skies: The Romance of the Skyscraper* the effect of a three-day seventy-mile-an-hour gale on a 450-foot-high building in Dallas. Exact measurements showed that before the wind dropped the building had leaned just ten inches out of plumb, a matter of about one-fortieth of an inch to the foot, not enough to be perceptible to tenants. Three days later, says Bossom, everything had straightened itself out again.

Certainly no structure, big or small, is absolutely rigid, nor should be. In very high winds, say Earle Shultz and Walter Simmons in *Offices in the Sky* (1959), the Empire State Building may sway two and one half inches from the vertical—a far cry from eight feet. Bossom was convinced that tenants may often be persuaded that a tall building is swaying during a bad storm either because inadequate weatherstripping lets in wind enough to cause some movement of pictures, china, etc.; or else periodic movements larger than those of the building itself create the illusion that the building must be moving much more than it actually is. He mentions a lamp, presumably pendant, in a New York skyscraper the amplitude of whose swing is some fifty times that of the tower itself; a very slight movement of the building would, under the right circumstances, thus create the illusion of considerable "swaying."

slanted eyes of Orientals. Although they may seem to, the eyes of Chinese, Japanese, and other Orientals do not slant; they are, in fact, closer to the horizontal than those of non-Orientals. The *effect* is produced by a low nose bridge and the Mongolian, or epicanthic, fold of the upper eyelid—one of the very few genuine "racial" characteristics, incidentally. Children of Caucasian parents often show the apparent Mongolian slant until the nasal bridge develops.

smart Yankee and dirty Jew. Among the more nonsensical manifestations of ethnic stereotyping is that those very qualities which, in the American tradition, lead to thigh-slapping approval when applied to the Yankee horse-trader change direction at once when applied to Jews.

Your Yankee horse-trader is smart; has to be watched every minute or he'll take advantage of you; knows just how to undercut the opposition psychologically; and always come out on top in any kind of deal. Good sound old American initiative and know-how; you got to give 'em credit, right?

But Abie the pawnbroker: ah, that's another matter. Apply exactly the same concepts to him, and what have you got? One of *them,* that's what. Maybe *nonsensical* isn't a strong enough word, come to think about it.

Smithsonian, the. The Smithsonian is an institution, not an institute. Perhaps the lack of euphony—all those *n*'s—has inspired the common error of calling it the Smithsonian Institute. It is not, by the way, named for someone called Smith; its founding was the result of a bequest by one James Smithson. And the most famous feature of the institution, its museum, is not, strictly speaking, a part of the Smithsonian Institution at all, but exists merely under its direction. The museum is, correctly, simply the United States National Museum.

smog. Most of us have the impression that smog, if not a new phenomenon, is certainly a new word. Actually smog was prevalent in Chicago and Pittsburgh by the turn of the century. The word itself was coined, according to the *Oxford English Dictionary*, by a Dr. Des Voeux, in 1905. It is what linguists call a "portmanteau" word, made by telescoping, of course, *smoke* and *fog.*

snakes. Few creatures excite such a mixture of awe, fear, and fascination as snakes. And few are the subject of so many myths and folk beliefs. One of the oldest is that it was a "snake" in the Garden of Eden which was responsible, in John Milton's words, for bringing "death into the world, and all our woe." But there is no reference to a snake in Genesis; it is, rather, a "serpent" that tempted Eve. Serpents, in antiquity, were not necessarily snakes; any creeping thing, especially if venomous or noxious, was called a serpent. In the fifteenth and sixteenth centuries, the term was applied to a variety of creatures, including both salamanders and crocodiles. (Admittedly the temptation of Eve by a crocodile does seem to verge on the ridiculous.)

Snakes do not swallow their young to protect them. But big snakes sometimes eat little snakes, often alive. The digestive juices of snakes are so quick-acting and strong—they can in a short time turn bone into powder—that any "young" swallowed are consumed, not protected. Nor are there any snakes with poisonous stingers in the ends of their tails. Some, like the red-bellied mud snake, or *Farancia abacura,* have sharp, spiny scales there; and if handled, the mud snake will strike with its tail. However, the scale is only about one sixteenth of an inch long and is not poisonous.

Quite obviously, another myth sometimes expressed—that snakes have been known to kill trees by striking them with the poisonous tips of their tails—cannot be true. Nor can any snake kill a full-grown tree either by striking it or biting it.

That St. Patrick drove the snakes out of Ireland is doubtless regarded by most people as a charming old tale not to be taken seriously. But it might be pointed out that many islands do not have and, so far as can be determined, never have had snakes. Nor do many take seriously the mythical glass snake, which upon being dismembered can reassemble itself; or the hoop snake, which is not mythical but certainly does not roll away, its tail in its mouth (it is said sometimes to roll after its victim, in which case the victim is supposed to run uphill). Nor can the coachwhip snake, *Masticophis flagellum*, whip its tormentors or enemies; it just looks like a coachwhip, and is entirely harmless. There is actually a legless lizard, not a snake (lizards have eyelids and ear openings, snakes do not), *Ophisaurus ventralis*, which will grow a new tail, as many lizards can, if the original tail is broken off. But it cannot reunite its original tail with its body, and if it is cut in half it dies.

Unlike the nonexistent glass snake, the milk snake, like the coachwhip, actually exists; but it does not milk cows. Even the most patient bovine is scarcely going to stand still for double rows of needle-sharp teeth. Actually, milk snakes are a great help to the farmer, for they feed upon the mice that feed upon the feed.

Black snakes (black racers, black rat snakes) are often said to be good to have around because they eat poisonous snakes. True, they sometimes eat smaller snakes, but not usually poisonous ones. In fact, black snakes get on so well with rattlesnakes and copperheads that they frequently hibernate in the same dens. And black snakes are often kept in captivity in the same cages as rattlesnakes and copperheads.

The puff adder (or puffing adder, hissing adder, or hognose, by all of which names and others the small American snake is known) is perfectly harmless. Contrary to what many think, it does not blow poisonous vapor at its foes nor can it inflict a wound; even if it could, the wound would not be envenomed, since the puff adder hasn't any venom sacs. All it does is try—most successfully—to look and sound very fearsome when aroused. The *African* puff adder is quite different. It's both big and venomous.

Some think that snakes cannot regurgitate their food because their teeth point toward the rear. This is nonsense. Snake teeth are generally very short; and snakes, especially if they are handled shortly after having eaten, can and often do regurgitate whole, large animals like squirrels and rabbits.

That the pilot black snake, *Elaphe obsoleta*, leads copperheads and rattlesnakes back to their dens in time of danger is one of those myths reflecting the human tendency to see the world of humankind reflected in the world of otherkind. The fact is that the pilot snake is simply more active than his lethal companions, with whom he often shares a den during the winter. In early spring, when the snakes come out of the den to sun during mid-day before actually leaving it, any sign of danger sends them scurrying back. The pilot snake just scurries faster; he isn't "leading" the others back, he's simply getting there first.

That snakes both charm and can be charmed belongs in the category of folk myth. Birds know snakes to be enemies; but sometimes they will try to decoy a snake away from the nest by approaching the snake closely. If the bird miscalculates the snake's striking distance, it will suffer the consequences not of having been "charmed," but of having been a poor judge of distance. And cobras are not "charmed" by flutes. Snakes do not, in fact, have ears; they sense vibrations in the earth rather than hear sounds as people do. The cobra sways in time with the flute because it is trying to get into position to strike at it. It is up to the charmer to keep the flute in motion so that the cobra cannot do so. He, too, had better be a good judge of distance or suffer the consequences.

There's no truth in the old folk belief that even if you cut off the head of a snake, it won't die until sunset. No doubt the belief arose because the reflex system of snakes continues to operate after death. In fact, in the higher animals this may also happen; all the organs do not "die" at once. But in snakes the tendency is more pronounced; a snake's heart may continue to beat, for example, for many hours after decapitation. It may even go right on beating after sunset, depending on when the snake was beheaded. But a headless snake is scarcely "alive."

Those cowboys or campers who encircle their sleeping bags with rope in the belief that snakes won't cross it are relying on a dangerous myth. Snakes don't at all mind crawling over ropes, as repeated experiments have proved.

As is true of flying fish, no snakes can actually fly, though some people believe they can. There is a species found in southeastern Asia and other locations that can glide for short distances by extending a webbed membrane running along each side of its body. But it cannot ascend, only descend by gliding.

A tale often told and often believed is the Fang in the Boot. Someone is bitten by a poisonous snake and dies. Years later, the man's son puts on the father's boot and, scratched by the still-embedded fang, dies. Occasionally the tale even involves the third generation: a grandson puts on the boot and is killed also. A large rattlesnake's fangs might be able to pierce a pair of thin leather boots and kill the first man, but that would be the end of it. Not enough venom would remain in the fang to kill anyone else. Even if it did, it would lose its potency with time and exposure.

As for snakes laying eggs, some do and some don't. Rattlesnakes, among many others, don't; so attribute it either to local ignorance or local joking, scare-the-tourist variety, if a Wyoming native warns you against rattlesnake eggs. (It's almost certain to be the latter; natives of Wyoming know where rattlesnakes come from.)

Finally, venomous snakes do not reserve their poison for their enemies, as is sometimes thought. They use it for a most practical reason: to kill their prey. They are themselves immune to their own venom if they swallow it.

snow as fertilizer. Contrary to a prevalent notion, snow does **not** "fertilize" any better than rain, both of which do bring certain elements from the air—nitrogen, for example. The advantage of snow over rain is that it may protect against frost damage, and may well provide a more uniform supply of moisture, without danger of erosion, as it melts.

solstices, summer and winter. It usually comes as a surprise to most people, but the dates on which the sun shines the longest in the Northern Hemisphere (summer solstice) or the shortest (winter solstice) are not invariably June 21 and December 21. The dates are June 22 and December 22 in years which precede leap years.

SOS. The universal symbol requesting aid, contrary to what is often said, doesn't stand for "Save Our Ship," or "Save Our Souls." It doesn't, in fact, stand for anything. It was selected because it is very simple both to remember and to transmit—three dots, three dashes, three dots. It is not, by the way, an oral signal, but strictly a Morse code one. The oral signal is *mayday,* perhaps selected because it sounds like the French *m'aidez,* or "help me."

South Sea Bubble. The South Sea Company was organized in England in 1711, was given a trading monopoly in the Pacific Islands and South America, and took over the national debt at 6 percent interest. It collapsed amid much scandal. Most people take it for granted that when the South Sea Bubble burst, that was the end of the South Sea Company. It is true that the stock dropped from 1,000 to 135 in four months, that "most notorious, dangerous and infamous corruption" was disclosed, and that the estates of the directors were confiscated by Parliament. However, the South Sea Company continued on until the end of the century, a span of some ninety years from its founding.

Spanish food. There is a widespread belief that Spanish food is hot and peppery. Actually the Spanish cuisine is rather bland, much less striking, for example, than the Italian. Probably the hot dishes from Mexico that are featured in so many parts of the United States are the causes of this misapprehension.

Incidentally, the Spanish people themselves are thought by many to be volatile. In Spain the people are conservative, kind to strangers, and not particularly excitable—except at bullfights.

Spanish moss. Some travelers in the South have looked up at branches festooned with Spanish moss and sadly concluded that this growth would inevitably kill the trees.

In the first place Spanish "moss" is not a moss at all. It is an epiphyte, that is an independent, nonparasitic plant that develops its own nourishment from the air, not from the tree. It can grow just as well on a telephone wire.

Even the great Linnaeus was dead wrong about one feature of the plant. So convinced was he that it eschewed moisture that he named it Tillandsia, after Elias Tillands, who is said to have harbored a great repugnance for water. (He walked a thousand miles rather than cross the narrow Gulf of Bothnia.) Actually Spanish moss does best in a moist environment.

"Spare the rod and spoil the child." This is neither a quotation from the Bible nor an anonymous proverb. It is to be found in Samuel Butler's *Hudibras,* published in the seventeenth century.

However, Prov. 13:24 gives, "He that spareth his rod hateth his son: but he that loveth him chasteneth him betimes," and the poet Menander says, "The man who has never been flogged has never been taught."

speeds of flying creatures. For many years it was taken for granted that certain kinds of birds and insects could achieve very great speeds in flight. Botflies, it was believed, would cruise at 400 m.p.h., and even get up to more than 800 m.p.h. Then someone pointed out that if this were true, people would be killed by speeding botflies; even a tallow candle will penetrate a board at such a velocity. Researchers have now concluded that no insect flies much over 24 m.p.h.—perhaps getting up to 36 m.p.h., for short intervals.

spelling. Spelling is no indicator of intelligence, or even of literacy or skill. F. Scott Fitzgerald, among many other notable writers, was a very bad speller. Highly intelligent people may be very poor spellers. What is often overlooked or unknown is that uniformity in spelling, or attempts thereat, is quite a recent development in English, linguistically speaking, springing from the rapid increase in printed material since Shakespeare's day. During that period of English literature commonly regarded as its summit, the time of Elizabeth I, nobody worried much about "correct spelling." Not even proper names were spelled consistently; of the few fairly certain examples of Shakespeare's actual handwriting we have, all of them his signature, not one is spelled exactly the same as any other. The spelling *Shakespeare* is, in fact, merely an agreed-upon convention.

Writing derives from speech, and spelling is simply an attempt to capture the sound of a word through conventional symbols. But no two people sound a word exactly the same way. Chaucer, like his contemporaries, spelled phonetically. But in the century following his death, printing came to England. And printing tends to fix the *forms* of words. There was no way to fix their *sounds* until the twentieth-century invention and spread of recording devices. However, since these devices merely reproduce, with varying accuracy, the various ways different people pronounce the same word, we still have not achieved uniformity of pronunciation—nor prevented it from changing over the years since Thomas Edison and Guglielmo Marconi. (It may be that radio and television have to some degree modified *regional variations* in speech; but this is another matter.)

Not until the middle of the eighteenth century did English spelling achieve something approaching uniformity; and even by then, pronunciations had changed markedly in many respects. And they have continued to change; Alexander Pope rhymed *tea* and *obey*, but today *tea* is obviously sounded much differently. However, it's *still* spelled the same.

Obviously, then, spelling is simply a formalized convention. Nor has it been really based on sound since Geoffrey Chaucer's day; one can come pretty close to achieving Chaucer's pronunciation simply by sounding all the letters, although there have been certain shifts in vowel values since his time. Bernard Shaw once amused himself by pointing out that *ghoti* can today quite logically spell "fish": *gh* as in *enough; o* as in *women; ti* as in *nation*. And so it can; but it doesn't. Shaw's attempts at a more logical spelling, however, were doomed to failure, as are all such attempts. For pronunciations will continue to change, spelling or no. *Coupe*—with or without the accent mark—was *coopay* not so long ago. Today's "logical" or "phonetic" spelling, fixed in form by the printing press, would become tomorrow's convention, whether it "made sense" or not. In any case, viewed from the long perspective of the history of our language, spelling—or, more precisely, making a fetish of it—is quite a Johnny-come-lately. One wonders how intelligence and literacy were judged back in the days when England's greatest literary genius was spelling his name *Shakspere* on one page of his will and *Shakspeare* on the next.

***Spirit of '76, The* (painting).** This famous picture, showing a boy and a man as drummers while a third man plays the fife, was not painted during the time of the American Revolution, was not originally called *The Spirit of '76*, and did not in fact represent soldiers in the revolutionary army when it was conceived.

The first version of the painting, done by Archibald Willard of Wellington, Ohio, a Civil War veteran, was apparently not intended as a serious work. It shows three Civil War recruits in civilian clothes parading in lighthearted fashion; it is actually more cartoon than anything else. On the advice of a friend, Willard did a much more elaborate and solemn variation, adding the revolutionary costumes, the wounded or dying figure in the foreground, and other touches.

split infinitive. It is widely thought that a prohibition against splitting the infinitive is one of the fixed and unvarying rules of grammar. Not only does the split infinitive have nothing to do with grammar (rather, with style or "rhetoric"), it is an old and honorable device used by many respectable writers. Even the purists would have to admit that the following sentence could read only as follows (without, of course, recasting the sentence and changing the words): "The Commission has been feeling its way to modifications intended *to better equip* successful candidates for careers." It is quite impossible to move the adverb any place else without making the sentence ambiguous.

spoiled priest. This term, both used by, and sometimes applied to, F. Scott Fitzgerald, does not mean either a priest who has had an excess of attention paid to him, or one who has slipped from the standard to which he is expected to adhere. The term refers merely to a candidate for the priesthood who fails to take his vows.

"Stardust." Hoagy Carmichael's lovely tune is so often heard in lush instrumental or vocal arrangements that it is hard to realize it was originally published as a piano solo: a ragtime piano solo, as a matter of fact. So perfectly wedded do tune and lyrics seem in "Stardust" that Carmichael is often thought to be author of both. He wasn't. The lyrics are by Mitchell Parish.

***Stars and Stripes* in American Revolution.** The numerous paintings, all of them long after the fact, which show Old Glory being flown by revolutionary troops—for example, the Howard Pyle picture of Washington and Steuben at Valley Forge—are in error. It was not until 1783 that Congress supplied Washington with any official stars-and-stripes flags. By that time, all the big battles were over.

stars in the United States flag as representing the various states. No particular star in the flag now stands for, or has ever stood for, any particular state. There were stars in the flag for years before the Constitution was adopted; indeed, until 1912 there was not even a legal order of arrangement for the stars. In fact, the notion that each state should have its own star was specifically rejected during debates over adoption of the Flag Act of 1818. As Quaife *et al.* say in *The History of the United States Flag* (1961), "The stars thus represent the States collectively, and no particular star has any regional or local significance."

Among other perpetuators of the myth is Edward Everett Hale, in his THE MAN WITHOUT A COUNTRY; as the old Philip Nolan lies dying, he points to the stars on the flag and says, "Tell me their names . . . . The last I know is Ohio . . . . But where are your other fourteen?"

stars seen in daylight from the bottom of a well or shaft. That someone who looks up at the sky from the bottom of a well or mine shaft can see stars in daylight is one of those persistent myths that survive, apparently, because no one bothers to check them out. Since it is the brightness of the daytime sky that hides the stars from view, looking up from the bottom of a well will scarcely reduce this brightness; if anything, it will make it all the more apparent by contrast.

statistics, use, misuse, and abuse of. Those who own Corvette automobiles in and around New York City must have felt a chill of fear recently upon reading, in a magazine devoted to sports cars, that the average life of a Corvette in a New York City parking space—before it gets stolen, that is, not bashed to pieces—is one hour. A reasonable inference would be never to park a Corvette in New York for any period of time beyond 59 minutes. The "statistic" is, of course, absurd.

The "average life" figure obviously had to be derived from owners of stolen Corvettes; one does not derive statistics on stolen cars from owners of cars which have not been stolen. So what the statistic actually means is that if a Corvette is going to be stolen at all, it is most likely to happen within one hour after it has been parked, which is scarcely surprising; even a dim-witted car thief knows that his chance of getting away with it decreases in direct proportion to the decreasing time he has available before the owner returns.

The only possible way to state with certainty the "average life" of any car parked on a New York or any other street would be to interview every owner who parked, whether his car was stolen or not, and then derive an "average life" figure. But of course this is an impossible task. Meanwhile, Corvette owners are frightened by a "fact" that turns out to have no validity whatever.

No matter how much reverence is paid to anything purporting to be "statistics," the term has no meaning unless the source, relevance, and truth are all checked.

Too commonly, gross figures are used without qualification. To speak with horror of the some 50,000 traffic deaths which have occurred yearly in recent times and then compare it with the lesser figures of a generation ago is to falsify the truth. Population growth and the increased number of vehicles on the road must, among other factors, be considered. If they are, it turns out that driving is a good deal safer now in the United States than it was in the 1930s.

Data purporting to compare the safety of various means of travel also need to be carefully assessed. Airline safety records are impressive—in terms of mileage. Expressed so, a commercial airliner appears to be far safer than a family automobile. But one's life is measured not in miles, but in time. A jet liner covering some 600 miles an hour has a very large built-in "statistical" advantage over the automobile which takes perhaps 12 hours to cover 600 miles. It would be quite proper to say that one is as safe—or as unsafe—in an automobile for one hour as in an airliner for five minutes.

If mileage traveled rather than time spent is the only criterion, then as of this writing American spaceships are far and away the safest mode of travel, having over the years covered millions and millions of miles with no injuries to their crews. (The only fatalities were on the ground.) A supersonic aircraft like the Concorde, which flies at nearly three times the speed of conventional jets, enjoys an equivalent "statistical" advantage.

Other factors need to be considered also, of course. The safety of an automobile journey is a *controllable* variable; one generally can choose whom to ride with, for example. This is obviously not so in airline travel. In fact, it is simply impossible to say that airline travel is safer than driving one's own car. One can only say that airliners travel more miles per fatality than automobiles.

But even here serious questions arise; there is no way to determine accurately what the total mileage of all automobiles in the United States is for a given year; no agency collects this information on a scientific basis. With scheduled airlines, one can come close to an accurate figure simply by consulting records of flights completed, records which are kept and available.

Only when someone is clever enough to derive a direct comparison, in terms of safety, between hours spent on airliners and hours spent driving or riding in an automobile will safety figures have any real meaning.

A common misconception is that as one continues to engage in hazardous activity, the chance of mishap increases with each experience. But this confuses generalized data with individual experience. Only the chance of death by old age increases with "experience," that is to say time and its contents, so to speak. Crop dusters live dangerous lives; but each flight is a separate experience. Statistically, every flight, every journey, each experience, starts with a clean slate. Indeed, if experience counts for anything, the chance of trouble decreases, not increases, as time goes on.

The built in bias of the statistics gatherer often interferes with objectivity, of course. And increased efficiency of the data gathering process may lead to false assumptions. A computerized data bank which makes easier the tiresome task of sending in crime reports will almost automatically show an increase in "crime" when it is installed. And it has been argued that some of the increases in crime reported from the ghetto result not from an actual increase, but from the fact that police departments, sensitive to the times, no longer tend to ignore murder, rape, and other serious crimes in ghetto neighborhoods. (In past years, the time and bother of a murder investigation could only too easily be avoided by listing a killing in a neighborhood with no social or economic clout as "accidental shooting." Case closed.)

Public utilities frequently use statistics to their advantage when determining their rate bases, regulated by law. If a power and light company has invested $100,000,000 in its plants and equipment and clears ten million dollars in a year, its profit—usually also regulated—is 10 percent. But the facilities built over the years could not be duplicated today at the same prices. So utilities would prefer to take the *replacement cost* as a basis, as if it were likely that its whole physical plant might be destroyed all at once and have to be rebuilt. This higher figure obviously makes it appear that the profit margin is lower.

Sports writers and sports pages contribute their confusions, of course. It sounds much better to say that a batter "hits .300" than to write that he hit about thirty percent of pitches thrown to him.

But perhaps the most profound misconception spawned by the worship of statistics is the concept of the "average." In its current sense, "average" goes back only to the eighteenth century. Today we speak of the average man, the average household, the average child, as if there really were such things. There are not. There cannot be. "Average" is purely a statistical abstraction; it has no existence in the real world.

In a village of one hundred where fifty people earn $50,000 a year and the remaining fifty earn nothing at all, the average income is $25,000. Of course, nobody earns that, or anything like it, in this admittedly simplified example. Still, $25,000 is the "average income." The only problem is that the average income earner does not exist.

Finally, the worship of statistics has had the particularly unfortunate result of making the job of the plain, outright liar that much easier. As recent events have proved once again, there are those, in high places as well as low, who do lie deliberately, with neither passion nor regret. And a lie cast in the form of a table or a graph or a row of figures is most effective of all. Not only does it look impressive; it demands positive effort to nail down as a lie. One must check sources, references, and their validity; the burden of proof has been shifted from the liar to his victim.

steam. You just think you can see it. Like most other gases, steam is invisible. Only when it cools enough so minute droplets of water condense is it visible. If one looks closely at the spout of a boiling teakettle, one can observe a small space of what looks like air between the spout and the mist. *That* is steam.

Still water runs deep. Another example of fatuosity rampant. (See EXCEPTION PROVES THE RULE.) Still water doesn't run at all, now does it?

Stonehenge. It used to be thought—and still is by many—that Stonehenge was erected by the Druids. The idea was promoted in the seventeenth century by John Aubrey, the biographer of Thomas Hobbes, and it has persisted ever since. Even now there is a modern sect called the Ancient Order of Druids which annually celebrates at Stonehenge the solstice sunrise.

Stonehenge, however, is a Bronze Age creation, going back to the second millennium B.C., whereas the Druids in Britain were of the Iron Age, arriving there in the middle of the third century B.C.—that is, more than a thousand years later.

storage battery. Despite the implications of its name, a storage battery doesn't store electricity. It stores chemicals which, under the right conditions, create electricity; in other words, it stores chemical energy, not electrical energy. Nor does recharging a storage battery put any electricity back into it; rather, electrical energy is changed into chemical energy and stored in the cells— the reverse, in other words, of what happens when the battery is supplying current.

The amount of voltage a storage-battery cell delivers bears no relationship to the size of the cell; in the common automobile zinc-acid battery, it's about one and one half volts no matter how large the plates are made to be. Four cells connected properly deliver about six volts; eight, about twelve volts. A battery as big as a house would do no more—in terms of voltage, or electrical "pressures," that is.

Current, or the *amount* of electricity delivered, is another matter. A battery as big as a house would last a very long time indeed before it ran out of juice.

The zinc in the common automobile-type storage battery is consumed, as current is created, by its chemical reaction with the other components. It is, thus, a fuel; if zinc were as cheap as coal and as common as waterfalls, batteries as big as—or bigger than —a house would no doubt be commonplace, and we would not need dams, nuclear reactors, or steam plants.

straightjacket. *Straight* and *strait* come from separate sources. The former is derived from the past participle of a Middle English word, *strecchen,* "to stretch." The latter comes from Middle English *streit,* meaning "tight, close, or narrow." (The word *strait* as used by geographers and mapmakers derives from this latter source.) Thus, the correct form is *straitjacket*.

Stratford-on-Avon. The birth and burial place of William Shakespeare is not usually so called by its present-day residents. They prefer Stratford-*upon*-Avon. Incidentally, there are other Avons than the familiar one; Bath is near its own Avon River, an equally beautiful stream.

strawberry. The straw in strawberry has nothing to do with the occasional use of straw in its cultivation. The word is most unusual in that although it is quite old—Aelfric used it about A.D. 1000—it has no cognate form in any other Germanic language. Theories about its etymology are only speculative; some propose that the resemblance of the long runners to straw may have inspired it; others, that its origin may lie in the fact that in past times strawberries were commonly strung on straws. But no one really knows.

Stutz Bearcat. The Stutz Bearcat is almost always associated with the Roaring Twenties—F. Scott Fitzgerald and John Held, Jr., *Vanity Fair,* and flappers. But the famous Bearcat does not belong to the twenties; it was distinctly old hat by then, having been introduced in 1914.

It couldn't have been much of a performer. The Stutz Bearcat weighed in at almost 5,000 pounds, with an engine whose maximum horsepower was 60.

subconscious mind. This is neither a Freudian term nor a Freudian concept, although it is often identified with Freud. In fact, in his "The Psychology of the Dream-Processes," a part of *The Interpretation of Dreams,* Freud specifically disavows it. Freud uses the term *unconscious* for what most people seem to think *subconscious* means.

subways (New York) and their "safety" doors. Even many New Yorkers, who should know better, believe that their subway trains won't start unless all doors are completely closed: an alleged safety feature. Of course this is not so; people can be, and sometimes are, caught in a door and dragged away, with consequences not pleasant to dwell upon.

suicide rate in the Great Depression. It is generally believed that after the Crash of 1929 financial men jumped out of windows in such numbers that there was an unprecedented number of suicides. Actually the suicide rate remained the same.

suicide, talking about. In the popular belief, those who talk about killing themselves can safely be ignored; if they talk about it, they never do it. Few folk-beliefs are more fallacious—or more potentially destructive. Those of suicidal tendency who talk about it are clearly reaching out for help. To deny them this help by ignoring them may well insure that what might have been forestalled will actually take place.

An analogous, and equally unfortunate, tendency is to regard those who worry about losing their minds as in no real danger; the ones who go crazy, in popular belief, are never those who express concern about it. This is equally nonsensical. No doubt most people, at one time or another, have fretted about their emotional adjustments, or even worried about "losing their minds." Still, it must be said that emotional breakdowns are no more likely to occur without warning signals than are physical breakdowns. In either case, ignoring the signals, especially on the part of others who might be of help, can be very dangerous.

suntan as a sign of good health. A suntan shows only that the skin has adopted a protective device against further damage by the ultraviolet rays of the sun, which are dangerous just like many other forms of radiation. It certainly is no indication of good health. In fact, during the Renaissance and Elizabethan eras it was a sign of the lower classes, who were constantly exposed to the sun in the outdoors. A suntan or sunburn, incidentally, can be acquired easily enough on a fairly cloudy day; thin clouds do not filter out ultraviolet rays.

surgeon general. *Surgeon general* is not a military title any more than is *attorney general,* although the surgeon general of the Air Force, of the Army, of the Defense Department, etc., does usually hold a general officer's rank. The top officer of the Public Health Service, which is not a military organization, is also called the surgeon general.

Susannah and the Elders. This is a favorite religious subject of many great painters, including Thomas Hart Benton. Many who have seen the numerous depictions of Susannah being spied upon have tried to look up the story in the Bible and wondered why they could not find it. It is not in the Bible but in the Apocrypha, Dan. 13.

suspension bridge, first iron wire. The first iron wire suspension bridge was not, as usually assumed, the Brooklyn Bridge. It was, rather, the Schuylkill River Bridge in Philadelphia, designed and constructed by Erskine Hazard and Josiah White in 1816. Admittedly, it wasn't much of a bridge, having a thirty-three-foot sag and able to support only a half dozen people at a time. But it was a true iron-wire suspension bridge.

Swanee River. Stephen Foster's great song "The Old Folks at Home," which begins, "Way down upon the Swanee River," is dear to the hearts of millions of Americans. Most of them have naturally assumed that the "Swanee River" was dear to Foster's heart. Hardly. In the first place he had never seen the river in his life; in the second place that is not exactly its name.

What happened is that Foster wrote the song in Pittsburgh in 1851, then began looking for a river's name that would sound well. At first he used the Pedee (or Pee Dee) River of North and South Carolina but decided that something more euphonious was needed. His brother then suggested, believe it or not, the Yazoo River. An atlas was consulted; Stephen discovered, and liked the sound of Suwannee, a river which flows through Georgia and northern Florida. But he needed a two-syllable name, so changed Suwannee to Swanee. Strictly speaking, thus, the Swanee River does not exist.

If Stephen Foster had seen the Suwannee, he might have been surprised at what he picked out. Only thirty-five miles of it are in Georgia, and they are in the Okefenokee Swamp country, so that the river's water is about the color of black coffee. From there on it meanders for more than two hundred miles through Florida to the Gulf of Mexico. Most of its length is in swamp and jungle —a home for snapping turtles and water animals—not through rich fields and lovely plantations.

That was not the first time this river's name had been corrupted. Originally it was the San Juan; this evolved into Suwannee, probably through local attempts to pronounce the exotic name.

swastika. Although it is almost universally identified with them, the swastika is far from original with the Nazis who made it infamous. Indeed, the swastika is a very ancient symbol, going back to prehistoric times. That the word is one of the few to be found in almost exactly its present form *(svastika)* in Sanskrit, the oldest written language in the Indo-European family, indicates how long the swastika has been around. Ancient Greek pottery was sometimes decorated with the swastika. It is not, thus, as often believed, an American Indian decoration stolen by Hitler.

Nobody knows for certain what the swastika stands for. Some theorize that it is a sun symbol. The Sanskrit word means something like "he is well," indicating that it stood for something good rather than something bad.

If you still like the design of the swastika in spite of what it came to be associated with, then it can be used in a way that will distinguish it from the Nazi version, at least to the knowledgeable: let the arms point to the left, or counterclockwise. The Nazi swastika always has the arms pointing to the right, or clockwise.

Non-Nazi swastika   **Nazi swastika**

syphilis. Most authorities assert that syphilis was imported to Europe in 1493 by sailors of Columbus who contracted it in the New World. Others maintain that it stems from remote antiquity and was widely dispersed around the world prior to Columbus. Actually it is not positively known where syphilis was distributed prior to 1493, or whether it was already to be found in Europe.

A false belief about the disease is that it may be innocently contracted through superficial contact. As it is a blood disease, this is possible only if there is an open wound or if infected blood or plasma is brought into contact with an uninfected blood system.

Another false belief is that syphilis is hereditary. It is not hereditary but congenital. That is, the disease may not be transmitted through the germ cells of the parents. (See HEREDITARY DISEASES.) However, the corkscrew organism characteristic of syphilis can, if the mother is infected, penetrate the fetus, with the result that the child is born syphilitic. During World War I it was a common but inaccurate assertion that Kaiser Wilhelm II had "hereditary" syphilis.

teeth and pregnancy. "You lose a tooth for every child"—a completely false old wives' tale. In fact, pregnancy doesn't cause calcium to be taken out of the teeth.

teething and healthy teeth. Early teething means healthy teeth or early teething means weak teeth—you can take your choice because the peasant prophecy went both ways depending on the source. In fact, the time schedule of teething has nothing to do with the health of the teeth. Just as some children walk early and talk early or late, others teethe early or late.

teething as a natural function. "Teething is a natural function and should be painless." In fact, teething is a very traumatic experience for the infant. It not only causes pain but has a histaminic effect, almost like an allergy, and so the child's nose and eyes run and he has coldlike symptoms with poor appetite and poor sleeping.

teeth straightening. "Teeth are straightened for cosmetic reasons." In fact, most orthodontic treatment is done for functional purposes so that the occlusion is proper and so that there won't be periodontal breakdown in the fifties, sixties, and seventies. Incidentally and at the same time one's looks are also improved.

telephone, invention of. Alexander Graham Bell was not the first to construct a device, however imperfect, for transmitting sounds by wire. (More accurately, sounds are changed to electrical impulses in a transmitter and then re-created at the receiver. The only device that actually transmits sound by "wire" is the common child's plaything made of two coffee-cans and a length of string.) Fifteen years before Bell's famous summons to his assistant ("Mr. Watson, come here; I want you"), Phillip Reis had invented a crude telephone in Germany. And Elisha Gray had patented a form of telephone in both Great Britain and the United States before Bell. (Gray did not, however, claim credit for inventing the telephone.)

In the United States, there were so many claimants for the honor of having invented the telephone that it took years of litigation before Bell's patent was finally upheld by the Supreme Court—in a divided decision. Certainly *Bell* deserves credit for having made the telephone practicable and for his foresight in prophesying the immense impact the telephone would have in the future.

Reis's instrument, whose principle Reis himself apparently did not fully understand, was unsuited for commercial development and was held by the German patent office, long after its invention, not to be a "speaking telephone." It did, however, transmit and reproduce the sound of the human voice, though not very well. Germans, nonetheless, consider him the "real" inventor of the telephone.

Tell it to the marines. This presumably American folk-saying, with its implicit assumption that one can get away with telling it to somebody else, but not a United States marine, could scarcely be more misapprehended by most people. It turns out to be an old Sir Walter Scott saying, and, in full, reads "Tell that to the marines—the sailors won't believe it."

Another old saying goes, "That will do for the marines, but the sailors won't believe it." and Lord Byron expresses, through one of his characters, a similar sentiment implying that marines are more gullible, not less, than others.

tenderfoot. It is natural to suppose that this word always referred to people—people new at the game, uninitiated and unhardened. Actually it originally referred to a cow, raised in a corral, and then turned out to fend for itself on the range in the West.

"Tennis, anyone?" This oft-quoted line is attributed by Bartlett to Humphrey Bogart; it is said to have been his only line in his first play, though the play is not otherwise identified. Bogart himself, however, denied ever having said it; his denial was a part of an ABC television program, "Play It Again, Sam," broadcast May 9, 1974. In his statement, obviously recorded some years earlier (Bogart died in 1957), he also denied ever having spoken the line "DROP THE GUN, LOUIS"—a fact known to Bogart fans who watch *Casablanca* whenever it is rerun.

Bogart aficionados also know that he does not say "Play it again, Sam," in *Casablanca.*

tenure. Particularly with reference to teachers and college professors, *tenure* is widely misunderstood as a guarantee against dismissal. It is no such thing. To be "on tenure" simply means that one cannot be dismissed *without cause.* In this respect, it differs not at all from the provisions unions generally insist upon in contracts with management. Without tenure, or similar provisions in union contracts, anybody can be fired any time for the most trivial or malicious of reasons—or no reason at all. But anyone who thinks that tenured teachers and professors are forever secure in their jobs is misinformed. There are many grounds on which tenured personnel can be discharged, including incompetence.

But prior to dismissal, there must be some kind of hearing at which both the charges and the evidence supporting them are presented; and quite obviously the person under attack is given the right to defend himself. Since this is exactly the procedure under which persons are tried when they are charged with offenses at law, it is a little difficult to understand why tenure should be so widely regarded as somehow foreign to democratic traditions. Quite the contrary; it is squarely in the mainstream of that American way the opponents of tenure seem so often to invoke.

Thanksgiving Day, first. "Our harvest being gotten in, our governor sent four men on fowling, that we might after a special manner rejoice together after we had gathered the fruit of our labors. The four in one day killed as much fowl as, with a little help beside, served the company almost a week. At which time, amongst us, and among the rest their greatest king Massasoit, with some ninety men, whom for three days we entertained and feasted, and they went out and killed five deer, which they brought to the plantation and bestowed on our governor, and upon the captain and others. And although it be not always so plentiful as it was at this time with us, yet by the goodness of God, we are so far from want that we often wish you partakers of our plenty." As James Deetz and Jay Anderson point out in "The Ethnogastronomy of Thanksgiving" (*Saturday Review of Science*, Nov. 25, 1972), this sole eyewitness description of the festival we now consider the first Thanksgiving—it's by Edward Winslow—nowhere mentions any giving of thanks. Indeed, it bears little relationship to the image of pious sobriety and heaven-directed gratitude we now assume the "first Thanksgiving" to have been. In Deetz's and Anderson's words, "What took place on that fall day some three-and-a-half centuries ago is best understood as the first *harvest festival* held on American soil, the acting out of an institution of great antiquity in the England the Pilgrims had left behind. It was a time for joy, celebration, and carousing, far removed from any suggestion of solemn religious concern."

As the authors go on to point out, the Pilgrims did not choose "a solemn day of thanksgiving" to "formalize their thanks to God." Rather, they opted for a day of "revelry, sports, and feasts" long known to them, back in England, as Harvest Home.

"That government is best which governs least." This quotation which occurs in the first sentence of Henry David Thoreau's *Civil Disobedience* is often attributed to Thomas Jefferson. Occasionally that notion is corrected by showing, rather, that it is from the masthead of the "Democratic Review," to which Thoreau contributed. Actually it is from Thomas Paine. Thoreau, it should be added, did not claim the remark as his.

The average IQ of the American public is that of a child of twelve. When this statement first began making the rounds, the IQ was generally regarded as something one was born with. It was considered an innate, not an acquired, characteristic, and could not be raised by training or education. The IQ of a child of twelve was exactly what it had been at birth, and would continue to be throughout life. (Psychologists have since discovered that education and training can influence a person's IQ.)

Thus the statement, intended to be pejorative, was quite meaningless.

The bride walked down the aisle. Don't lay odds on it. What she almost certainly walked "down," or through, was the nave. The aisles of a conventional church or cathedral are the longitudinal sections along either side, separated from the central 'portion, or nave, by pillars.

The human body completely renews itself every seven years. As a moment's thought demonstrates, this common saying is transparent nonsense. Certainly a living body is always changing. (So is a dead one, as a matter of fact.) But some parts change faster than others. The number seven must have been chosen because of its "magic" significance or (presumed) properties.

The man that hath no music in his soul . . . . This is not the way Shakespeare puts it in *The Merchant of Venice* (act 5, sc. 1, l. 83ff.) . The correct quotation is "The man that hath no music in himself / Nor is not mov'd with concord of sweet sounds, / Is fit for treasons, stratagems and spoils. . ."

The Negro has no rights which a white man is bound to respect. Poor Chief Justice Taney! True, he said this, in effect; but in so saying it he specifically disavowed the sentiment. Here is the full context:

> It is difficult at this day to realize the state of public opinion in regard to that unfortunate race which prevailed in the civilized and enlightened portions of the world at the time of the Declaration of Independence, and when the Constitution of the United States was framed and adopted; but the public history of every European nation displays it in a manner too plain to be mistaken. They had for more than a century before been regarded as beings of an inferior order, and altogether unfit to associate with the white race, either in social or political relations, and so far unfit that they had no rights which the white man was bound to respect.

As Chief Justice of the United States in 1857, Taney did write the Dred Scott decision. But it seems unfair to quote the remark above out of a context which includes the phrase "that unfortunate race," etc.

"The only thing we have to fear is fear itself." Often thought to have been spoken first by Franklin D. Roosevelt at his inauguration in 1933, these words, or others very like them, had been spoken by Montaigne in the sixteenth century ("The thing of which I have most fear is fear"), Francis Bacon in the seventeenth ("Nothing is terrible except fear itself"), and the duke of Wellington and Henry David Thoreau in the nineteenth ("The only thing I am afraid of is fear"; "Nothing is so much to be feared as fear"). Even further back, Prov. 3:25 has "Be not afraid of sudden fear."

"The public be damned!" William Henry Vanderbilt denied that he ever said this, although he was so quoted by a reporter for the Chicago *News* in 1882 and is widely believed by many today to have said it.

"There are more things in heaven and earth, Horatio, / Than are dreamt of in your philosophy." Hamlet's remark to Horatio (act 1, sc. 5, lines 166–67) is about as often misunderstood as it is quoted. Hamlet is not accusing Horatio of narrow-mindedness; *your* in this context is used as it was very commonly used in Elizabethan times, and not too uncommonly today: a substitute for the definite article. ("Now, you take your Rolls Royce—*there's* an automobile!")

Philosophy was a part of all university curricula in Shakespeare's day, and Hamlet and Horatio have been college classmates at Wittenberg. Hamlet is simply saying that philosophy as a field of study has its limitations; the emphasis in the speech does not fall upon *your,* nor is it placed there by actors who know their business—and their Shakespeare. The stress is on the word *philosophy.* A reasonable paraphrase of Hamlet's remark would be, "There are more things in heaven and earth, Horatio, than our philosophers have dreamed of."

"There are no second acts in American lives." This famous remark by F. Scott Fitzgerald is almost universally misinterpreted as meaning that there are no second *chances* in American lives. But Fitzgerald, an experienced playwright and scenarist, surely was not accustomed to thinking of plays as being written in two acts. In the format he knew best, the most common today, the second act is the one that builds or develops the plot and prepares the audience for the resolution or denouement in the third and final act. It would seem certain that what Fitzgerald meant is that American lives rush too quickly to their resolutions whatever they may be; there is no time to explore possible solutions, to build, to progress in orderly fashion. Like Jay Gatsby, he seems to be saying, Americans are fated to rush pell-mell from beginning to end, with no middle—a violation of Aristotelian principles in terms of the techniques of the drama; and only too often, in American life itself, a tragic rush toward a denouement which shocks or destroys because there has been no time to prepare against it.

There but for the grace of God go I. The quotation that is now so frequently used is an adaptation. The original was uttered in the sixteenth century by John Bradford (1510?–1555) as he observed a group of criminals being taken to their execution. He said, "But for the grace of God, there goes John Bradford."

"They shall beat their swords into plowshares." This rendering of Isa. 2:4 contains an anachronism introduced by the translators. The plowshare belonged to the type of plow invented in the seventh century A.D. in order to turn the heavy turf of Europe. It was unknown in the East at the time those words were written.

Thin Man, the. In spite of the role so charmingly played by William Powell in the fine old movies based on Dashiell Hammett's fine old detective novel, there is no such character in the book. To say more would be telling.

This is my son and heir. Strictly speaking, not possible. Heirs are created by death. In fact, no one can make anyone else his heir, only his "devisee."

"This [not "the"] world is a comedy to those that think, a tragedy to those that feel." This quotation is usually attributed to Bernard Shaw. It was actually said by Horace Walpole in 1776.

Three Wise Men. There is no mention in the Gospels of the number of wise men who brought gifts to the infant Jesus. The wise men did not find Jesus in a manger. They did not follow the star from where it first appeared to Bethlehem.

The Christmas story is told in Matt. 2 and Luke 2, and Matthew is the only book that mentions the wise men at all. He says simply that "there came wise men from the east to Jerusalem." The idea that there were only three wise men crept in no doubt because the gifts included three types of treasure: "gold, and frankincense, and myrrh." When the Bible story was translated into stone in the churches (and later into other media) it was most natural to portray one wise man for each of the three kinds of gift. There could have been many men and many gifts.

It was not the wise men who visited the manger, in spite of the numerous medieval and Renaisance paintings. Matthew clearly says, "and when they were come unto the *house* [or *inn*]." It was the shepherds, not the wise men, who (in Luke 2:16) "came with haste, and found Mary, and Joseph, and the babe lying in a manger."

The wise men had the guidance of the star in finding Jesus, but not for their entire journey. Again according to Matthew, they saw the star in the east, and walked to Jerusalem (which was to the west). There they asked where to find him "that is born king of the Jews." Herod heard about their arrival and asked the chief priests and scribes where Christ was to be born. They told him Bethlehem because the prophet had so written. Then Herod told the wise men about Bethlehem and told them to go and look for the child. They left, headed south, of course. At *this* point the star went before them and guided them to the house, or inn, where it stopped.

thumb sucking. "Thumb sucking causes bad bites." In fact, children need the sucking action until the age of three to develop the muscles and bones of the face and also for psychological health. Most bad bites that have been blamed on thumb sucking come from a faulty swallowing pattern called a tongue thrust. In this pattern, begun at birth, the tongue goes forward, snakelike, during the thousands of swallows a day instead of moving in a normal upward and backward direction.

thumbs up. Romans did not give a thumbs-up sign in the arena as an indication that the downed gladiator should be spared death. If the members of the audience wanted the loser slain, they extended their thumbs with fists clenched; if they wanted him spared, however, they simply clenched their thumbs in their fists so they did not show at all.

time shown on dummy or display clocks. A persistent American myth has it that display clocks are set at 8:18 because that is the hour Abraham Lincoln died—or, sometimes, the hour at which he was shot. Actually, Lincoln was shot shortly after 10:00 P.M. and died at 7:30 the next morning. In England, the notion persists that display clocks read 8:18 because that was the hour Guy Fawkes was caught—or the hour he planned to blow up the Houses of Parliament, depending on one's sympathies. The obvious reason is the true one: 8:18 is both a symmetrical arrangement and the one that leaves the most room for advertising.

tip (gratuity). The notion that *tip* originally was an acronym for "To Insure Promptness" appears to be pure folk-etymology. In the sense of giving money to someone, the word goes back several hundred years; the *Oxford English Dictionary* does not attempt an etymology, though hesitantly suggests that as "rogues' cant"—that is, the "inside" language of common rogues and thieves—it may have come from another meaning, "to touch lightly."

In any case, since a tip is almost always given after, not before, service, the popular explanation of its origin does not make much real sense.

" 'Tis better to have loved and lost / Than never to have loved at all." Although they are usually applied to traditional relationships, these famous lines from section 27, stanza 4, of Alfred, Lord Tennyson's long poem *In Memoriam* do not refer to love between man and woman. They were written, as was the whole of *In Memoriam,* with reference to Arthur Hallam, Tennyson's close friend, whose premature death at twenty-two was a shattering experience to the young poet (Tennyson himself was in his early twenties when Hallam died) .

To answer a question no proper Victorian would have thought of raising, Tennyson was not homosexual. Quite contrary to the usual impression, he came from a family whose head, Tennyson's father, took to the ministry because he had been disinherited, and who ended up a drunk. One of Tennyson's brothers spent his life in what was then called an insane asylum; still another was a dope addict. Tennyson met Hallam at Cambridge; he seems to have found in Hallam the kind of father-figure he may have missed at home.

Certainly one may safely assume that had there been the slightest suggestion of "impropriety" in the relationship between Tennyson and Hallam, Queen Victoria would scarcely have appointed Tennyson Poet Laureate as a direct result of the publication of *In Memoriam* in 1850. (Tennyson did not, incidentally, inherit a peerage; he became Alfred, Lord Tennyson only in 1884, eight years before his death.)

tobacco in Europe. According to one common belief Columbus saw the Indians of the Western Hemisphere smoking tobacco in 1492 and Raleigh introduced tobacco into Europe about a hundred years later.

Actually the tobacco plant came to Europe by a quite different route. It was brought to the continent of Europe as early as 1558 by a Spanish physician named Francisco Fernandez, who had been sent out by King Philip II of Spain to investigate products of Mexico. It was received as a cure-all, with supposedly extraordinary healing powers. In 1559 the French ambassador to Portugal Jean Nicot, sent seeds to his queen, Catherine de Médicis, for the plant had been brought into Spain that very year from Santo Domingo. For this service Nicot's name became immortalized in the Latin botanical name for tobacco, *Nicotiana,* and of course in our word *nicotine.*

Some say that Sir John Hawkins was the one to bring tobacco to England, in 1565, when Raleigh was only thirteen years old, for Hawkins sailed to Florida and described in his diary the smoking of tobacco there.

It is fairly certain, however, that Sir Ralph Lane and Sir Francis Drake, returning in the summer of 1586 from the first unsuccessful attempt to colonize Roanoke Island, North Carolina, brought back tobacco and smoking implements to Raleigh, organizer of the expedition. Raleigh got the Elizabethan courtiers to smoke tobacco for pleasure and the habit spread rapidly.

Thus tobacco failed as a medicine and succeeded as a vice.

To gild the lily. Not from the Bible, and in any case a misquotation. What Shakespeare has Salisbury say in *The Life and Death of King John,* usually referred to simply as *King John,* is the following (act 4, sc. 2, lines 9–16; italics, of course, added) :

> Therefore, to be possess'd with double pomp,
> To guard a title that was rich before,
> *To gild refined gold, to paint the lily,*
> To throw a perfume on the violet,
> To smooth the ice, or add another hue
> Unto the rainbow, or with taper light
> To seek the beauteous eye of heaven to garnish,
> Is wasteful and ridiculous excess.

tomahawk, as American Indian invention. Though the word *tomahawk* certainly derives from the language of the Algonquian Indians of Virginia, it did not originally mean the weapon of war so familiar to readers of western novels and viewers of western movies. When John Smith introduced the word to the English vocabulary—he spelled it *tomahak*—he defined it as simply meaning "ax," although he later remarked that the term was also applied to the native war club and the iron hatchet. Only with the passing of the years did the word *tomahawk* come to be used exclusively for the metal war hatchet, a linguistic process scholars sometimes call "specialization." (*Liquor* once was merely a synonym for *liquid; meat* in older times meant food in general, as in "meat and drink"; and in Chaucer's time *girl* was commonly used for a young person of either sex.)

Since the American Indians of colonial times were not metalworkers, it is obvious that the tomahawk as now defined could not have been of Indian origin, and in fact it was not. It was, rather, made by white artisans for trade with the Indians, who accepted it enthusiastically; it spread rapidly to tribes in remote areas not even yet known to the whites.

Another common belief, fostered in modern times by the popular TV series starring Fess Parker as Daniel Boone and Ed Ames as his Indian sidekick, is that the tomahawk was regarded primarily as a "throwing" weapon. In fact, it was rarely thrown in combat, and for an obvious reason: a weapon thrown is likely to be a weapon lost. Or, worse, picked up in case of a miss and used against the thrower.

tooth decay. Generations of Americans were brought up on the advertising slogan, "A clean tooth never decays." And they believed it. This is not true, however.

In fact, despite our vast scientific knowledge we do not yet know what the fundamental reasons for tooth decay are, and we know no satisfactory way to prevent it. Yet tooth decay is the most common affliction of the human race, and at least 90 percent of the people in the United States suffer from it.

Wild animals, even meat-eating animals, do not have cavities, and it used to be thought that cooked foods were man's undoing. Then it was thought that candy and soft drinks were the chief cause, and that vast cavities were the just punishment of any little child who did not brush his or her teeth twice a day and go to the dentist every six months. Yet millions of people who have brushed their teeth morning and evening every day of their lives and never missed a dentist appointment have mouths full of fillings. On the other hand there are plenty of stories about people who have perfect teeth and never brushed them nor ever went to the dentist. Are they true? Yes, there are many cases of fine teeth with little care. They are especially numerous in Mediterranean countries where carbohydrates are a feature of the diet.

We do know that acid is the immediate cause of tooth decay. The acid is produced by the bacteria that live on the teeth. The bacteria produce it from the starch and sugar that remain in the mouth. Thus diet becomes a factor, but not the only factor. Cleanliness of the mouth (brushing the teeth) is certainly another factor. Heredity is still another factor. The composition of the saliva is a factor. The body's metabolism is sometimes a factor, for there are many cases of people working under great nervous strain whose teeth almost seemed to disintegrate from within.

The sad fact is that a clean tooth can decay, and it is even sadder that we do not know how to prevent it.

training and "discipline." The notion that toughness breeds disciplined invincibility dies hard. Yet Sparta did not defeat Athens; quite the contrary. Nor did the Prussian-trained goose-steppers of Germany succeed, in two dreadful attempts, in defeating the "soft" democracies. But it has been hard to come by any kind of real proof that the methods of a brutal sergeant or drill instructor may be less efficient in turning out good troops or other men who must act under pressure than those based on understanding and compassion.

Recently, however, in Los Angeles, an assistant sheriff named Howard H. Earle determined to try to settle whether stressful or nonstressful training would result in better policemen. Half of a class of seventy-four was given the traditional, hard-nosed, punishment-oriented course favored, at that time, by the academy for rookie policemen in the Los Angeles county sheriff's department. The other half (the men were matched by age, marital status, education, and prior military or police experience) was given nonstressful training.

According to Earle, the results were quite counter to what might have been expected. "The non-stressed," said Earle as quoted in *Time* (July 31, 1972), "outdid the stressed in everything . . . . They even wore their uniforms better." A second such experiment involving one hundred rookies yielded the same result.

tribes of people with tails. There are none. A famous hoax, which has since been debunked, was spawned in the Philippines after the Spanish-American War; it involved the "discovery" by an American army exploring party of an Igorot tribe all of whom had tails. It was said, and believed by many, that the tribe was to be kept isolated until it died out. A faked postcard purportedly showing a member of the tribe was widely sold.

Stories of men with tails are not new; Marco Polo claimed to have found some. But no scientific evidence has ever revealed a "tribe" with tails. Individuals sometimes are born with tails, because the human embryo does have a tail and it sometimes survives after birth. It does not, however, contain vertebrae.

true and valid. Not synonyms to one trained in logic or philosophy or both. A conclusion is "valid" in logic if it follows properly from the preceding premises. It is "true" only if it coincides with reality—admitting that this is not always easy to determine.

The following syllogism is quite valid:

Blacks are ignorant and shiftless.
Henry is a black.
Therefore, Henry is ignorant and shiftless.

Though not stated in formal syllogistic form, the following argument is also quite valid:

Since Jews are an inferior race, Hitler's treatment of them was justified.

It should be obvious at once that confusing truth with validity can have—has had, over the centuries—quite monstrous consequences. To put it another way, a series of statements can be entirely "logical" as the term is customarily used—and yet lead to monumentally false conclusions. Thus, to attack the "logic" of a racist, for example, is quite futile. If one believes blacks and Jews to be inferior beings, then a "logical" consequence of such belief is suppression, segregation, even mass murder. If one is convinced, as many were in Salem in the late seventeenth century, that witches exist and are in league with Satan to destroy whatever is good and replace it with evil, then tracking them down and destroying them is clearly the proper course of action; that is to say, the conclusion is valid, since it follows logically from the assumptions which precede it.

Clearly, then, it is the *assumptions* (or hypotheses or major premises, to use more technical terminology) which must be challenged, not the "logic," when one is dealing with problems like racism and bigotry. There was nothing illogical about slavery, since it was based on the assumption that slavery was all that Negroes were suited for. It was wrong because the assumption was wrong, not because it did not make sense. It made perfect sense, especially to slaveholders.

But it is often difficult to find the assumption lurking behind the (quite valid) conclusion, because seldom do we take the trouble to cast our arguments in syllogistic form. Most often, the assumptions take the form known to logicians as "begging the question," which is merely a fancy way of describing the process of taking for granted the very point which demands proof if one is to come to a conclusion which is *both* valid and—much more important— also true.

For instance, a common racist argument takes some such form as the following: Surely, you don't want people like that as neighbors (or guests or employees), do you? To which the quite "logical" answer is, Why, of course not. You have been trapped by the oldest device in argumentation. And, unfortunately, there is no way out but to insist upon going back to fundamentals, which is much less spectacular than the kind of clever legalism which begging the question, basically, is. ("Have you stopped beating your wife?")

The only answer to the question of whether you want "people like that" as neighbors, in other words, is to say "People like what?" It is the only way to flush the real issue out of the bushes. If the answer is "Why, ignorant and shiftless people," then probably both truth and validity are implicit; few of us prefer as neighbors the ignorant and shiftless over the educated and industrious. But the final step must then be to place the burden of proof upon the question-begger: What evidence do you have that blacks are invariably ignorant and shiftless? (Some are, no doubt; so are some WASPS, Jews, Chinese, Poles, American Indians, and so on and so on.) Such evidence cannot, obviously, be adduced; there are too many blacks who clearly are *not* ignorant and shiftless to enable the point to be made.

In summary, it is not our conclusions that betray us. It is our major premises. We tend to think that deductive reasoning—that is, from the general to the specific—is all there is, because in truth we must rely heavily upon it. One must take others' word for the general principle that in an encounter between an automobile and a pedestrian, the latter loses; we cannot afford to check it out personally. But deduction depends on, and must always go back to, induction: that is, the examination of individual facts or cases, enough of them to enable some kind of sensible—not "logical" or "valid"—conclusion to be drawn.

Truman, President: middle name. The late President Truman's full name was Harry S Truman—no period after the *S*, which stood only for itself and was itself Mr. Truman's middle "name." Nor is his case unique; middle-initials-only are not, admittedly, common; but they are by no means all that rare, although when encountered they do tend to lead to bitter arguments between careful reporters and their editors or proofreaders.

It took years for newspapers and press associations to achieve that *S*-without-a-period with reasonable consistency. Then came the publication of Margaret Truman's biography. Its title? *Harry*

S. Truman. With the period. Ms. Truman herself preferred the common, if inaccurate, version over having to answer the inquiries that might have resulted had the period been left out. And, as Ms. Truman is reported to have said, that *S* does really stand for something: presumably, itself.

Apparently even Mr. Truman tired of the battle sometimes; there are reproductions of his signature on record—with a period after the *S*.

tulip. So closely is the tulip now identified with the Netherlands that it is often thought to be of Dutch origin. This is hardly the case, for it comes from Central Asia, where it flourished on the steppes.

The Turks prized the tulip and were cultivating it assiduously by the sixteenth century—and perhaps long before. ("Tulip" derives, ultimately, from the Turkish for "turban.") In the mid–sixteenth century Augerius Gislenius Busbequis, the Austrian ambassador to the court of Suleiman the Magnificent, who was Sultan of the Turkish Empire, brought back bulbs for his garden in Vienna. From there it reached Western Europe, and by 1562 Antwerp had received a whole cargo of bulbs from Constantinople. In 1634–37 the famous tulipomania gripped all of Holland. Rich and poor alike speculated in the bulbs, and there are records of single bulbs selling for $750, $1,500, and $4,000.

The Netherlands is, to be sure, headquarters for tulip bulbs, though growers and fanciers in Belgium are equally ardent.

turkey (Thanksgiving variety). What Americans traditionally eat on Thanksgiving today is not the same kind of bird the Pilgrims knew. Though related, today's turkey actually arrived by way of the conquistadores, who sent back to Spain a type bred by the Aztecs. From Spain it got to England, thence back to the United States only a century or so ago. What the Pilgrims had was wild turkey, almost extinct in New England when the Aztec-Spanish-English bird fortuitously made its appearance, or reappearance, on the American continent. Its comeback, however, thanks to conservationists, has been so spectacular that some think there are more wild turkeys in the United States now than there were at the time the Pilgrims landed.

We need not feel sorry that the Pilgrims did not have the advantage of selective breeding; many consider the wild turkey more flavorful than the domestic variety, perhaps because its natural diet is acorns, seeds, and berries rather than somebody's bland synthesis of commonplace grains. The wild turkey is smaller, however, weighing in at some twelve to fourteen pounds on the average.

Twain, Mark. It is usually assumed that this most famous of American pseudonyms originated with Samuel L. Clemens, who made it famous. (And who also, in an apparent attempt to defeat the copyright laws, tried to make it a trademark.) Clemens, however, did not take the credit for this pen name; according to his account in Chapter 50 of *Life on the Mississippi* (1883), it had originally been used by a Captain Isaiah Sellers, an old riverboat pilot who wrote a rather ponderous column for a New Orleans paper. Clemens wrote a parody of the column which apparently hurt the old man's feelings. Perhaps partly in expiation, Clemens adopted the name following the old pilot's death.

However, Milton Meltzer, in *Mark Twain Himself* (1960), maintains that Sellers never used the name "Mark Twain," although Clemens obviously thought that he had.

Twain, Mark, birthplace of. Although he is often identified with these locations, Mark Twain was born neither in Hannibal, Missouri, nor on the banks of the Mississippi. His birthplace was the tiny village of Florida, Missouri, at the forks of Salt Creek. Twain —then known, of course, as Samuel Langhorne Clemens—moved westward to Hannibal with his parents only when he was almost four years old. Hannibal and the Mississippi certainly were major influences in Twain's life and on his work, but he was not born within sight of either.

Tyler as president. Not until 1967, it might accurately be said, did John Tyler legally become the tenth president of the United States. When William Henry Harrison died in 1841, nothing in the Constitution provided that the vice president should *become* president in case of the latter's death, disability, or removal by impeachment. It provided, rather, that the "powers and duties" of the president "shall devolve on the Vice-President."

Tyler, however, took over not only the powers and the duties;

at once he started to refer to himself as president, although there was no Constitutional authority for him to do so. At the time, many insisted upon referring to him as acting president, but finally Tyler's usage prevailed and every subsequent vice-president followed his precedent.

In 1967, as a result of the assassination of President Kennedy and speculations as to what might have ensued if he had been disabled rather than killed, the Twenty-fifth Amendment was finally approved. It provides that the vice-president will serve as acting president in case of the president's temporary disability. If the president dies, resigns, or is removed, then the vice-president "shall become President." Thus what amounted to an illegal assumption by Tyler in 1841 was at last legitimized.

Typhoid Mary. It is widely believed that Typhoid Mary had not, herself, ever suffered from the disease which she spread for so many years in so many places. But she had it, all right. Like other carriers, she recovered—but continued to harbor the germs of the disease. It is even possible for carriers not to know they have been ill, if the symptoms are not obvious, or are ignored or overlooked.

U

UFO's. It would surprise most people to learn that sightings of Unidentified Flying Objects are not confined to recent times.

According to *The UFO Controversy in America* by David Michael Jacobs (1975), the first documented sightings were in 1896–97! Cigar-shaped forms resembling airships were reported from coast to coast.

The "modern era" of UFO's began about fifty years later. The CIA got into the act during the wave of sightings in 1952 and concluded in their report that "UFO's" posed no threat to national security. A new wave of sightings occurred in 1973–74.

***Uncle Tom's Cabin* (the play).** Not many are aware that the first attempt at dramatizing Harriet Beecher Stowe's famous novel (whose full or "official" title, by the way, is *Uncle Tom's Cabin, or Life Among the Lowly*) failed miserably in spite of the enormous popularity of the book. (It sold over three hundred thousand copies during the first year of publication, a number representing some three million in terms of today's population.) An actor named C. W. Taylor was the first to try his hand at a stage version. It was denounced by the New York *Herald* and lasted only eleven performances.

But then another actor who was also a playwright—George L.

Aiken—attempted it; his version was an immediate hit and was to remain so for many years. It is the Aiken version which has been played so often and in so many places.

Nor is it by any means so bad as most people assume. True, the dialogue is often enough stilted and sentimentalized, and the ascension of Eva into heaven in a tableau at the end of the play would certainly inspire guffaws on Broadway today.

On the other hand, the characters do come alive; and the play is not by any means so simplistic a treatment as its detractors assume. Not all the Southerners in the play (or the book) are bad, nor all the Northerners good. Indeed, Simon Legree, the epitome of white-master brutality, is a Yankee. And Ophelia, another New Englander, is the very prototype of a latter-day liberal who would not want others to abuse "Negroes" but wouldn't have anything to do with them herself. And in spite of the excessive religiosity which runs through the play, St. Clare, a Southern character who does have good instincts, although they are flawed by a kind of moral atrophy, reacts in disgust against invoking the Scriptures to justify slavery. He makes the point that if slavery were to cease being profitable, the pulpit would soon enough find other Scripture to justify its abolition.

Finally, when Eliza makes her famous escape, she does not hop from ice floe to ice floe; in the words of the stage direction, "ELIZA appears, with HARRY, on a cake of ice, and floats slowly across. HALEY, LOKER, and MARKS on bank, observing PHINEAS on opposite bank."

The discerning may note another significant absence. There are no bloodhounds. None, in fact, are mentioned in the script; the only time the word occurs is when Eliza, just before her crossing, says "Powers of mercy protect me! How shall I escape these *human* [italics added] bloodhounds?"

United States Chamber of Commerce. Has no connection whatever with the United States government. There is no law (United States Steel Corporation, e.g.) that says "United States" cannot be used as part of the name of a purely private operation, though admittedly it may sometimes tend to deceive. (The official name of the United States Chamber of Commerce is actually the Chamber of Commerce of the United States of America.)

up to par, to be. Customarily taken to mean performing as usual, nothing special, just getting along O.K., this expression does not mean the same thing to a golfer. *Par* is defined in the rule book as the score that an expert golfer—not an average golfer—would be expected to make for a given hole; or errorless play, without flukes, under ordinary weather conditions, and allowing for two strokes on the putting green. *Par,* in other words, is "perfect" golf —no errors. To be up to par is to be considerably better than ordinary.

V

Vengeance is mine, saith the Lord. Few biblical quotations—this one is from Rom. 12:19—are so universally both misquoted and misunderstood. Almost always cited as lending scriptural authority to human vengeance, in fact it says exactly the reverse, as the context makes plain (verses 17–21 inclusive) :

> Recompense to no man evil for evil. Provide things honest in the sight of all men.
>
> If it be possible, as much as lieth in you, live peaceably with all men.
>
> Dearly beloved, avenge not yourselves, but rather give place unto wrath: for it is written, Vengeance is mine; I will repay, saith the Lord.
>
> Therefore if thine enemy hunger, feed him; if he thirst, give him drink: for in so doing thou shalt heap coals of fire on his head.
>
> Be not overcome of evil, but overcome evil with good.

As is obvious, the emphasis in the quotation falls upon the word *I:* "*I* will repay, saith the Lord." Far from being a call to human revenge, the passage is reminiscent of the so-called Sermon on the Mount (Matt. 5) , with its famous injunction to turn the other cheek.

village smithy. Contrary to popular belief, it isn't the blacksmith who stands under that spreading chestnut tree in Longfellow's famous poem. It's his shop, which is what *smithy* means. Longfellow himself knew the difference; in case you've forgotten, that well-worn first stanza goes as follows.

> Under a [not "the"] spreading chestnut tree
>   The village smithy stands:
> The smith, a mighty man is he,
>   With large and sinewy hands;
> And the muscles of his brawny arms
>   Are strong as iron bands.

virgin forest. Many tend to think of a virgin forest as one that has existed since time immemorial without alteration. But there can scarcely exist today a true "virgin forest"; there can hardly be any forest in the world which has not at one time or another been leveled by a lightning-caused fire.

Volstead Act. During Prohibition, many people thought that the Volstead Act was the same thing as the Eighteenth Amendment, and Andrew Volstead was the target of much blame and acrimony. Contemporary cartoons depicted him as something between the world's greatest killjoy and a villain.

Of course the Eighteenth was an *amendment to the Constitution* (ratified by at least two thirds of Congress and three fourths of the states) whereas the Volstead Act was an act of Congress to provide for *enforcement* of the Eighteenth Amendment. The act's provisions were indeed drastic, and President Wilson vetoed it, to no avail.

Mr. Volstead's concept of a nonintoxicating liquor was definitely on the safe side. Anything containing more than .5 percent of alcohol by volume was deemed intoxicating. Just before the repeal of the Eighteenth Amendment it was decided that any beverage containing up to 3.2 percent of alcohol was not intoxicating.

Walden and Thoreau. If one were to sum up the popular image of Henry Thoreau, with particular reference to his life at Walden Pond, something like the following would no doubt emerge: Thoreau was a recluse, largely self-educated, who spent most of his life in the woods far from human companionship or civilization. He was self-supporting, a vegetarian living off his land, who wrote little except for his masterpiece, *Walden;* finally, he was a man so dedicated to his principles that he went to jail rather than support the government in what he regarded as an imperialist venture, the Mexican War of 1846.

It would scarcely be possible to construct a less accurate portrait than that above. Only the last statement has any truth in it, and it needs to be heavily qualified. True, Thoreau spent one night in jail, for refusing to pay his poll tax. But someone paid it for him the next morning, and the affair was ended; Thoreau never spent another night in jail in his life.

Far from being a recluse at Walden, Thoreau enjoyed an active social life. Walden Pond is within walking distance of Concord, Thoreau's home town—and home also of Ralph Waldo Emerson and the Alcotts. According to Walter Harding in *The Days of Henry Thoreau* (1966), "hardly a day went by that Thoreau did not visit the village or was not visited at the pond." Difficult as it may be to reconcile with the popular image, Thoreau had as many as twenty-five or thirty people at his cabin at once; on August 1, 1846, the antislavery women of Concord held their annual commemoration of the freeing of the West Indian slaves on the doorstep of Walden; Emerson, William Henry Channing, and Caleb Stetson spoke to the assembled group. Emerson, who owned the land upon which Thoreau built his cabin, was, in fact, a frequent visitor. And Thoreau returned his calls, perhaps when he tired of cooking for himself. Bronson Alcott, says Harding, spent nearly every Sunday evening for several months visiting with Thoreau at his cabin. And that was during the *winter* of 1846–47.

Thoreau neither was, nor in fairness claimed to be, entirely self-sufficient at Walden, if by that is meant that he made or grew for himself everything that he needed. It took a fair amount of cash money to support his experiment; he gives us a detailed accounting in the famous opening chapter of *Walden,* "Economy." He was not a vegetarian; he spent almost as much for pork in eight months, in fact, as he spent for apples. He even went so far once as to try eating a woodchuck.

The stay at Walden did not take so large a chunk out of Thoreau's life as is usually assumed. He lived at the pond from July 4, 1845, until September 6, 1847—something over two years. Moreover, he was hardly self-educated, being a Harvard graduate, class of 1837.

Nor was he a "one-book" man; indeed, he was the author of thirty-nine manuscript volumes, although only two were published in his lifetime. He knew Greek, Latin, and English literature thoroughly, and was a subtle, conscientious, sophisticated stylist. Whatever else Thoreau was, he was no untutored rustic, no Grandma Moses of Transcendentalism.

None of which is to depreciate in any way the profound and enduring appeal Thoreau holds for so many, particularly in his account of his stay at Walden Pond. That the real Thoreau was so different from the popular image certainly detracts nothing from his accomplishments.

Wall Street, name of. Tourists often think Wall Street got its name because of the way high buildings seem to "wall" it in. But this is not so. The street was so named because there actually was a wall across Manhattan Island, designed to keep the Indians from the small city then huddled on the tip of the island.

warm beer in England. It is often said that the English like to serve and drink their beer warm. This is not exactly true; commonly, beer is served in England at room temperature. No one who has spent much time in England is likely to confuse this with "warm."

warning tags on upholstered furniture, mattresses, etc. There is no way of knowing how many battered and threadbare tags listing the materials used still adhere to chairs, mattresses, sofas, and pillows because the tags read, "Not to be removed under penalty of law." But there was never a law forbidding the *consumer* to remove the tag; only the seller. In recent years, the phrase "except by the consumer" has appeared on many such tags because of the widespread misconception that nobody at all could take them off without risking the wrath of legal authorities.

warranties, purpose of. Popular belief to the contrary, warranties are not designed to protect the customer; rather, they serve to limit the manufacturer's or dealer's liability. Particularly is this true of "express" warranties (warranties that are express or specific in their coverages), such as those of automobile manufacturers. No such warranty is any kind of guarantee of customer satisfaction.

Without an express warranty, there may exist what courts have held to be an "implied" warranty, much broader in its coverage. Thus, it is very much to the interest of automobile—and other—manufacturers to spell out just what they will allow themselves to be held accountable for. That is why a warranty will almost always include a statement to the effect that it stands in place of any other guarantee of any kind, "stated or implied."

Thus, those who take seriously that CAUTION: FILL OUT AND MAIL WARRANTY CARD AT ONCE often do themselves out of quick replacement or repair, especially the former, when something turns out to be wrong. Once the warranty card has been detached and mailed, the matter is out of the dealer's hands; he is now stuck with what amounts to a used item; the warranty card is a part of a new item's "package." If, for example, the buyer changes his mind and wants another model, or a different color, it is a simple matter to trade it for the different model or color, assuming, of course, that the item being traded has not been used (or at least shows no evidence of having been used) ; many dealers are quite willing to do this, particularly if the decision is to exchange the item for another model that costs more. If, that is, the warranty card hasn't been detached and mailed.

Even if the item turns out to be defective, the buyer is probably better off if he has not sent in the warranty card. The defect may be a simple one, easily fixed by the dealer. If so, surely this is better than having to take or send the item to an "authorized repair station" with the delays and frustrations this process so often entails.

Even if a major defect turns up, you may be better off going back to the dealer with warranty card intact. Let *him* send the defective item to that "authorized repair station," replacing it at once, if you can persuade him to do so. After all, he's the one that sold it to you.

warts. Perhaps because warts do sometimes disappear spontaneously for no reason yet discovered, a vast mystique has surrounded them, no doubt helped along by the occasional juxtaposition, by coincidence, of "treatment" and disappearance. But there is no particular mystery about the cause of warts; it's a virus. Handling frogs does not cause warts. Nor does masturbation or anything else, except that virus. Warts are infectious, and may also tend to be contagious. There are various methods of treating them, none involving incantations, stump-water, or the light of the full moon.

washing and/or mending the United States flag. Nothing in law or custom forbids cleaning the flag when it is dirty, though for some reason the notion persists that a dirty flag must be destroyed. Similarly, a flag can certainly be mended. Public Law 829, generally referred to as the Flag Code, merely states that a flag should be destroyed "in a dignified way, preferably by burning," when it is "in such condition that it is no longer a fitting emblem for display." Note also that burning is not the mandatory means of disposing of flags which are no longer usable, merely the recommended means. Many of the "rules" about the American flag have been set forth by flag organizations rather than by statute.

Washington Crossing the Delaware. This famous painting is by a nineteenth-century American painter, German-born Emanuel

Leutze. He actually did the painting in Düsseldorf and used the Rhine as a model. It contains at least two historical errors. The flag occupying the center position has thirteen stars and stripes, a design which was not adopted until 1777, whereas the crossing was in 1776. Also the boats are wrong. Washington had collected Durham boats from the Pennsylvania side. These were good-sized —some forty to sixty feet long—in contrast to the rather inadequate craft depicted. Perhaps we should allow the painter some artistic license, but it must be pointed out, too, that the soldiers would not have been holding their guns with barrels pointed upward, thereby catching the sleet that was falling, and Washington would certainly not have stood in the bow of the boat in so dramatic—and unseaworthy—a pose.

After landing, the army started its march to Trenton at four in the morning. They arrived after daybreak. It is not true that the Hessians were all drunk or paralyzed with hangovers; regular guard duties had been carried out. It is true, however, that Colonel Rall of the Hessians had indeed celebrated Christmas convivially and gone to bed very late, and was sleeping soundly in his nightclothes when one of his officers banged on the door. Later, as Rall lay dying, he was undressed; and found in one of his pockets was an unread note from a Loyalist, tipping him off on Washington's movements hours before the attack.

"Was this the face that launched a thousand ships, / And burnt the topless towers of Ilium?" Although these are thought to be Marlowe's best-known lines, they are not original with Marlowe in terms of the concept. In Lucian's "The Dialogues of the Dead" (Lucian died about A.D. 190) occurs the following, as translated by M. O. Macleod:

Hermes

This skull is Helen.

Menippus

Was it then for this that the thousand ships were manned from all Greece, for this that so many Greeks and barbarians fell, and so many cities were devastated?

water as a liquid. Not always. It's just as much a solid (ice, snow) or a gas (steam, water vapor) as it is a liquid. And it has, incidentally, the extraordinary characteristic—only bismuth shares it

—of being *less* dense as a solid than as a liquid. Which is a good thing; otherwise, ice in times of freeze would sink to the bottom of every lake or stream, and the resultant flooding would be almost beyond imagination. (Oddly, water has a greater density at 3.90° C., or about 39° F., than at any other temperature above or below.) (See LIQUIDS PUMPED UPWARD INTO A TANK.)

Waterloo. The battle was not fought at Waterloo. It was fought about four miles away at a point between the two villages of Pancenoit and Mont-St.-Jean. However, Wellington stayed in Waterloo the night before the battle, and returned there afterward to write his victory dispatch, as his friend Alexander Gordon, one leg blown off, lay dying on Wellington's bed.

The turning point actually occurred when the Prussian troops arrived to reinforce Wellington's men. The duke rallied his forces to make a great charge against Napoleon's army, fighting fiercely and hopelessly, with Napoleon's famous Imperial Guard in the front lines.

As night fell, an English officer sent a message to the commander of the guard to surrender. History says that he replied, "The Guard dies but never surrenders." What he really said was "Shit" (in French, *merde*).

water running out of bathtubs or basins. It is often said that the whirling action of water as it drains from tub or sink always takes the same direction because of the rotation of the earth. Sometimes it is added that this direction is opposite in the Southern Hemisphere. This is a myth easily enough demolished by simple observation.

waterspouts, composition of. Except for the small variety which resembles the "dust devils" commonly seen on land, waterspouts are primarily composed of freshwater, not seawater. In effect, a major waterspout is a tornado at sea; its moisture content is largely from the parent cloud and surrounding air, though it may suck up some seawater near its base.

Watt, James—and the steam engine. James Watt did not invent the steam engine nor did he claim to have done so. His improvements on the Newcomen steam engine of his youth, notably the separate condenser, were so important that he can certainly be given credit for greatly improving its efficiency. But this is scarcely the same as "inventing" the steam engine.

Watusis, height of. The common notion that the Watusis, or Tutsi, are a race of seven-footers any one of whom a basketball coach would be glad to recruit is quite false. No doubt encouraged, if not spawned, by the film *King Solomon's Mines,* this popular belief has truth only if applied to certain members of the court and some royal dancers, who even so, scarcely reach seven feet, though they may run to six feet, three inches or so. But these are "a specific, highly inbred clan," according to the United States Government's *Area Handbook for Burundi* which puts the average height of the Tutsi at five feet eight inches.

Wayne, John—as war hero and marine. As surprising as it may seem, John Wayne, the very prototype of the tough combat marine, has never served in the armed forces. And, in fact, he has to date played a marine in combat only twice: in *Sands of Iwo Jima* and *Flying Leathernecks.* (A third movie in which he appears as a marine is a comedy set in the States: *Without Reservations,* with Claudette Colbert.)

weather signs and prophecies. Every autumn there is a crop of prophecies about the relative severity of the coming winter based on the activity of squirrels gathering nuts, the markings of woolly-bear caterpillars, etc. These are neither supported by scientific knowledge nor evidenced by the weather itself. Meteorologists are aware of certain long-term trends, expressed as average temperatures, etc., but predicting the weather of a given season is beyond the competence of both men and caterpillars. In 1974 there were no less than three extraordinary weather features in certain food-producing areas of the United States, of importance to the whole world in terms of food supplies: an unusually wet spring, an unusually dry summer, an unusually cold fall. Not one of these factors was publicly predicted.

Webster's Dictionary. Although the phrase is often heard and seen, there isn't any such thing. Like any identifying label or title, *Webster's* cannot be copyrighted. And, like *aspirin,* it cannot be

registered as a trademark—much to the regret, no doubt, of the
G. & C. Merriam Company of Springfield, Massachusetts, which
regards itself as the legitimate successor to Noah Webster.

Thus, anyone at all can publish anything he chooses to call a
dictionary, and then proceed to title it *Webster's Dictionary*. It
may be, and sometimes is, cheaply printed and abominably edited.
But no one can stop the publisher from identifying it as *Webster's*.

As a matter of fact, Noah Webster himself did not call his dictionary *Webster's Dictionary*. He called it simply *The American
Dictionary*.

"We learn by doing." Made famous in the twentieth century by
John Dewey, these words were first said by Aristotle: "For the
things we have to learn before we can do them, we learn by doing
them, e.g. men become builders by building and lyre-players by
playing the lyre" (W. D. Ross translation). Nor does the phrase,
as used by Dewey, mean, in context, what his critics infer from it:
random and aimless classroom activity which only by accident results in any meaningful consequence.

As Prof. Ralph A. Smith of the School of Education at Portland
State University reminds us, these are Dewey's actual words, from
Democracy and Education:

> One may learn by doing something which he does not under-
> stand; even in the most intelligent action, we do much which we
> do not mean, because the largest portion of the connections of the
> act we consciously intend are not perceived or anticipated. But
> we learn only because after the act is performed we note results
> which we had not noted before.

"Hence," as Professor Smith points out, "one may learn by
doing, but only if what he is doing is meaningful to him." If one
were to criticize Dewey's statement at all, it would not be on the
ground that Dewey said anything either unlikely or so very remarkable, but because he does take a good many words to express
the obvious. Certainly he did *not* say that doing and learning are
the same thing, as so many of his critics maintain.

welfare cheats and chiselers. Few myths are so stubbornly rooted
as that a high percentage, even a majority, of those "on welfare"

are perfectly able to work if they want to; that they are freeloaders at public expense. Along with this belief go the notions that many welfare mothers continue to bear children so that their payments will be increased, that large numbers of public assistance cases are better off financially not working than working, and that "once on welfare, always on welfare."

An odd paradox of the welfare mythology is that it inherently contradicts itself. The assumption underlying the false beliefs cited above is that "respectable" people are always happier working than not working and will gladly accept any employment offered them. But if this is so, then the belief that those on welfare inhabit a kind of paradise denied those who must grub out a living cannot also be true.

There have been and are, without question, cases of welfare fraud; in no segment of human society has moral perfection yet been found. Priests have stolen from collection boxes, and certainly it is a matter of public record that some people of the highest social standing may cheat on their income taxes. It may well be that a search through records of the various states would turn up welfare recipients who own new Cadillacs; indeed, it would seem more unlikely that this has never happened than that it had. But one swallow does not make a summer, and if an expensive color TV set is found in a hovel—and there must be one such somewhere—this scarcely is persuasive evidence of large-scale fraud.

Many studies have been made of welfare problems, real or imagined. Perhaps three recent studies, covering a representative range (one by the Oregon Department of Human Resources; another centered on Detroit, a joint project of the University of Michigan and Pennsylvania State University; the third by the United States Census Bureau) may help to pierce through the commonest misconceptions regarding "welfare."

In summary, this is what the Oregon study found. "Once on welfare, always on welfare" turns out to be far from the truth. Of ADC (Aid to Dependent Children) cases, half had been on welfare less than a year; over half of these had never before received any kind of public assistance. Three fourths had been on ADC for two years or less. In terms of adult assistance—and note that these figures include old age, blind, and deaf clients—the median figure in no case exceeds four years.

As to cheating, four tenths of one percent are referred for prosecution; in even fewer cases has fraud actually been established. A persistent myth is that ADC families are always large, and that they have more children simply to get more money. As a matter of fact, in Oregon welfare families are getting smaller, not larger; and over 60 percent have only one or two children. Since the monthly "raise" per child amounts to $27, it seems hardly likely that "children for welfare" is much of a business proposition. Nor are most welfare children illegitimate; the percentage, in fact, was less than 12 percent—or, put in positive terms, 88 percent of welfare children were quite legitimate. In fact, the welfare illegitimacy rate in this state is declining *faster* than the illegitimacy rate for the population as a whole.

Most important, perhaps, are the figures which belie the "able-bodied loafer" myth. In Oregon, as in many other states, childless adults are not even eligible for welfare. Of those who do get assistance, one fifth are either over sixty-five, or totally disabled, or blind. Another fifth are mothers who are caring for children, most of them preschoolers at home. Over half are children averaging about eight years of age. Of the rest, 5 percent are in a temporary bind, and the rest are fathers looking for work.

The Detroit study, which involved both low wage earners and welfare recipients, showed that most of what the public thinks about welfare recipients is a stereotype with little basis in fact, and that since a good deal of policymaking is based on the same stereotype, programs designed to get people off welfare or out of poverty only too often get nowhere.

With respect to personal characteristics or background, the study found, there are few differences between low-income welfare recipients and low-income nonrecipients. In neither category did work alter very much either economic resources or the life situation. And, quite counter to popular belief, there were more male welfare recipients who worked more than half the time than there were nonwelfare males who did. In other words, the idea that receiving welfare invariably weakens the will or "softens the character," so that those who get it no longer want to work, is untrue. Among women, a majority of both recipients and nonrecipients worked at least half the time.

Characteristics tending to keep people in poverty, whether working or on welfare, included rural origins with poor educational opportunity; migration to the city or elsewhere; lack of skills and training. And all these problems were compounded for racial minorities and women. Good jobs for such people were not usually available no matter how great the desire to work; as a result, many accepted welfare but without, apparently, losing the desire to work; there simply was no work available for them.

Also contrary to stereotype, and confirming the Oregon data, is that welfare women in Detroit do not have large numbers of children. They do tend to be the only workers in their families—and they work for the lowest of wages. The study concludes that since there appear to be no significant differences between the working poor and the welfare poor, the problem is not to get people off welfare, but to get far more people out of an economic dead end.

A final myth, disputed by the Census Bureau study, is that large numbers of rural blacks migrate from low welfare benefit states to northern cities in order to "go on welfare," where they "load up the rolls." In fact, in six northern cities blacks born and raised in the city are more likely to be on welfare than those who have moved there.

It should finally be mentioned that invariably a substantial majority of all welfare cases consists of those wholly incapable of supporting themselves no matter how much they might wish to do so: the blind, the aged, the sick, the paralyzed.

Westminster Abbey, burial in. Burial in Westminster Abbey is not a privilege reserved for those of noble blood or exalted reputation in literature or statecraft. There are no fixed rules or regulations; the deans of the Abbey determine who shall be interred there. Jack Broughton, whose distinction is that he was a champion prizefighter in the eighteenth century, was buried in Westminster Abbey.

Westminster Cathedral. Travelers in London often ask for Westminster Cathedral when they are really looking for Westminster Abbey—or as Londoners are wont to say, "the Abbey."

There is a Westminster Cathedral; it is a modern edifice built at the turn of the century, the most important Roman Catholic church in England. A cathedral is the most important church of a diocese, and is presided over by a bishop. The cathedral of the bishop of London (Church of England) is Saint Paul's, a church designed by Christopher Wren.

Westminster Abbey as an example of medieval architecture ranks with the finest cathedrals, but it is not called a cathedral, being an abbey church. (Elizabeth I accorded it a dean.) Its proper name is Collegiate Church of Saint Peter in Westminster but no one ever calls it that, either.

whalebone. Not, as sometimes assumed, from the skeletons of whales—not, in fact, bone at all, but a horny substance found along the whale's upper jaw.

"What time does the next swan leave?" Backstage at the opera there is a classic story about Wagner's *Lohengrin*. In the first act Lohengrin is supposed to arrive on stage in a boat drawn by a swan, but on one occasion the overzealous stagehand pushed the boat onto the stage before Lohengrin could climb aboard. With perfect composure the tenor turned to the stagehand and asked, "What time does the next swan leave?"

When Lauritz Melchior was prominent in the role, the remark was attributed to him. Walter Slezak, writing about his father, the famous tenor Leo Slezak, attributed the remark to *him,* and entitled his book *What Time's the Next Swan?* Research discloses that the story was first told about the very first tenor to sing the role of Lohengrin, Joseph Tichatschek (1807–1886) .

wheat found germinating in Egyptian tombs. A persistent story has it that wheat grains found in King Tut's, or other ancient Egyptian tombs, sprouted and grew when planted. If so, none of the persons who were involved in discovering, exploring, or studying the tombs knows anything about it. There have been many experiments, often involving seed obtained from museums, to determine maximum viability. The extreme for wheat is about thirty-five years, though some seeds—notably the legumes—may sprout after a century or more.

wheel and fire, invention of. Enshrined in popular mythology are the forever-to-be-anonymous geniuses who first gave their fellow humanoids the wheel and fire. But the wheel could scarcely have been invented; round shapes are common enough in nature. It was the *axle* that made the wheel useful. As for fire, surely it antedated man's emergence as an inventive animal; cataclysmic volcanic eruptions, not to mention lightning and its effects, wracked and lighted the face of the earth while man was yet evolving from primitive forms. (Even in fundamentalist terms, God created "light" before He created man.)

whence. Although the most frequent use of this word is in the expression *from whence, whence* doesn't mean "when." It doesn't mean "where." It means *"from* where." Thus, *from whence* means "from from where," literally at least.

whiskey as antidote for snakebite. Whiskey actually makes the effects of the venom worse. Alcohol acts at first as a stimulant, which is just the reverse of what one needs when there's venom in the bloodstream; then it acts as a depressant, reinforcing the effect of the venom, itself a depressant, which has now been circulated more rapidly as a result of the whiskey. One may, of course, pour whiskey on the bite itself in the hope that its alcohol content will help to sterilize the wound. But this would merely tend to inhibit any infection that might result from bacteria in the snake's mouth, much the lesser danger; it would have no effect on the spread of the venom.

An old wives' tale given unfortunate currency in both the book and the movie *The Yearling* is that snakebite can be treated by putting a piece of liver from a freshly killed animal or bird over the bite. There's no truth in it.

Whistler's mother. Not what Whistler called his famous picture. His name for it was *Arrangement in Gray and Black.*

white elephants. Everybody knows how the expression "white elephant" originated; the king of Siam would present a white elephant, which was regarded as sacred by certain cultists, to a courtier upon whom the king wished to confer financial ruin. Only trouble is, there's no evidence that any king of Siam ever did any such thing.

"Who reads an American book?" When Sydney Smith asked this sardonic question, he was not really going after American books or authors, but rather after one aspect of America that few would care to defend. Here is the actual ending of the magazine article which contained this famous question. It was, surprisingly, a review of something called *Statistical Annals of the United States,* by one Adam Seybert, which set Smith off, in 1820, in the pages of the *Edinburgh Review.*

> In the four quarters of the globe, who reads an American book? or goes to an American play? or looks at an American picture or statue? What does the world yet owe to American physicians or surgeons? What new substances have their chemists discovered? or what old ones have they analyzed? What new constellations have been discovered by the telescopes of Americans? What have they done in mathematics? Who drinks out of American glasses? or eats from American plates? or wears American coats or gowns? or sleeps in American blankets? Finally, under which of the old tyrannical governments of Europe is every sixth man a slave, whom his fellow-creatures may buy, and sell, and torture?

"Who reads an American book" is obviously just the first in a rising crescendo of questions leading to quite another point. It is rather a shame that the savage irony of that last sentence has been so often unrevealed because American authors were so sensitive.

Whitney, Eli, and interchangeable parts. Although Eli Whitney invented the cotton gin, it was not that accomplishment that made him rich. So great was his ingenuity that he produced a working model of the gin in ten days, only to have it stolen and imitated by others.

Whitney made much more money a few years later, when he set up a factory (1798) in New Haven, Connecticut to manufacture firearms with interchangeable parts—so it had been thought until recently. Whitney is usually credited with having originated the idea of standard, interchangeable parts—which is the very foundation stone of mass production. However, a recent study of a number of Whitney guns revealed that the parts fitted only the guns they were made for, whereupon it was inferred that Whitney's factory did not, in fact, employ that important concept. In all fairness, Whitney most likely did originate the idea and employed it in his manufacturing process. However, before the advent of precision machinery it was difficult to produce parts that were exactly identical, with the result that some hand fitting had to be done.

widow's walk. The railed-in platform on the roof of many an American house is called a widow's walk, and most people be-

lieve that seamen's wives went there to watch for the ships that
would bring their husbands home.

Actually, it was there to help in the fighting of chimney fires.
About three hundred years ago when the chimney was often
placed in the middle of the house instead of at the end, it was
necessary to have quick access in the event of the all-too-frequent
fire in the chimney. So a roof scuttle—an opening with a lid on
it—was put in and the platform with railing followed. In fact
widow's walks may be seen hundreds of miles from the sea.

wild horses of the western plains. There is a colorful and persistent legend to the effect that by 1600 the Great Plains were well
stocked with herds of wild horses, which the Plains Indians had
only to catch and tame. These horses, it is thought by many, were
descendants of animals brought to the Texas plains by De Soto
and Coronado.

De Soto's horses, however, did not include any mares. The five
male horses that were released were killed by Indians the very
same day, and there is no record of any of the other horses surviving. The records of the Coronado expedition are meticulous and
they do include the listing of three mares, but there is no indication that they were taken eastward into the buffalo country.

Furthermore, for a whole century thereafter Spanish explorers
were traversing the Plains without so much as mentioning any
horses at all—wild or domesticated. It was not until 1705 that wild
horses were reported, and this was years after the Indians had gotten domesticated horses from the Spanish.

The source of the Indians' horses was unquestionably the Spanish colonies in what is now New Mexico. There were twenty-five
mission farms surrounding Juan Oñate's colony and there Indian
boys learned not only to work with the livestock, but to ride
horses and handle them. From this permanent base horses and the
horse culture spread out among the Indian tribes long before
white men came across the Mississippi from the East.

wine, temperature to be served at. Those who know, or profess
to know, about wine are forever reminding American hosts and
hostesses that red wines are properly served at room temperature.
But room temperature, in the great wine-growing areas of Europe,
is by no means the seventy degrees or so to which Americans often

heat their houses. It is more likely to be some where in the neighborhood of sixty to sixty-five degrees. Thus, if one is really determined to serve French red wine at the "proper" temperature, it
should be at least slightly chilled—in the United States, anyway.

winter in Scandinavia. The popular notion that Finns, Swedes,
Danes, Norwegians, and Icelanders suffer through bitterly cold
winters is very far from the truth. Advertisements which make so
much of what a car in Sweden must undergo during the cold
months certainly are not relevant to the area where most Swedes,
at least, live and drive. The average January temperature in
Stockholm is 27 degrees Fahrenheit. (In Duluth, it's 9 degrees,
in Minneapolis 12 degrees.) Those Swedes who, it is said, emigrated to the north central United States because the climate was
said to be so much like Sweden's must surely have experienced a
shock to discover the 30-below days which are common enough
there; Stockholm would be immobilized at such an unheard-of
temperature.

Helsinki's January average is 23 degrees, Oslo's 25 degrees, Co-
penhagen's 32 degrees, with Reykjavik's about the same as Copen-
hagen's—"Iceland" is a considerable misnomer.* True, in remote
northern areas of the Scandinavian peninsula, there's plenty of
cold weather: enough to challenge Rapid City or Helena. But no
important Scandinavian city undergoes anything like the extremes
that the patient residents of St. Paul or Superior must endure.
And, also true enough, the winters in Scandinavia are long, yes;
and temperatures in the national capitals though not, as said, particularly low, do tend to stay pretty much the same. Finland's
principal harbors freeze for so long and so solidly not because of
extreme cold, but simply because such cold as there is—typically,
just a few degrees below freezing—tends to persist, seldom rising
during the winter to a point of thaw.

But don't go to Helsinki in January, if that's what you have in

---

* In case any should question Iceland (or, as sometimes happens, even Finland)
as a "Scandinavian" country, it should be pointed out that Icelanders and Finns
certainly consider themselves Scandinavian, and somewhat resent the tendency to
confine the application of "Scandinavia" to Sweden, Norway, and Denmark. Even
though the language of the Finns is not, like the others, Germanic, all five of the
countries consider themselves bound by common cultural ties. (Finland is bilingual:
Finnish and Swedish are both official languages.) All five countries use national
flags of identical design, only the colors differentiating one from another.

mind, steeled against the kind of Arctic weather Duluth provides, for you aren't likely to find anything even remotely approaching it.

wisdom teeth impacted. "My wisdom teeth have to come out because they are impacted." The patient is describing a tilted or malposed tooth. The word *impacted* is totally misused—it means "confined within," like a tooth that is totally within gum and bone tissue.

Incidentally, the saying "All wisdom teeth have to be extracted" is another bit of misinformation. At least 50 percent of the wisdom teeth or third molars erupt into vertical positions that are completely normal and useful.

witchcraft trials in Salem. The popular notion that witches were burned is quite false. In fact, no witches were burned at any time in Salem or anywhere else in America. Nor were witches by any means all women; in fact, they were not all even human beings. Two dogs were actually put to death in Salem for "witchcraft." The means of execution in all cases, including the unfortunate dogs, was by hanging, with one exception: an old man named Giles Corey. Corey, in an instance of bravery under torture scarcely paralleled in American history, "stood mute," or refused to plead either yes or no to the charge against him. Under the law, this meant that his heirs would not be deprived of his property, which would have been sold at auction had he confessed or been found guilty. (Had he denied the charge, he would almost surely have been convicted.) Corey's death was by "pressing"; heavy stones were placed upon his chest in an attempt to force him to plead. He was crushed to death; it is said that his last defiant words were "More weight!"

Nor was the witchcraft hysteria confined to Salem; Andover, Massachusetts, was caught up in it before the affair had run its course, and at least one witch was found in Maine. Salem was not, as a matter of fact, even the first to hang a witch. An old woman in Boston had confessed to witchcraft and been hanged in 1688, four years before the first execution in Salem.

It is often thought that all one needed to do was to cry "Witch!" and the accused was as good as hanged. This was by no means the case; more than once, a "respectable" member of the community got off scot-free. The mother-in-law of one of the judges, Jonathan

Corwin, was, as a matter of fact, repeatedly accused, but never even arrested.

Often forgotten, if ever known, is the fact that all of the witches were cleared of all charges within a matter of less than twenty years. In an Order of Compensation dated October 17, 1711, and signed by Governor J. Dudley, all convictions were reversed, and compensation provided for the heirs of those who had been hanged.

It should finally be noted that Salem represented no aberrant hysteria in a rude, far-off, and uncivilized community. Belief in witchcraft was well-nigh universal in the "civilized" world of the seventeenth century. As Theodore Morrison notes in the introduction to David Levin's *What Happened in Salem* (1952) :

> . . . in European countries both Catholic and Protestant, thousands of "witches" had been executed. Despite important advances toward modern science, few people had thought of criticizing current theology in the light of the newest scientific discoveries. No one used Newton's law of gravitation to challenge Cotton Mather's remarks about the aerial activities of "legions of devils." The "invisible world" was still, for most people, a real one. Even the few articulate critics of the Salem trials did not deny the existence of witchcraft; they attacked the methods used by the Salem judges. The intellectual leaders and, so far as we know, the mass of the people read their Bibles literally, accepting without question the Mosaic pronouncement (Exod. 22:18): "Thou shalt not suffer a witch to live."

witch hazel. Despite the name, witch hazel has nothing to do with the true hazel and very little to do with witches. No one knows exactly where the name came from, but most likely the first settlers in America confused it with the hazel they knew in Europe, to which, in its leaves and young fruits, it bears a superficial resemblance.

The hazel tree belongs to the birch family, bears edible nuts and was once credited with great magical powers. Hazel rods could be used to discover thieves, murderers, water, and gold. The wands would protect against evil spirits; a couple of hazel nuts in the pocket would prevent toothache.

Our witch hazel is a shrub rather than a tree. Its fruit is four brown seeds in a pod. The pod explodes when ripe and shoots out the seeds as much as ten or twelve yards. They are not edible.

Its powers were considered to be medicinal and by some still are. A decoction made from the bark was thought by the New England Indians to alleviate internal bleeding and help to prevent dimming of the eyes. Commercially, extract of witch hazel, liberally mixed with alcohol, was sold as a soothing liniment for sprains and sore muscles, but as with many such remedies, its effectiveness was in the alcohol rather than the extract.

Witch hazel wands have been used for "witching" for water, but that is not where the name came from. It may come from the Old English *wic,* which derives from an Old Teutonic form *wik-,* "to bend."

wolves. For several thousand years man has been making up stories about wolves: The she-wolf that suckled Romulus and Remus; werewolves, men who turn into wolves at night and feast on human flesh; Red Riding Hood; Mowgli, in Kipling's *Jungle Books,* who was reared and taught by benign wolves.

No one believes these stories, but a great many people do believe:

> 1. That wolves are among the most ferocious of creatures, wicked enemies of men who continually band together in huge hunting packs, sometimes numbering hundreds, and kill and eat human beings, and
> 2. That wolves, nevertheless, sometimes adopt children and bring them up with their pups.

These beliefs are false.

Recent scientific studies have demonstrated that the wolf is not particularly ferocious. Basically he is friendly and more sensitive than the dog, with a complicated and subtle social organization.

Wolves do not customarily hunt in large packs. Their howling is not a hunting cry, and does not frighten other animals. Like all animals they get their food the easiest way they can, and with the least risk. Thus much of their prey is mice, squirrels, and rabbits; but also, unfortunately from man's point of view, lambs and calves. It is chiefly in winter that wolves form packs to hunt larger game. The pack is of moderate size—very often merely a family group consisting of an old couple and their mature offspring.

Stories of wanton attacks by wolves on human beings are nonsense. There is not a single verified case in North America of a wolf attacking a human, much less eating one. Mammalogists agree that if a wolf ever attacked a person it would have to be one infected by rabies, not uncommon among wolves, foxes, etc.

The stories of wolves as foster parents seem to be almost irresistible to many people, and they have cropped up from time to time since antiquity. For example, in 1926–27 within a space of ten months there were three accounts—all in India—of children allegedly reared by wolves. However, no case has ever been authenticated by scientific observers, and there have been no such reports for a long time.

Stories of children reared by wolves are not only common; they are only too often taken seriously, sometimes by persons as renowned as the famous Dr. Arnold Gesell. He apparently swallowed *in toto* the account by a Reverend J. A. L. Singh, of Midnapore, India, of the "wolf-reared waifs of Midnapore." Dr. Gesell repeated the story in the January 1941 issue of *Harper's* magazine. People have continued to believe the tale ever since; it has been incorporated into textbooks, reprinted in newspapers and magazines, and is even the subject of Dr. Gesell's *Wolf Child and Human Child.*

Yet, upon examination, the whole story turns out to depend entirely on the unsupported—and quite unscientific—observations of the Reverend Mr. Singh.

Man is still exterminating wolves: shooting, trapping, and poisoning them. It remains to be seen whether the few remaining wolves in the United States will be allowed to survive. If not, one thing is certain; the stories about wolves and their man-killing ferocity will survive long after the wolves themselves are all dead.

X

Xmas. Often regarded as a newfangled and vulgar abbreviation, this word has its origin in very ancient times indeed. In the Anglo-Saxon Chronicle, written near the beginning of the twelfth century, the Old English word for Christmas begins with X. Whether or not the X in *Xmas* is meant to symbolize the Cross, as some say, it is true that the Greek word for "Christ," from which the English derived, begins with the Greek letter *chi,* or X. X is thus a quite proper abbreviation for "Christ."

Y

"Yankee Doodle." The origins of this prerevolutionary marching song are veiled in mystery, but what puzzles most people is why, when Yankee Doodle stuck a feather in his cap, he called it "macaroni"—of all things.

The reference is not to an article of food but to the Macaroni Club, founded in the mideighteenth century and consisting of fops and effete young men who wished to bring continental elegances to England. Hence the humorous incongruity of Yankee Doodle, trotting into town on his pony, sticking a feather in his hat and calling it "macaroni."

It is not known for sure how the club got its name, but quite possibly the members affected foreign dishes, such as macaroni, hitherto unknown in England.

Fairly obviously, "Yankee Doodle" must originally have been meant to slander the American revolutionary troops—but got defiantly, perhaps sardonically, taken over by the very objects of its satire.

Yellowstone Park, location of. Widely assumed to be in Wyoming, Yellowstone Park actually includes parts of both Montana and Idaho.

Ye Olde Gifte Shoppe. Usually thought of as introducing a touch of Olde Englande, the *Y* in such signs as mentioned above is really a variant of an earlier symbol called the "thorn," characteristic of Old English manuscripts, which looks as though it could not decide whether to be a *p* or a *b* and ended up somewhat resembling both (*þ*). In later years, but still some hundreds of years ago, early printers used the letter *y* to stand for the thorn. The sound for which the thorn stood was the sound represented today by the combination *th,* as in *the.* So all that *Ye* stands for, when used as above, is merely the commonest, most prosaic of English words: *The.*

Yes or No, witness must answer. In spite of the widespread belief to the contrary, witnesses in court may not be required to answer Yes or No to any question the examiner, or crossexaminer, chooses to put. True, a witness may be required to answer with a simple Yes or No a question which *can* be so answered. But he certainly has the right not to incriminate himself by responding Yes or No to a question such as the classic "Have you stopped beating your wife?"

"You cannot bring about prosperity by discouraging thrift." "You cannot bring about prosperity by discouraging thrift. You cannot strengthen the weak by weakening the strong. You cannot help the wage earner by pulling down the wage payer. You cannot further the brotherhood of man by encouraging class hatred. You cannot help the poor by destroying the rich. You cannot keep out of trouble by spending more than you earn. You cannot build character and courage by taking away man's initiative and independence. You cannot help men permanently by doing for them what they could and should do for themselves."

There must be many people who think Lincoln said this, judging from the number of times it is attributed to him. Extensive research, however, has failed to turn it up in any collection of Lincoln speeches or letters. Lincoln did make the following two remarks, according to Fred Kerner (ed.) in *A Treasury of Lincoln Quotations* (1965):

> I take it that it is best for all to leave each man free to acquire property as fast as he can. Some will get wealthy. I don't believe in a law to prevent a man from getting rich; it would do more harm than good. . . . I want every man to have the chance—

and I believe a black man is entitled to it—in which he *can* better his condition; when he may look forward and hope to be a hired laborer this year and the next work for himself afterward, and finally to hire men to work for him!

Speech at New Haven, Connecticut
March 6, 1860

That some should be rich shows that others may become rich, and hence is just encouragement to industry and enterprise. Let not him who is houseless pull down the house of another; but let him labor diligently and build one for himself, thus by example assuring that his own shall be safe from violence when built.

Reply To New York Workingmen's Democratic
Republican Association
March 21, 1864

These are scarcely the same as the words which are so often attributed to Lincoln; but perhaps they are what started it all.

You can't change human nature. This favorite saying of those generally farther right than left on the political spectrum does not really stand up to close examination, if "change" is taken to mean here what it means in any other concept: modify, not radically alter or reverse. What human nature is must, obviously, be revealed by what human beings do. And they have certainly changed what they do within historical memory and in many important respects.

In terms of what we generally refer to as Western culture, for example, Bergen Evans reminds us in his *The Natural History of Nonsense* (1946) that cruelty to animals was a matter of custom until only about a century ago; in his words, "the torturing of animals for fun was universal in Christendom." Until quite recently in history, another universal assumption was that the stranger is *automatically* an enemy. And while traces of this assumption undoubtedly persist, we have come a long way from the time, not so long ago, when everyone armed himself against those he met on the road, or might so meet; and the burden of proof was on the stranger that he meant no harm.

The concept of law—even if you will, of law and order; the gradual development of the state as an outgrowth of narrow tribal loyalties; those concepts of compassion even for those in other lands which, perhaps more often than we realize these days, do operate (that Castro's Cuba should send, as it did, aid to earth-quake-stricken Managua though Nicaragua is Cuba's bitterest foe would simply be incomprehensible to the Greeks or Romans, who would have regarded the destruction of an enemy capital as the quite proper and just work of the gods) ; the emergence, imperfectly implemented as we know they only too often are, of the ideals of racial equality and justice (lest someone adduce the Greeks, let it be recalled that Plato's notion of justice was everyone's knowing his place—and keeping it) —if these do not indicate a change in human nature within historical memory, then what in the world does?

"You can't fool Mother Nature." Unless one wishes to discard a vast amount of progress in the treatment and prevention of disease, one *must* fool Mother Nature. Vaccines against poliomyelitis, smallpox, and a host of other once-dreaded diseases work by deceit, in a sense; the body is "fooled" into producing the necessary defenses before the disease actually strikes.

Z

Zen diet and vegetarianism. Many believers think that the Zen macrobiotic diet, which in its extreme form involves nothing but brown rice, is a safe way to adhere to the principles of vegetarianism. This is a dangerous myth according to Dr. Jean Mayer, professor of nutrition at Harvard.

Dr. Mayer makes it plain that he is not scoring vegetarianism in general—as long as it allows for sufficient variety to provide the protein, vitamins, and minerals we need. But the vegetarian who not only refuses to eat meat, but even draws the line at all animal by-products (milk and eggs, for example) as well as fish, and who refuses to supplement his or her diet by vitamin pills because they are "chemicals," is taking a very considerable risk, particularly with reference to the vitamin B-12. In Dr. Mayer's words:

> Many individuals have insisted to me—sometimes with considerable anger—that they and their children have been on a total-vegetable diet for years with no ill effects. But, I repeat, the symptoms of B-12 deficiency take many years to show up. And once they do, they can't be reversed.
>
> Unless the vegetarian's diet allows milk, there is also a danger of calcium insufficiency. Calcium deficiency is a particularly severe problem for nursing mothers; without ample calcium in their

diet, they have to steal calcium from their own bones to make breast milk. And as in the case of B-12 deficiency, the resulting damage occurs slowly and may be entirely unsuspected until the latter years, when the victim becomes highly susceptible to brittle bones and disabling fractures.

Added to the burden of inadequate calcium may be a shortage of vitamin D, which is necessary if the body is to utilize what calcium it does get. All small children (except those who live in year-round sunny climates) need vitamin D supplements during the winter, and this is even more true of children on low-calcium diets. They will not get sufficient vitamin D if their vegetarianism prohibits them from having D-fortified milk, fish liver oils or vitamin supplements.

zeppelin. Zeppelins are neither blimps nor merely dirigibles. They are steerable lighter-than-air craft with rigid frames. Any steerable airship is a dirigible; but only a zeppelin (after Count Ferdinand von Zeppelin, 1838–1917, its inventor) is both steerable and rigid.